A CONC
OF R...

MB20065

BY PAUL FOWLES

BILL'S
MUSIC
SHELF

Visit us on the Web at www.melbay.com or www.billsmusicshelf.com

Paul Fowles was born in the North of England, where he still lives.

For more than twenty years, he has been a reviewer and feature writer for Classical Guitar magazine, a post that has taken him to musical events throughout the world.

He is also director of the Manchester Guitar Circle, one of England's longest-established instrumental music societies.

With special thanks to:

Phillip Houghton and Heinz Böhler,
for sharing their wisdom and insight

Graham and Elizabeth Wade,
for their support and encouragement
at all stages of this project

Contents

Foreword

This book, intended for the general public, music students, and enthusiasts of all ages, explores the entire history of rock music, from its origins up to the twenty-first century.

Paul Fowles, guitarist, teacher and writer, has created a fascinating guide to a musical phenomenon which has captured the imagination of young people throughout the world.

Paul's expertise and wide researches over many years have enabled him to cover every aspect of this subject with a true authority. He writes with immense knowledge and insight, and also with passion and humor, about a subject which is central to the international artistic culture of the last five decades.

I would like to express my gratitude to William Bay and all his staff at Mel Bay Publications Inc. for making this book possible and to my wife, Elizabeth, for her invaluable editorial assistance during the preparation of this work.

Graham Wade
General Editor – *ALL ABOUT MUSIC SERIES*

Preface

Sometime in the mid 70s, the British DJ Bob Harris played *Shakin' All Over* by Johnny Kidd and the Pirates on his regular show for BBC Radio One. Over the fade-out, Harris commented that *Shakin' All Over*, first released in 1960, had been 'one of the first true rock singles'.

For Harris (b.1946), the 70s represented the highpoint in a long and distinguished broadcasting career that has continued into the twenty-first century. After serving his media apprenticeship as founding co-editor of the listings magazine *Time Out*, Harris had joined the BBC as one of a new breed of DJ whose role was perceived as that of expert rather than entertainer. Sharing this elevated status at the BBC was his older contemporary John Peel (1939–2004, real name: John Robert Parker Ravenscroft). But Harris was the one who, as permanent anchorman on the now legendary *Old Grey Whistle Test*, had conquered the fortress of network TV. Peel's uncompromising late-night show on Radio One always retained its unequaled capacity to predict and even shape future developments in music, but Harris was one of the first rock pundits to have regular access to the most powerful of all broadcasting platforms.

First transmitted in 1971 on the 'serious' channel BBC2, *Whistle Test* was the very antithesis of its BBC1 counterpart *Top of the Pops*, in which chart acts mimed to their latest hit record before a studio audience of self-consciously gyrating teenagers. On *Whistle Test*, bands and solo artists performed live in the studio. Between the live sets, tracks from forthcoming albums were played to a visual montage of silent movie footage and vintage cartoon animations, the pace of the on-screen action reflecting the tempo and character of the music. Harris conducted in-depth interviews with musicians and producers, his laid-back and unthreatening delivery earning him the nickname 'Whispering' Bob. The show's surreal-sounding name added considerably to its cult status, the rather prosaic explanation being that it was a reference to the doormen (or, according to some sources, the cleaners) at Tin Pan Alley publishing houses, who were known as 'old greys'. Songwriters would play their latest offerings to the 'old greys', whose ability to whistle the tune after one hearing was considered a valuable indicator of the song's hit potential – the 'old grey' whistle test.

The early 70s was the era in which the growing division between pop and rock became fully defined. One audience bought singles, the other bought albums. One lived for the 'here and now', the other had both respect for and an insatiable interest in the artistic heritage that had brought their music to its present state. By this time, rock was a wide church, with subcategories such as country-rock, folk-rock and jazz-rock established and universally recognized. Ethnic styles such as reggae were also welcomed to the fold: it was due, in part, to enthusiastic support from the rock audience that Bob Marley (1945–1981) became a world star.

All this grew from the seeds of the 60s, in which creativity in all aspects of popular culture had reached unprecedented heights. From early in the decade, the separate lineages of pop and rock had started to emerge, bringing with them some problems of terminology. No survey of rock music would be complete without an appraisal of the Beatles, but would it not seem more appropriate to describe Liverpool's most celebrated sons as a pop group *par excellence* rather than a rock band? A similar question might be asked when categorizing the Beach Boys, whose teenage ideal of sun, sand and sexual aspiration emerged from a vocal and instrumental texture of often underestimated complexity. These two key examples illustrate that, despite the perceived antagonism that still exists between pop and rock, the two historical lines were always interdependent.

No doubts about categorization arise when evaluating such quintessential rock patriarchs as the Rolling Stones, the Who, the Doors or the Mothers of Invention. Likewise Cream, the Grateful Dead and the Velvet Underground, not to mention the dashing figure of Jimi Hendrix, who has become to rock music what Shakespeare is to English literature.

As the 70s arrived, all had played their part in shaping an art form that grew from pubescent entertainment into one of the principal monuments of twentieth century culture. Some would remain at the epicenter for decades to come, others had already moved on.

What prompted Harris to say what he did about *Shakin' All Over* was never fully explained, but there can be little doubt that it was this record and others like it that signaled the natural maturing of the liberated and increasingly affluent lifestyle of 50s youth. The song was derived from the twelve-bar blues and driven by an adenoidal lead singer expressing mildly erotic imagery against an ever-present guitar fill. It unquestionably had its roots in the existing conventions of Rock & Roll. And yet *Shakin' All Over* was not a strict twelve-bar and the beat was considerably slower than the frantic and exuberant performances that had previously emanated from Memphis and elsewhere. As the handsome and charismatic Kidd (1939–1966, real name: Frederick Heath) caressed the microphone, clipped guitar lines were doubled at the octave by a gently throbbing electric bass, creating a brooding, almost menacing, pulse. *Shakin' All Over* was without doubt an early manifestation of what was to become the highly developed genre of rock music, as distinct from fundamentalist Rock & Roll.

The song soon acquired friends in high places, and remains to this day one of a select few cover versions performed and recorded by the Who. After various live outings, *Shakin' All Over* appeared on the classic *Live at Leeds* album in 1970. Despite the passage of time, the revered team of Daltrey, Townshend, Entwistle and Moon made no significant changes to the original.

So it was that a British song would frame the decade in which rock music on both sides of the Atlantic became a global force derived from the teenage social conventions of 1950s America...

— 1 —

Beginnings

The white man's fascination with black musical forms and the very persona of the Negro entertainer has been central to popular culture for at least two centuries. The stage act of Al Jolson (1886–1950, real name: Asa Yoelson) was by no means without precedent, the 'blacked up' minstrel being a frequently encountered vaudeville character. Such apparitions also became fashionable in Victorian England, G.H. Elliott (known as the *Chocolate-Colored Coon*) still treading the boards as recently as the 1950s.

The birth of jazz brought together various ethnic strands within American society and, over a remarkably short period of time, spawned a musical language of unprecedented diversity that still appealed to the masses. From the 1920s onwards, jazz had transformed from exuberant but unsophisticated improvisations, reminiscent in both spirit and content of the New Orleans marching bands, into a complex and wide-ranging genre whose leading exponents were a more or less equal mix of black and white. With the growth of the 'big bands' in the 1930s, the jazz musician was perceived as a highly trained professional, often expected to be a reliable 'reader' as well as being fully adept in the art of improvisation.

One of the few points on which most observers seem to agree is that Rock & Roll, like jazz, started as an all-American phenomenon. A synthesis of the existing styles of blues, country, gospel and jazz, it is also generally accepted as the first music to represent the newly-defined 50s concepts of youth culture and teenage rebellion. None of Rock & Roll's antecedents ever quite achieved this subversive status in its own right, although jazz enjoyed a mildly insubordinate late flowering as a favored idiom of the Beatniks. But by the time Jack Kerouac's anti-hero Dean Moriarty was hailing the British jazz pianist George Shearing (b.1919) as a living deity, a large part of Shearing's audience would be ageing armchair radicals with gray goatee beards.

Rock & Roll in its formative years was a club whose members were subject to a strict upper age limit, the terms and conditions stipulating the absence of parental approval. So it was pleasingly ironic that one of its earliest stars should look like the portly father figure in a cosy 50s sitcom...

BILL HALEY

Born – Detroit, 6 July 1925
Died – Harlington, Texas, 9 February 1981

William John Clifton Haley spent his early professional career in country music. Before acquiring his trademark hollow-bodied electric, Haley had used an acoustic guitar to accompany his wholesome vocal style, complete with yodeling. His backing band became known as the Comets, a reference to the celestial connotations of Haley's surname, at a relatively late stage in their development. In a former incarnation, they had suffered the rather less inspired collective title of the Saddlemen.

An often overlooked fact is that *Rock Around the Clock* failed to make a huge impression when released in 1954, Haley's first major hit being the follow-up *Shake, Rattle & Roll*. Significantly, this latter song was a cover version of an earlier release by the black R&B artist Big Joe Turner (1911–1985), emphasizing a new and vital influence in Haley's work.

With the benefit of half a century's hindsight, *Rock Around the Clock* seems an anodyne creation. Resplendent in tartan dinner jackets and indulging in puerile but harmless stage antics, Haley and his team came over as a novelty act whose apparent aim was to raise a smile rather than shock the establishment. The record's most truly distinguished component was the guitar solo. Performed by Danny Cedrone (1920–1954, real name: Donato Joseph Cedrone), rather than Haley's regular guitarist, Frannie Beecher, this brief burst of period virtuosity was so intricate as to only just keep pace with the not overly energetic rhythmic pulse. Leaning strongly in the direction of jazz and utilizing the round, plummy guitar tone favored by many senior jazzers to this day, this miniature epitaph to

Cedrone's tragically short career took the former Saddlemen a decisive step beyond their rustic roots.

What brought *Rock Around the Clock* into the public arena was its being selected to accompany the opening credits in the 1955 movie *Blackboard Jungle,* a subsequent ascent of the singles chart on both sides of the Atlantic occurring within a few weeks of general release. The content of the movie, in which Glenn Ford plays a teacher given a rough ride by his unruly high school class, might also explain why the generation that begat these troublesome teens became a little uneasy in the presence of the avuncular Haley, even though he looked pretty much like one of their own and, by now in his thirty-first year, was not that much younger.

Haley went on to enjoy a number of lesser hits and achieved classic status just one more time with *See You Later Alligator* (1956). He also scored a first with the movie *Rock Around the Clock* and its hastily-prepared sequel *Don't Knock the Rock* (both 1956), anticipating the endless line of celluloid 'tie-ins' that was soon to feature in the merchandise catalog of every rocker considered worthy of the financial investment. By this time, Haley's long-term future was assured by almost unlimited potential for reissues, compilations and personal appearances on the nostalgia circuit. But his days as an unlikely *bête noire* were numbered. Someone ten years Haley's junior who both looked and sounded the part was fast learning the trade in a Memphis studio that would become as much of a Rock & Roll legend as the musicians who recorded there…

ELVIS PRESLEY

Born – East Tupelo, Mississippi, 8 January 1935
Died – Memphis, 16 August 1977

Elvis Aaron Presley came from a poor rural background, his parents moving to Memphis as he reached his teens. Few scriptwriters could have improved on the true tale of how he first entered the music business at the age of 18 by cutting a private disc for his mother's birthday. The fact that he happened to choose the recently established Sun studio owned by the enterprising Sam Phillips (1923–2003) was a vital first step on the career ladder, Phillips recognizing the shy but charismatic youth as the 'white boy who sings like a black man' he had been hoping to find. Phillips was already involved in recording local black artists, but was aware of the limited airplay their records were likely to receive due to the political climate. Hence his willingness to invest time and money in the talented but inexperienced Presley.

With his thick dark hair and finely chiseled features, Presley was the All-American Boy who carried an air of defiance while remaining less scary and primeval than many of the Rock & Roll icons set to emerge over the next few years. In short, he was the marketing man's dream, Phillips pocketing the then colossal sum of $35,000 when Presley moved to RCA after just two years with Sun. The deal was brokered by the former country and western promoter Col. Tom Parker (1909–1997, real name: Andreas Cornelius van Kuijk), who was by that time in charge of Presley's career and remained an influential and often controversial figure in the singer's future success.

During his time at Sun, Presley released his first generation of classic recordings, starting with the famous reworking of Arthur Crudup's *That's All Right Mama,* which secured a reported 5000 advance orders after its first play on the Memphis station *WHBQ*. Presley also acquired his legendary backing team of Scotty Moore (b.1931) (guitar) and Bill Black (1926–1965) (bass). Following the success of *That's All Right Mama,* both gave up their places with local band the Starlite Wranglers to work permanently with Presley.

The RCA deal transformed Presley from a regional phenomenon into a national, shortly to be international, star. An impressive round of high-profile TV appearances ensured the success of his first RCA single, the smouldering and bluesy *Heartbreak Hotel* (1956). Later the same year came the high-octane pairing of *Hound Dog* and *Don't Be Cruel* on the same disc, closely followed by unashamedly sentimental *Love Me Tender.*

If *Hound Dog* and *Don't Be Cruel* represented proof positive of Presley's status as a key figure in Rock & Roll's first wave, *Love Me Tender* showed the diversity of his vocal style. Derived from the 1861 ballad *Aura Lee* by W.W. Fosdick and George R. Poulton, *Love Me Tender* was the title song from the first of many Hollywood vehicles for Presley's box office potential. Originally to be titled *The Reno Brothers,* this Civil War narrative featuring Richard Egan and Debra Paget was rewritten at the eleventh hour to include an acting role plus four songs for Presley. When Presley performed the song on the *Ed Sullivan Show,* RCA faced the logistical challenge of rush-releasing a single to meet a tidal wave of advance orders, said to be in the region of 850,000.

Love Me Tender was by no stretch of the imagination a great song, the new lyrics by Ken Darby (credited to Darby's wife, Vera Matson) adding no significant contemporary spice to a pleasant but hardly arresting original. But this, more than any other early Presley release, demonstrated his capacity to grow professionally beyond the 50s. By the time many of his once-celebrated contemporaries were reduced to reliving their glory days before an ageing and dwindling audience of diehards, Presley was able to spend the 60s and early 70s moving increasingly towards the bland but lucrative world of easy listening, performing to packed houses at cabaret-type venues in Las Vegas and elsewhere. By his final years, Presley was targeting much the same audience as the soporific crooner Perry Como (1912–2001), seen by many in the 50s as representing the complacent face of popular music that Rock & Roll was out to get. It was with bitter irony that, near the end of Presley's life, Como's popularity enjoyed an Indian summer with a best-selling cover version of the sugary but sincere *And I Love You So*. The song was written by Don McLean (b.1945), whose most famous title *American Pie* is an extended allegory depicting the decline of Rock & Roll following the death of Buddy Holly (see Chapter 2).

But even though Presley's work would eventually descend into professionally packaged mediocrity, he spent the rest of the 50s releasing classic songs that for many still symbolize the essence of Rock & Roll. What James Dean and Marlon Brando achieved in the movie industry, Presley achieved in music.

19

CHUCK BERRY

Born – St. Louis, 18 October 1926

If Presley was early Rock & Roll's defining performer, Charles Edward Anderson Berry remains arguably its most influential formative instrumentalist. A dusky figure with a pencil mustache, he was by no means a conventional pin-up but had stage presence by the truckload. He was also one of Rock & Roll's first guitar heroes, his catchy and inspired licks being shamelessly copied by generations to come. Having been pointed in the direction of the Chicago blues label Chess Records by the revered senior figure of Muddy Waters (1915–1983, real name: McKinley Morganfield), Berry's debut single *Maybellene* achieved national success in 1955 and earned him the coveted Billboard award for *Most Promising R&B Artist.* Credited as a joint composition to Berry, Russ Fratto and the pioneering Rock & Roll DJ Alan Freed (1922–1965), whose position in the media undoubtedly contributed to its success, *Maybellene* was followed in 1956 by *Roll Over Beethoven,* possibly Berry's most covered song apart from *Johnny B. Goode.* A string of US hits followed, plus the mandatory movie roles in *Rock, Rock, Rock* (1956) and Freed's *Mr. Rock & Roll* (1957), this latter title was recycled in 1999 as a dramatized documentary of Freed's career.

Although Freed is widely credited with inventing the term Rock & Roll, it is known to have existed long before the 50s in black American slang as a euphemism for sexual union. Early uses of the term in music are common, *My Man Rocks Me (With One Steady Roll)* having been recorded by Trixie Smith (1895–1943) as far back as 1922. When Freed first adopted the term in the early 50s, he used it as a reference to the black 'do-wop' vocal groups he was promoting at the time.

Despite his fall from grace after the so-called *Payola* scandals of the early 60s, said to have been a contributing factor in his early death at the age of 43, Freed remains a seminal figure in the history of Rock & Roll. The 1973 album *Moondog Matinee* by The Band is a tribute to Freed's early broadcasting alias, taken from his theme tune *Blues for a Moon Dog* by Todd Rhodes (1900–1965).

Unlike Presley and Haley, Berry's success during the 1950s was mostly limited to the USA. His own legal problems, culminating in a period in jail during 1962/3, cannot have helped his export potential. But in any case, despite his unique brand of showmanship, complete with the much-imitated 'duck walk' (said to have first been a ploy to hide the wrinkles in a rayon suit he wore at a New York performance in 1956), Berry's work was always perceived abroad as being more for the connoisseurs. His status among serious musos was illustrated by his 1958 appearance at the Newport Jazz Festival, a remarkable accolade for anyone associated with teen culture.

His first UK Top Ten hit did not happen until 1963, when *Memphis Tennessee* was reissued as a 'spoiler' against a now largely forgotten cover version by the British singer Dave Berry (no relation). The ploy proved successful, *Memphis Tennessee* by "Dave Berry and the Cruisers" peaking at No.19.

But by this time, Chuck Berry was a revered figure in the approaching British R&B boom, with the Beatles, the Rolling Stones and countless lesser bands openly acknowledging his influence.

From the mid-50s onwards, Rock & Roll expanded its territory as new and talented exponents entered the arena. To take just one early and significant example, Carl Perkins (1932–1998) had tasted national success with the original version of his own song *Blue Suede Shoes* before it was adopted by his Sun Records stablemate, Elvis Presley. Had Perkins' career not been put on hold by a 1956 car accident (en route to appear on a TV show presented by the recurring figure of Perry Como), many believe the history of Rock & Roll would have been radically different. Sam Phillips himself is often quoted as having stated that Perkins had at least the same star potential as Presley.

Gibson ES-335

Meanwhile, such wild characters as Little Richard (b.1932, full name: Richard Wayne Penniman) and Jerry Lee Lewis (b.1935) were producing a growing inventory of classic recordings. Unlike Berry, Haley and Presley, Penniman and Lewis used the piano as their self-accompanying instrument. The symbolic element of this choice of hardware is considerable. Such chrome-embellished totems as Chuck Berry's famous red Gibson ES 335 (first available to the public in 1958) were both audibly and visibly a different tool from the hand-crafted guitars by Hermann Hauser and José Ramírez used by that most iconic and patrician classical guitarist of the era, Andrés Segovia (1893–1987). But the concert grand pianos used and at times abused by Penniman and Lewis were essentially the same as those being caressed by Arthur Rubinstein (1887–1982) and other world-ranking classical pianists at the Carnegie Hall and elsewhere. For Lewis, Penniman et al, the static nature of the instrument proved no obstacle to its visual possibilities, the sturdy construction providing a secure base for innumerable onstage acrobatics.

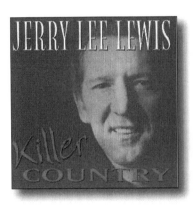

An instrument whose background in popular music was at the time considerably more pivotal and diverse than the newly emerging guitar, the piano also provided a harmonic backdrop for the less energetic but equally influential figure of Fats Domino (b.1928, real name: Antoine Dominique Domino).

But as Rock & Roll's first wave neared its conclusion, new and younger talents with ideas of their own were set to enter the arena…

— 2 —

Rock to Pop – 50s to 60s

❧

On 3 February 1959, Rock & Roll suffered its first major casualty. At just 22, Buddy Holly (born Charles Hardin Holley in Lubbock, Texas on 7 September 1936) may be seen as a primary manifestation of Rock & Roll's even more youthful second wave. His death in a plane crash that also claimed the lives of the Big Bopper (Jiles Perry Richardson) and Ritchie Valens (Richard Steven Valenzuela) brought to an abrupt end a fast-track career that had already generated a string of major hits, starting with *That'll Be The Day* in 1957. Holly's singles had typically been equally successful on both British and US territory, *It Doesn't Matter Anymore* proving a poignantly titled posthumous UK No.1.

Softer and more lyrical than the performances of many of his contemporaries, his recorded legacy may be seen as representing either a taming or a refining of Rock & Roll's once uncompromising language, his Texan roots emerging in a mix that was arguably more country than blues. Holly's geeky, bespectacled appearance also made him one of the first premier league rockers of whom Mom and Dad might just approve. A much mourned talent whose long-term potential will never be known, Holly is perhaps best seen as an architect of that less assertive genre that would become pop music.

On 17 April 1960, a second Rock & Roll tragedy occurred. A native of Oklahoma but raised in Minnesota and later California, Eddie Cochran was just 21 when the Ford Consul taxi he was travelling in at the end of his first British tour went out of control and crashed near Chippenham, Wiltshire. Fellow rocker Gene Vincent (1935–1971), remembered primarily for his 1956 hit *Be-Bop-A-Lula,* was also on the tour and sharing the cab. Vincent survived the accident, as did Cochran's fiancée, the rising songwriter Sharon Sheeley (1940–2002). Cochran died from multiple head injuries within a few hours. In a recording career that ran for just three years, he released such significant and much covered hit songs as *Summertime Blues, C'Mon Everybody* and *Three Steps to Heaven.* An able exponent of the multi-track techniques pioneered by guitar legend

Les Paul (b.1915, real name: Lester William Polfus, also spelt Polfuss), Cochran left a considerable quantity of unreleased experimental studio footage, the existence of which suggests his star was still very much in the ascendant. He also made a youthful appearance in the movie *The Girl Can't Help It* (1956), seen by many as one of the more palatable 'rocksploitation' features.

Occupying ground close to that of Holly and Cochran were the clean-cut figures of Don and Phil Everly (b.1937 and 1939 respectively). Hailing from Kentucky, the Everly Brothers developed their bittersweet vocal harmonies from an early joint apprenticeship in country music. Starting with *Bye Bye Love,* they turned out an average of two hit records a year over the second half of the 50s, their productivity starting to slow after the international success of *Cathy's Clown* in 1960. Like Holly and Cochran, they were a major presence in the UK charts. Whatever their records may have lacked in dynamic energy was made up for in melodic invention and slickness of execution. The once staple diet of a pounding 12-bar was already taking its place in history.

Although the piano had played a major part in the first wave of Rock & Roll, the guitar soon claimed the position of main supporting instrument and, from *Rock Around The Clock* onwards, the most usual medium for the featured soloist.

This led to a sub-genre that arrived in 1958 with *Rebel Rouser* by Duane Eddy (b.1938). A protégé of Tucson DJ Lee Hazlewood (1929–2007), Eddy was a country-picker who had modeled his early style on Chet Atkins (1924–2001). With *Rebel Rouser,* Eddy hit on a formula of low *tessitura* and high reverb that he would retain for the rest of his career, his 1959 LP *Have Twangy Guitar, Will Travel* being one of remarkably few memorable album titles of the era.

The guitar instrumentals of the early 60s were an almost inevitable by-product generated by 50s Rock & Roll. It was also one of the first areas where American and British acts would chart a parallel course, the all-American Ventures and the staunchly British Shadows even occasionally sharing the same repertoire. Although Eddy had no serious British counterpart, there can be little doubt that the 1959 UK hit *Guitar Boogie Shuffle* by Bert Weedon (b.1920) was a commercially motivated response to Eddy's success. In fact, *Guitar Boogie Shuffle* was a reworking of the 1945 hit *Guitar Boogie* by Arthur Smith (b.1921), who subsequently became known as Arthur "Guitar Boogie" Smith. A modest talent whose subsequent career has essentially been that of a cabaret entertainer, Weedon has nonetheless been immortalized in his instructional publication *Play in a Day*, which provided a whole generation of his compatriots with their first step towards mastering the basic skills required to learn the guitar.

This last point uncovers an important stimulus generated by the guitar instrumental. Although it took considerable skill to emulate precisely the neatly crafted lead parts delivered by Hank Marvin (b.1941, real name: Brian Robson Rankin) of the Shadows and Bob Bogle (b.1934) of the Ventures, it was quite feasible for the aspiring amateur guitarist at least to capture the essence of what they did.

The straightforward melodic lines and absence of extended improvisations enabled anyone with a fair command of the instrument to copy their prized vinyl with reasonable accuracy. Having struggled for years to puzzle out Cedrone's 20-second innings on *Rock Around the*

Clock, the bedroom plucker could now produce a recognizable outline of the complete *Walk Don't Run* or *Wonderful Land* with relative ease.

Identifying a niche market, the Ventures retained their audience for more than four decades by faithfully serving up the tunes people came to hear. They are still in business at the time of writing, the only significant change since the early 60s being Bogle's decision to move from lead guitar to bass, exchanging roles with Nokie Edwards (b.1935, real name: Nole Edwards), thus making it difficult for even the most seasoned enthusiasts to be sure of who played what on which recording.

First entering the public arena as backing group to Cliff Richard (b.1940, real name: Harry Rodger Webb) in the late 50s, the Shadows were originally known as the Drifters, the need for a new collective title arising due to the growing international prominence of the identically named black American vocal group, formed in 1953 by Clyde McPhatter (1932–1972) and later a training ground for soul singer Ben E. King (b.1938, real name: Benjamin Earl Nelson). After their first UK No.1 with *Apache* in 1960, the Shadows enjoyed a string of UK hits while still on Richard's payroll. Their mass appeal started to fade after 1963, although they remained active, with various line-up changes, until the late 60s. After an embarrassing stint as the unfunny sidekick on Richard's BBC TV show, Marvin suffered further humiliation by agreeing to reform the band for the 1975 *Eurovision Song Contest*, performing the excruciating *Let Me Be The One.*

This dreadful song deservedly lost to the magnificent *Ding-a-Dong*, one of the greatest Eurovision self-parodies in the history of that tragi-comic event, skilfully delivered by a group named Teach-In, representing the Netherlands. In the meantime, Marvin had teamed up with former Shadows Bruce Welch (b.1941, real name: Bruce Cripps) and John Farrar (b.1946) to form the acoustic guitar/vocal trio Marvin, Welch and Farrar. Once optimistically described as Britain's answer to Crosby, Stills and Nash, the project yielded more favorable results than might have been expected, but never really caught on with the public. Currently enjoying semi-retirement, Marvin can rest secure in the knowledge that there is still an audience out there for what he did best.

A further role of the guitar instrumental in which the Shadows, for obvious geographical reasons, played no part was that of precursor to the rise of surf music. The Ventures are still seen by many as chief exponents of the 'surf guitar', their extensive back catalog containing a cover version of the surf anthem *Wipeout,* recorded by the more specifically targeted California band the Surfaris in 1962. An often overlooked figure is Dick Dale (b.1937, real name: Richard Monsour), billed as 'King of the Surf Guitar'. With his band the Deltones, Dale enjoyed a brief heyday in the early 60s, his clipped, metallic guitar style being rather more raw and challenging than that of many of his contemporaries. Despite several attempted comebacks, Dale spent many years in obscurity until his 1962 hit *Misirlou* was used in the 1994 movie *Pulp Fiction.* He finally became known to UK audiences in the late 90s when his quirky and staccato instrumental *Let's Go Trippin'* was adopted by John Peel as the theme for his non-musical radio chat show *Home Truths.*

It goes without saying that surf music in its vocal form was represented by the Beach Boys, together with lesser talents such as Jan and Dean, not to mention the inimitable Trashmen (of *Surfin' Bird* fame/ notoriety). Applying falsetto vocal harmonies to an underlying Rock & Roll structure, their early hit *Surfin' USA* being directly lifted from Chuck Berry's *Sweet Little Sixteen,* the music came to represent a sun-drenched lifestyle to which fans the world over aspired. Led by the unstable genius of Brian Wilson (b.1942), the band went on to release such sophisticated and award-winning albums as *Pet Sounds* (1966), even though the unavoidable retention of the original name prevented the band entirely shaking off their adolescent fun-loving image.

Their status in the pantheon of rock music will always be somewhat controversial. Paul McCartney is said to have held their work in high regard, whereas the mischievous, albeit practically inaudible, reference to surf music in the last line of *Third Stone From The Sun,* possibly suggests Jimi Hendrix did not. Hendrix is also credited with the onstage rebuke 'This ain't no surf music...', following the announcement that the Beach Boys had cancelled their scheduled appearance at the *Monterey Festival* in 1967. A decade later, Frank Zappa lampooned the whole genre brilliantly and mercilessly with *Let Me Take You To The Beach* from the 1978 album *Studio Tan.*

Despite the success of Cliff Richard and the Shadows, the British music scene throughout the 50s was dominated by American imports, a favorite trivia question being to name a British Rock & Roll single other than Richard's *Move It* (1958). Perceived as a rather less than convincing Elvis soundalike, Richard was nonetheless a competent professional whose 'not very angry young man' image was easily tolerated by parents and grandparents alike. His boyish good looks also ensured a large, mostly female, teenage fanbase. He remains to this day a respected showbiz figure and was knighted in 1995.

Move It notwithstanding, Britain would have been almost entirely bereft of homegrown Rock & Roll and its derivatives, had it not been for the curious phenomenon of Skiffle. Developed from the 'jug band' tradition of the Southern States, Skiffle started out as a strictly acoustic genre, often relying on makeshift instruments. A universally recalled feature of the British skiffle movement was the use of a washboard as a source of both percussive sounds and engaging visuals. The material performed was mostly of American origin, such British narratives as the unforgettable 1960 Cockney hit *My Old Man's a Dustman* by Lonnie Donegan (1931–2002) being the exception rather than the rule. Although this was inevitably the title that would grab the headlines, Donegan's regular fare was transatlantic acquisitions, including *My Dixie Darling* and Leadbelly's *Rock Island Line*. Likewise future Skiffle historian Chas McDevitt (b.1934), whose group featuring Nancy Whiskey (1935–2003, real name: Anne Wilson) scored two UK hits in 1957 with *Freight Train* and *Greenback Dollar*.

Although Skiffle was never destined to become the most refined of languages, its place in the history of rock music is significant for two reasons. Firstly, it provided the training ground for numerous fledgling talents that would come to fruition in the 60s. Liverpool band the Quarrymen, featuring a young John Lennon, are an obvious example. Secondly, it provided an early public platform for both British and American folk music, a then relatively unexploited resource in the mainstream popular arena. It seems unlikely that the California based folk group the Kingston Trio would have scored such a major UK hit in 1958 with *Tom Dooley*, had Donegan's interpretation of the same song not been in the charts at the same time.

Through its lightweight and unpretentious ethos, the British Skiffle movement highlighted a vast traditional heritage that was to play a key supporting role in the history of rock...

— 3 —

Roots and Radicals – The Folk Connection

Although the breadth and diversity of the global folk tradition is almost incalculable, the universality of traditional music and dance as an active pursuit is often over-estimated. Not all Spaniards express themselves through the medium of the flamenco guitar, any more than all Englishmen spend their weekends morris dancing.

By definition, almost any tune that is not the acknowledged work of a named composer may be categorized as folk music. But by the early twentieth century, use of the term 'folk song' would typically be a reference to an identifiable species of sentimental or nostalgic ballad, either urban or rural in origin. It was not uncommon for new songs to be written in a style that imitated the genre, these pastiches often being mistaken for traditional fare. Fosdick and Poulton's American Civil War ballad *Aura Lee,* referred to in Chapter 1, may be seen as one such example.

From the 60s onwards, the adjective 'folksy' would become one of unmitigated condemnation, although the British trio the Springfields appear to have used it without irony on their 1962 album *Kinda Folksy,* together with the spin-off EPs *Kinda Folksy Nos.1, 2 and 3.* Best remembered for their 1963 hit *Island of Dreams*, the Springfields also provided an early platform for the huge talent that was to become Dusty Springfield (1939–1999, real name: Mary Isabel Catherine Bernadette O'Brien), one of the classiest British singers to emerge in the 60s, and among the finest female interpreters of the suave songwriting team of Burt Bacharach (b.1928) and Hal David (b.1921).

From the late 40s onwards, the grittier side of folk music reached the attention of a new breed of left-wing intellectual. Inspired by poignant narratives of hardships and injustices from the past, these educated reformers soon saw the possibilities of applying a similar language to the ills of the present day. The protest song had arrived. An undisputed father of the movement was Pete Seeger, drawing much of his early musical and lifestyle inspiration from the *Dust Bowl Ballads* of Woody Guthrie (1912–1967). The Harvard educated son of a violin teacher and the noted musicologist Charles Seeger (1886–1979), he was born in New York on 3 May 1919.

Between periods spent traveling across America in the guise of a banjo-toting hobo, Seeger was engaged in serious research with folk music guru Alan Lomax (1915–2002) at the Library of Congress. In 1949, he formed the Weavers folk group. His previous group, the Almanac Singers, had been a joint venture with Guthrie. Alongside such traditional songs as *Goodnight Irene* and *On Top of Old Smokey,* the Weavers gradually became a vehicle for more recent writing, although such gentle offerings as Leadbelly's *Kisses Sweeter Than Wine* gave few hints as to what was to follow.

Seeger is often credited as the sole creator of the protest chant *We Shall Overcome*, but he was in fact just one of a 'committee' of four, the other members being Guy Carawan, Frank Hamilton and Zilphia Horton. The song was published in 1963 by Ludlow Music Inc. of New York, and it is anybody's guess how they approached the task of collecting royalties from the myriad unscheduled performances that have taken place ever since. Other Seeger perennials included *Where Have All The Flowers Gone?*, co-written with Joe Hickerson (b.1935), *Little Boxes*, often attributed to Seeger, but actually by Malvina Reynolds (1900–1978) and *If I Had a Hammer*. Composed as *The Hammer Song* for a Communist Party rally in 1947, this later became associated with the wholesome yet politically active Peter, Paul and Mary, and a worldwide hit record for Trini Lopez (b.1937, full name: Trinidad Lopez III).

Seeger's political affiliations led to an appearance before the House of Un-American Activities Committee (HUAC) in August 1955, his willingness to admit his beliefs, combined with a firm refusal to name his comrades, leading to a twelve month prison sentence that was only averted following a storm of international protest. Proof positive that Seeger's growing band of disciples had the capacity to practice what he preached.

Seeger's opposite number in the UK was the singer, songwriter, actor and playwright Ewan MacColl (1915–1989, real name: Jimmie Miller).

Although his Celtic roots were genuine, MacColl was an Englishman, born to Scottish parents in Salford, Lancashire. *Dirty Old Town,* MacColl's most enduring original song, refers to specific locations in Salford and initially formed part of his 1946 theatrical work *Landscape With Chimneys.* MacColl was widely read but, unlike Seeger, did not benefit from a university education, a short career in various manual jobs ending when he formed an agit-prop street theater group named the Red Megaphones (later renamed Theater of Action) during the 1930s. After his brief marriage to the dancer Jean Newlove (his second wife) ended in 1956, MacColl's long term relationship with Peggy Seeger (b.1935), half-sister of Pete, created a family link within the protest song's senior generation. It was this lasting union that inspired MacColl to write the lilting ballad *The First Time Ever I Saw Your Face*, a worldwide hit in 1972 for jazz and soul singer/songwriter Roberta Flack (b.1937).

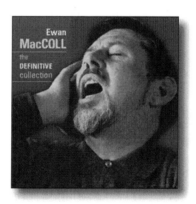

By the early 60s, a second generation of protest singers emerged, with America taking the lead. As might be expected, they were louder and more outspoken than their elders. Even Seeger himself is portrayed as an icon of the soft center left in *Love Me, I'm a Liberal* by the largely forgotten figure of Phil Ochs (1940–1976).

But it was another Jewish American boy who brought the protest song into the mainstream of 60s life…

BOB DYLAN

Born – Duluth, Minnesota, 24 May 1941

Robert Allen Zimmerman was raised in middle-class comfort. His childhood in the mining town of Hibbing, Minnesota, where his family had moved when he was six, appears to have been one of modest prosperity. Usually described as Reform Jews, the Zimmermans upheld the traditional practices of their religion, the young Robert learning Hebrew in preparation for his Bar Mitzvah. The family's lifestyle was financed by Abraham Zimmerman's secure positions with first the Standard Oil Company and then his brothers' furniture business.

In common with many of his contemporaries, the adolescent Robert Zimmerman played Rock & Roll in high school, most sources citing Little Richard as his main role model. But by the time he was preparing to drop out of the University of Minnesota, he had shifted his allegiances to Woody Guthrie. It was around this time that the name and persona of Bob Dylan started to take shape, the early spelling of 'Dillon' emphasizing the likely absence of Welsh poet Dylan Thomas (1914–1953) from Zimmerman's train of thought. The name, in its finalized form, was legally adopted in 1962.

After moving to New York's Greenwich Village, already the heart of the protest movement, in 1959, Dylan honed his craft on the café circuit before signing with record producer John Hammond (1910–1987) of CBS in 1962. A jazz and blues specialist who is often credited with discovering Bessie Smith (1894–1937) and Billie Holiday (1915–1959), Hammond undoubtedly took a risk with Dylan, whose whining voice, erratic breath control and idiosyncratic pronunciations cannot have been an easy sell in the early 60s market. But Hammond's gamble paid off, Dylan's self-titled 1962 debut album receiving a favorable response, although the single *Mixed Up Confusion* c/w *Corinna, Corinna,* neither of which appeared on the first album, was not a big hit.

But it was the second album, with its then ultra-cool title *The Freewheelin' Bob Dylan,* that established him as a world force. Containing such classics as *Blowin' In The Wind, A Hard Rain's A-Gonna Fall* and *Don't Think Twice, It's All Right* this was surely the album that set the agenda for Dylan's long and productive career, its groovy cover shot of Dylan with his then girlfriend, the artist Suze Rotolo (b.1943), being as much a symbol of the era as the disc it contained. Much more was to follow. If the 50s had been virtually devoid of memorable LP titles, Dylan made up for that deficiency almost single-handed. Not everyone can remember which song appeared where, but *Highway 61 Revisited, Blonde On Blonde, John Wesley Harding* and *Nashville Skyline* entered the lexicon of the time as permanent fixtures. Dylan's current discography contains well in excess of 40 albums, the precise figure depending on how the bootlegs are calculated. Always an unpredictable talent, even Dylan's much raved about skills as a lyricist are far from unblemished. As Ian MacDonald points out in his article *Wild Mercury: A Tale of Two Dylans,* '…one never knows whether a Dylan line is there merely to sound good, provide a rhyme or fill a hole in the verse'. No litmus tests exist for the first and third assertions, but the second is demonstrably true. Dylan's penchant for forcing a rhyme via distorted pronunciation, or creating one by writing just anything, both show up in the song *Joey* from the 1975 album *Desire.* In this romanticized account of the life of mobster Joey Gallo (1929–1972), we are informed at the outset that the subject of the song was 'Born in Red Hook Brooklyn, in the year of who knows when' and that he 'opened up his eyes to the sound of an *accordi-enne'*. At the climax of the song, Dylan announces that Gallo met his untimely demise 'in a clam bar in New York' and that the assassination took place 'as he lifted up his fork'. This really was stretching it, quite apart from the fact that Dylan, having researched his subject, would be fully aware of the year in which Gallo was born.

But despite this occasional poetic slackness, Dylan has always reigned supreme in his mastery of the soundbite and his unfailing ability to stay one step ahead of the game. By the time Barry McGuire (b.1935) was entering the charts with the 1965 single *Eve of Destruction* – a protest rant so crude that it is impossible to say whether it was meant as a parody or just turned out that way – Dylan was already moving away from the guitar/voice/harmonica format that McGuire replicated in this rudimentary creation by the New York songwriter P.F. Sloan (b.1945, real name: Philip Schlein). Contemporary accounts describe how *Eve of Destruction* became a rallying cry in calls for the US voting age to be reduced from 21 to 18, although some might have considered it reason enough to raise the age to 35.

Dylan's 'Judas' incident of 17 May 1966 is well-documented, although precise details of what took place vary between accounts. What is known is that, when Dylan was about to perform *Like A Rolling Stone* as the closing item in his set at Manchester's no longer active uptown venue the Free Trade Hall, someone in the crowd, generally accepted to have been John Cordwell (1944–2001), yelled out the offending appellation. Contemporary commentators tell of how Dylan's followers were becoming increasingly uneasy about his all-new 'electric' sound, complete with Fender Stratocaster and heavily amplified backing group. There had even been unconfirmed reports of a threat to blow up the Sheffield venue where he was booked to play on the same tour. It is therefore easy to jump to the conclusion that Cordwell's outburst was a knee-jerk reaction from a fan who objected on principle to anything other than the tried and trusted acoustic Dylan.

But in a much later interview with the BBC's Andy Kershaw (b.1959), Cordwell strenuously denied this. Describing himself and his companions as 'bit players on the Manchester folk scene', Cordwell emphasized that they were 'trying to move it away from its traditional finger-in-the-ear woolly jumper roots'. Scarcely the words of a hardline fundamentalist. Cordwell went on to explain that he was not in the best of moods that night because the lyrics had been obliterated by 'dreadful' sound quality, but he objected most of all to Dylan's newly developed 'on stage posturing and rock star arrogance', an attitude seen as betraying the audience whose faithful support had been the key to his success.

In the company of this early incarnation of The Band, drawn from the Hawks, backing group to Ronnie Hawkins (b.1935), Dylan had, for better or worse, finally bridged the divide between folk and rock. This said, his own work never quite fitted into the hybrid genre known as 'folk-rock'. That term would be initially applied to American groups such as the Byrds, remembered mainly for their electric arrangements of Seeger's *Turn, Turn, Turn* and Dylan's *Mr. Tambourine Man*, early manifestations of a style later to become known as 'jangle pop'.

The hugely talented partnership of Paul Simon and Art Garfunkel (both b.1941) became reluctant early exponents of folk-rock, their first major hit *Sounds of Silence* (1965) being 'electrified' in the studio by CBS producer Tom Wilson (1931–1978) without their knowledge. Simon's songwriting skills and often underrated acoustic guitar mastery, combined with Garfunkel's celestial vocal lines, soon drew a massive audience from the worlds of folk, rock and easy listening. Their ethereal setting of *Scarborough Fair* remains one of the most sublime contemporary arrangements of traditional English song.

Needless to say, the Byrds were by no means the only band to cover Dylan's work. So sought after was his writing that some acts had hits with Dylan songs previously only available as bootlegs. One was the 1968 UK hit *Mighty Quinn* by the band bearing the name of bespectacled keyboard player Manfred Mann (b.1940, real name: Manfred Lubowitz). In the same year, *This Wheel's On Fire* by Julie Driscoll (b.1947), backed by the Brian Auger Trinity, also entered the UK charts. Both songs appear on Dylan and the Band's much discussed 1967 *Basement Tape*. These informal sessions were not released by Columbia until 1975, having by this time been 'remixed' to mono and subjected to various later overdubs. Some material from the *Basement Tape* surfaced on the 1969 Dylan bootleg known as *The Great White Wonder,* whose illicit sales were said to have technically qualified for a Gold Disc. *Mighty Quinn* was soon to appear on the 1970 Dylan release *Self Portrait,* but *This Wheel's On Fire* only emerged with the official 1975 double album bearing the now plural title *The Basement Tapes*. Driscoll's source for the song was not widely disclosed at the time, although it was believed that keyboard player Brian Auger (b.1939) was one of a select few recipients of an acetate copy of the Dylan recordings. Although *This Wheel's On Fire* was to be Driscoll's only UK hit single, her musical career has continued to the present day under her married name of Julie Tippetts, her long-time partner and musical collaborator being the English jazz pianist Keith Tippett (b.1947). The decision to adopt the original spelling of Tippetts is puzzling, her husband having dropped the final consonant at an early stage in his career.

Perhaps the greatest Dylan cover of all grew out of an understated and seemingly rather obscure song from the *John Wesley Harding* album of 1968. With its descending three-chord *ostinato* and enigmatic imagery, *All Along The Watchtower* was hardly an obvious candidate for a hit single, let alone a titanic rock anthem that, in its revised setting, would be considered by many as one of the finest studio recordings to emerge from the short but unequaled career of Jimi Hendrix. Recognizing the potential in Dylan's original, Hendrix increased the tempo and added drums, bass and layers of guitars including, unusually for Hendrix, a metal-strung acoustic. This last instrument is widely believed to have been played by Dave Mason (b.1946) of Traffic, although no credit appeared when the song was released on the Hendrix two-LP magnum opus *Electric Ladyland* later in 1968. A hit for Hendrix on both sides of the Atlantic, *All Along The Watchtower,* apart from being possibly the most breathtaking 3'58" of the entire 60s, represents a triumphant coming together of the two most influential musical languages of the era.

Although this union of Dylan's songwriting and the pace-setting instrumental skills of Hendrix was a defining moment, the parallel worlds of folk and rock were to retain their independent paths, regularly meeting along the way. By the end of the decade, a whole new folk-rock scene would develop in Britain, with bands such as Steeleye Span, Pentangle and Fairport Convention performing their own material alongside inspired and elaborate settings of traditional songs, jigs and reels.

The latter's 1969 release *Liege and Lief* is arguably the definitive album of classic British folk-rock. Using more traditional instruments but performing fewer traditional songs was the Incredible String Band, led by the exuberant pairing of Mike Heron (b.1942) and Robin Williamson (b.1943). One of several acoustic acts to find favor with the rock audience, the ISB used everything from sitars to Celtic harps, their eclectic mix reaching its highpoint in *The Hangman's Beautiful Daughter* from 1968.

But before there could be folk-rock, the first seeds of rock had to germinate…

— 4 —

R & B – A Transatlantic Trade

For a nation that prides itself on innovation, Britain's early contribution to rock music was not noted for its wealth of original thought. Skiffle was essentially recycled Americana, Rock & Roll was a straight import and the guitar instrumental yielded only one high-ranking British exponent in Hank Marvin. Even in the newly awakened interest in folk music, where Britain's rich tapestry of tradition should have given it a natural advantage over the younger nations, America was widely perceived to have led the way until at least the mid-60s.

This bulk importation of raw material continued during the years that Britannia ruled its domestic club scene, if not its airwaves, in that most Stateside of idioms, R&B. Dating back to the late 40s and generally attributed to Jerry Wexler (1917–2008), the term Rhythm & Blues had been compressed to its initials long before it became standard currency in the British capital more than a decade later. It has to be conceded that the British R&B boom was short-lived and is arguably most notable for what it led to, but there can be no doubt that London was a major center of activity in those formative years of the early 60s.

What exactly distinguished R&B from the more contemporary urban guises of straight 'blues' has never been easy to define. Whichever yardstick you choose, be it tempo, instrumentation, melody or harmony, you sooner or later hit an exception. But everyone who was there at the time knew that R&B was what took place at such London haunts as the

Marquee Club and the Flamingo. Interestingly, British R&B drew much of its nascent support from a scene previously dominated by 'trad.' jazz. It was a radical decision on the part of established jazzman Chris Barber (b.1930) to arrange UK dates for such key figures as (Big) Bill Broonzy (1893 or 1898–1958), Brownie McGhee (1915–1996), Muddy Waters and the extrovert New Orleans pianist and singer Dr. John (b.1940, real name Malcolm Rebennack, also known professionally as the 'Night Tripper'). This led Barber's mature audience into what was then exotic and uncharted territory, the reported response not always being entirely favorable from the more conservative factions.

Even before the heyday of Barber's blues tours, the Roundhouse pub in Soho was playing host to the Thursday evening proceedings of the Blues and Barrelhouse Club. These informal sessions were organized by Cyril Davies (1932–1964) and Alexis Korner (1928–1984), who were also the principal performers. As Britain's first widely recognized exponents of the genre, both were invited to appear with Barber's band (Davies on harmonica, Korner on guitar) when he introduced R&B into his own sets from 1960. Encouraged by the success of the blues tours, Barber ended his shows with a short sequence featuring Davies, Korner and the singer Ottilie Patterson.

Having by now acquired their own following from both within and beyond Barber's audience, Davies and Korner judged that the time was right to go it alone with their own pioneering outfit Blues Inc., the choice of the American legal form being either an acknowledgement of their source of ideas, or possibly just an acceptance that 'Blues Ltd' did not have the same ring. But despite their popularity in some quarters, Davies and Korner were aware that their brand of amplified music was not universally appreciated on the jazz circuit. This was understandable, since even Muddy Waters had apparently suffered an initially cool reception from a British audience more attuned to the acoustic 'delta' blues.

In a bold step that showed considerable confidence in R&B's long-term viability, Davies and Korner opened the Ealing Blues Club in March 1962. Originally intended as a platform for their own performances, Davies and Korner's venue soon became the meeting place for a growing network of enthusiasts, the corresponding rise of the Flamingo and the Marquee widening the range of places to go.The ever-changing line-up of Blues Inc. reads like a Hall of Fame. The drummer on the opening night was Charlie Watts, and bass player Andy Hoogenboom would shortly be replaced by a young Jack Bruce. Watts himself soon gave up the drum stool to Ginger Baker. The departure of singer Art Wood to form the Artwoods led to the arrival of John Baldry (1941–2005, later known as 'Long' John Baldry), whose rich bass baritone was later utilized to considerable commercial effect in the period tear-jerker *Let The Heartaches Begin* (UK No.1, 1967). When Davies left to form his own band, taking with him Baldry and pianist Nicky Hopkins (1944–1994), Korner recruited alto sax player Graham Bond (1937–1974), who later fronted the Graham Bond Organization (or Organisation). Davies and Korner's penchant for American-sounding corporate titles had clearly made its mark.

As the personnel came and went, a nucleus of club regulars with their own musical aspirations sat in on the sessions. These included Paul Jones (b.1942, real name: Paul Pond). Jones later found fame as lead singer with Manfred Mann before embarking on a hugely successful career in TV acting, while reliving the old days with the imaginatively titled Blues Band. At a table near the clean-cut and handsome Jones could sometimes be seen three slightly sinister-looking characters. One styled himself Elmo Lewis, although his real name was Brian Jones (no relation to Paul). The others were Keith Richards, an art student from Kent, and a London School of Economics undergraduate named Mick Jagger...

THE ROLLING STONES

While the line-up of Blues Inc. altered almost from session to session, the Rolling Stones soon emerged as a band that would see remarkably few changes over the next four decades. Until the departure of Jones just a few weeks before his death in July 1969, the permanent team of Jagger (b.1943) (lead vocal, harmonica), Jones (1942–1969) (guitar), Richards (b.1943) (guitar), Watts (b.1941) (drums) plus Bill Wyman (b.1936, real name: William George Perks) (bass) had remained essentially unchanged since 1963. Prior to that date, the band had evolved around the nucleus of Jagger, Jones and Richards.

Early members included Ian Stewart (1938–1985) (piano) and Dick Taylor (b.1943) (guitar/bass). Taylor went on to form the Pretty Things, remaining aboard for his new band's first four albums. Stewart was not replaced for the simple reason that he never actually left, his position as 'associate member' continued until shortly before his death. It appears to have been Watts, not Wyman, who was last to join. The mature and experienced jazz drummer reportedly needed much persuasion.

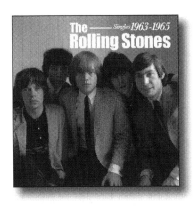

With the membership stabilized, the band secured a residency at the Crawdaddy Club in Richmond, establishing a cult following within a short time of arrival. It was here that they first came to the attention of the then unknown rock promoter Andrew 'Loog' Oldham (b.1944). A gifted publicist with only limited prior knowledge of music or the music business, Oldham was largely responsible for cultivating the menacing image that would get the Stones noticed and later prove a valuable weapon against the Beatles. Oldham also reportedly made the decision to demote Stewart, simply because he did not fit the image. The mysterious plight of Stewart, the 'sixth Stone', is a study in itself, although fellow band members publicly acknowledged his contribution by including an excerpt of him playing *Key To The Highway* as a 'hidden' track on the 1986 album *Dirty Work*.

From 1963 onwards, the story unfolds with movie script rapidity. The first single *Come On* was released in June 1963 to coincide with their TV debut on *Thank Your Lucky Stars*. By September, they were the support act on a 'package' tour, comprising the Everly Brothers, Little Richard and doyen of rock & roll guitar heroes, Bo Diddley (1928–2008, real name: Otha Ellas Bates, later known as Ellas McDaniel).

A truly patrician figure in the history of rock, Diddley's influence is acknowledged in numerous cover versions and such overt tributes as the Animals' recording of *The Story of Bo Diddley* and, much later, *Bo Diddley is Jesus* by the Jesus & Mary Chain. The precise derivation of his adopted name is the subject of some debate, a favorite explanation being that 'bo diddley' is a Southern black slang phrase meaning 'nothing at all', as in 'that ain't bo diddley'. This being the case, it would appear the term is a close relative of the expression 'diddly squat', itself a sanitized version of a more excremental original. In November 1963, the Rolling Stones' second single, an 'authorized cover' of Lennon and McCartney's *I Wanna Be Your Man*, entered the UK Top 20. Although the Beatles' own version appeared during the same year on the *With The*

Beatles LP, the song had first been offered to the Stones, via Oldham. The Stones' disc thus predates that of the Beatles by a few weeks. According to Beatles lore, it was the efficiency with which the Liverpudlians were able to complete the song on demand that motivated Jagger and Richards to start writing their own material.

When the Stones toured with Phil Spector's exquisitely photogenic Ronettes in early 1964, they were no longer just the support act. It was during that year that *Not Fade Away* became their first UK Top Ten hit and also their first US chart entry. A self-titled debut album followed, presenting an R&B retrospective that started with *Route 66* and ended with *Walking the Dog*. By summer 1964, *It's All Over Now* was at the top of the UK chart and would shortly make its mark in the US, their gradual penetration of the US market successfully concluding its first wave with *(I Can't Get No) Satisfaction* in 1965. History must surely pay tribute to Oldham for achieving so much over so short a period, his marketing flair being supported from the outset by an eye for a saleable product whose quality would further improve with time.

After four decades as world superstars, the Stones' longevity remains one of the ongoing phenomena of rock music. Unlike their supposed arch rivals the Beatles, the Stones survived not only beyond the 60s but beyond the millennium. This said, the Stones tended to come off second best in marketing wars with Liverpool. The *Aftermath* album of 1966 was at least partly overshadowed by the release of *Revolver*, while the initially lukewarm reception for *Their Satanic Majesties Request* (1967) was hardly alleviated by the euphoria that surrounded *Sgt. Pepper*. But the Stones never lost their capacity to attract new followers, the 'lips and tongue' icon from their own record label adorning many a school bag in the early 70s. It was their departure from Decca in 1970 that led to the globally revered *Cocksucker Blues*, a 'contractual obligation' song that Decca refused to release and were never expected to. The offending title was later reused in a documentary film directed by Robert Frank (b.1924), chronicling the Stones' 1972 North American tour.

Throughout their history, a regular diet of wild living and occasional brushes with the law has kept the Stones in the headlines, while a consistent output of high-octane mainstream rock has ensured their credibility as musicians remains unassailable. The murky business of Jones' death by drowning at Cotchford Farm in Sussex (Jones' country retreat and the former residence of *Winnie The Pooh* creator A.A. Milne) remains to this day a favorite topic of investigative reporters and has, if anything, added to the mystique that surrounds the band. Jones' replacement, Mick Taylor (b.1948), sounded the part but never looked quite right, even though his six year tenure earned him credits on such important middle-period albums as *Let It Bleed, Exile On Main Street* and *Goat's Head Soup*.

After Taylor announced his departure in December 1974, Ronnie Wood (b.1947) from the Faces was widely tipped for the job and duly appointed. A quality rock guitarist of the old school, whose strength lies in solid and imaginative fills rather than lengthy fret-burning solos, Wood was an obvious co-driver for the similarly inclined Richards.

The only regrettable outcome of Wood's high-flying new career was that it effectively meant the end for the Faces who, having risen from the ashes of the Small Faces minus lead singer/guitarist Steve Marriott (1947–1991), enjoy a unique position in British rock history as possibly the nation's greatest ever good-time pub band. Anyone who understandably denigrates the ensuing glitzy showbiz career of the Faces' inimitable lead singer Rod Stewart (b.1945) should listen again to such classic 70s vinyl as *Stay With Me, Pool Hall Richard* and *You Can Make Me Dance Sing or Anything*. Hidden beneath this last song was the splendidly ironic group 'composition' *As Long As You Tell Him*, one of the most engaging makeshift B-sides of all time.

If ever a rock band became an institution it was the Rolling Stones. Even the potential stigma of Jagger's knighthood (2003) was preempted by a successful paternity suit issued by the Brazilian model Luciana Gimenez Morad (b.1969), an episode both admired and envied by Jagger's fellow sexagenarians.

The Stones were by no means the only success story of the R&B boom. Traveling to London from the banks of the Tyne in 1964, the Animals, fronted by singer Eric Burdon (b.1941) but centered on the keyboard skills of Alan Price (b.1942), was possibly the only band from the Northeast to achieve national recognition before the emergence of the folk-driven Lindisfarne in the early 70s. Presenting material drawn from mostly American sources, including soul pioneer Sam Cooke (1931–1964), the Animals achieved immortality with Price's arrangement of the traditional *House Of The Rising Sun,* featuring the most copied guitar riff until *Stairway To Heaven* burst on the scene a decade later. Performed by a youthful Hilton Valentine (b.1943), this simple but compelling arpeggio figure provided a fixed framework for Burdon's powerful vocal and Price's central organ solo. A future collaborator with Price was the Lancastrian singer and keyboard player Georgie Fame (b.1943, real name: Clive Powell), whose residency at the Flamingo attracted a cult following for his unique and extrovert brand of R&B.

An outfit who seemed poised to emulate the success of the Stones and even deputized for them at the Crawdaddy was the Yardbirds. Built around the voice and harmonica of Keith Relf (1943–1976), the Yardbirds boast the remarkable distinction of having had (in chronological order) the mighty triumvirate of Eric Clapton, Jeff Beck and Jimmy Page as lead guitarist. Commercial success did not elude them, *For Your Love,*

Heart Full of Soul and the double A-side *Evil Hearted You/Still I'm Sad* all reaching the UK Top Ten in 1965.

But it was not to last: the band's high profile members all had plans for the future that did not include being a Yardbird. Even so, their short catalog of hit singles has worn better than those of many of their contemporaries, a somewhat desperate attempt to keep the ball rolling by collaborating with hit manufacturer Mickie Most (1938–2003, real name: Michael Peter Hayes) being best forgotten out of respect for an esteemed and influential band.

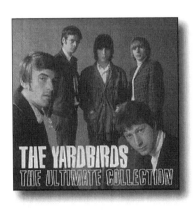

The remaining products of R&B tended to be less high profile. Chris Farlowe (b.1940, real name: John Deighton), leader of the Thunderbirds, who reached UK No.1 in 1966 with a heavily orchestrated version of Jagger and Richards' *Out Of Time*, was one of relatively few to achieve chart success. Others, sporting such classic period names as the Dowliners Sect and Zoot Money's Big Roll Band, relied more on their secure reputations as live acts.

A postscript to the decline of R&B in the mid-60s was the mini blues boom, piloted by the much discussed team of John Mayall's Bluesbreakers. Perceived as something of a retro figure even at the time, Mayall (b.1933) nonetheless provided a testing ground for the first wave of British guitarists who could compete on equal terms with American legends whose surname was usually King (Albert, Freddy and, of course, B.B.). The Bluesbreakers' LPs may seem dryly fundamentalist to the twenty-first century ear, but the historical significance of a band that played host to guitarists Eric Clapton, Peter Green and Mick Taylor, not to mention drummers Mick Fleetwood and Aynsley Dunbar and, briefly, bass player Jack Bruce, can scarcely be overstated. And before all these future luminaries came along, Mayall's lead guitarist was the youthful Bernie Watson (b.1949, according to one usually reliable source). This was apparently the same Bernie Watson who had served his apprenticeship as one of the Savages, backing group to the unique and ultimately tragic extrovert eccentric Screaming Lord Sutch (1940–1999, real name: David Edward Sutch). Watson is widely believed to have rebranded himself in the 70s as Bernard Watson, classical guitarist with the Omega Quartet.

But as London's nightlife reverberated to indigenous interpretations of America's musical heritage, a related but distinctly British sound was emerging from a maritime city near the top left-hand corner of England…

Liverpool and London

The port of Liverpool lies on the Lancashire coast, 35 miles west of Manchester. Skirting the south and west boundaries of Liverpool is the gaping estuary of the Mersey, opening into the Irish Sea. In sport, industry and culture, Liverpool and Manchester have been both partners and rivals. Since the Industrial Revolution, communications between the two cities have become advanced and efficient. As early as 1760, work had started in Manchester on the Bridgewater Canal, which eventually connected the two cities via its link to the Leeds and Liverpool Canal. Co-operation was further enhanced by the growth of the railway network, although the opening of the Manchester Ship Canal in 1894, making the city an inland port, went someway towards reducing Liverpool's role in the trading infrastructure. Nowadays, it is possible to drive from central Manchester to the suburbs of Liverpool in less than 30 minutes on the M62 motorway, one of the most heavily used British roads outside London.

Strange, then, that other Lancastrians still seem to regard the natives of Merseyside as a somewhat exotic species, and that Liverpool's 'scouse' accent remains such a distinctive mode of speech, even in the twenty-first century. Shared only by the inhabitants of the Wirral peninsula on the opposite side of the Mersey, this lyrical mix of Lancastrian and Irish, the latter component being drawn from Liverpool's large immigrant community, can be distinguished from the Mancunian brogue within the first few syllables. In stark contrast to this, it would surely require one of

Professor Higgins' most gifted students to spot a corresponding distinction between the speech patterns of a genuine Cockney (i.e. someone born and raised in London, within the sound of Bow Bells) and those of a speaker from a similar socio-economic background raised 35 miles away. Even the term 'scouse', which refers to a type of stew or 'hotpot' (with or without meat, depending on the budget), remains unique to Merseyside, although similar dishes exist throughout Lancashire and Yorkshire.

All this might go some way towards providing a reason why the whole Merseybeat phenomenon could be confined to just one city within a densely populated region of such a small island. Needless to say, Manchester had its own music scene in the 60s and would enjoy its time in the spotlight two decades later. But the environment into which John Lennon (1940–1980), Paul McCartney (b.1942), George Harrison (1943–2001) and Richard Starkey (b.1940, soon to become Ringo Starr) emerged was as specific to Merseyside as the way in which they spoke.

From the earliest recorded encounter between John Lennon and Paul McCartney, which took place after a skiffle group calling themselves the Quarrymen had performed at the Woolton church fête in July 1957 (Lennon was rhythm guitarist, McCartney a member of the public), every date and detail of Beatle history has been scrupulously documented. Their apprenticeship in the nightclubs of Hamburg, with bass player Stuart Sutcliffe (1940–1962) and drummer Pete Best (b.1941), and their residency at Liverpool's Cavern Club have been picked over in the minutest detail, as have Sutcliffe's death at the age of 21 and the controversial dismissal of Best in favor of Starkey. Responsibility for the dismissal is often placed at the door of manager Brian Epstein (1934–1967), although debate continues to this day.

What matters is that, when they signed with producer George Martin (b.1926, knighted 1996, often referred to as the 'fifth Beatle') at EMI/Parlophone in June 1962, having been famously rejected by Dick Rowe at Decca, the Beatles were a fully professional team, whose reliable but by no means exceptional performing skills provided a secure outlet for what was to prove an unequaled songwriting partnership of their two leading members. They also had an image that was more conventionally photogenic than the creatures emerging from the R&B clubs, the buttoned-up suits and comic strip haircuts being developed from creative input widely credited to Epstein, although it has been suggested that an earlier stylistic influence was Sutcliffe's arty German girlfriend, Astrid Kirchher (or Kirchherr) (b.1938).

Unlike the Rolling Stones, they went straight in with an original song (notwithstanding the unfortunate but now highly collectable *My Bonny* with Tony Sheridan from January 1962), *Love Me Do* by Lennon and McCartney achieving a UK No.17 in autumn 1962. The self-penned follow-up *Please Please Me* from January 1963 reached No.2 and, three months later, *From Me To You* made it to the top, as did every UK Parlophone single until the double A-side *Penny Lane/Strawberry Fields Forever* (No.2, 1967).

Their debut LP, also titled *Please Please Me*, was a mainly Lennon and McCartney platform, although some titles (e.g. *Twist and Shout*, a Rock & Roll derivative of the traditional *La Bamba*) were drawn from other sources. Subsequent albums, like the singles, sold in ever-increasing numbers. *With The Beatles* from late 1963 was released amid the build-up to their conquering of the States in February 1964, while *A Hard Day's*

Night from later that year marked their movie debut. Although an obvious cashing in on the band's seemingly unlimited earning potential, this imaginative portrayal of 'life as pop stars', directed by Richard Lester, made it a rather more highly regarded exercise than the earlier celluloid offerings of Elvis Presley et al.

As success followed success with *Beatles For Sale, Help!, Rubber Soul* and *Revolver,* the band reached what many regard as their masterpiece with *Sergeant Pepper's Lonely Hearts Club Band* in 1967. Not so much a concept album as a collection of songs framed by the *Sergeant Pepper* theme, the cover design by Peter Blake (b.1932, knighted 2002) alone guaranteed classic status. That surreal group photograph is still instantly recognized by almost anyone in the western world, the band resplendent in garish military uniforms reminiscent of the colorful Victorian characters on a tin of *Quality Street* chocolates.

The satirical mind of Frank Zappa soon spotted the potential for ridicule. His 1967 album *We're Only In It For The Money* (with the Mothers of Invention) showed a similar cover shot with the man himself, complete with imperial mustache, dressed in a girly frock. The following year, Zappa's occasional collaborator Captain Beefheart (b.1941, real name: Don Van Vliet, originally Don Glen Vliet) took a swipe at both Britain's top-earning musical exports with *Beatle Bones 'n' Smokin' Stones* from the album *Strictly Personal*.

The songwriting excellence and innovatory studio sounds of *Sergeant Pepper* are beyond question, although it is perhaps wise not to be too reverential towards an album that contains such lightweight offerings as the mock-retro *When I'm Sixty-Four* and the token 'Ringo vocal' *With A Little Help From My Friends*. The latter provided raw material for the manic cover version by Joe Cocker (b.1944, real name: John Robert Cocker), which remains one of the great hard rock parodies of all time, complete with a scorching guitar fill provided by the ubiquitous Jimmy Page (see Chapter 8).

From *Sergeant Pepper* onwards, tensions within the group became the subject of endless speculation. Even so, the songs kept on coming, albeit in packages of ever-increasing stylistic diversity or wayward inconsistency, depending on your point of view. The 1968 two LP set known thereafter as the *White Album* featured the cheery *Ob-La-Di Ob-La-Da* (UK No.1 for the Marmalade in 1968) alongside the wannabe *musique concrète* of *Revolution No.9,* a track that, following the advent of the programmable CD player, probably no longer gets played at all.

In the meantime, there had been the disappointing launch of the record label and Beatle umbrella organization Apple Corps, whose first signings included such minor catches as Mary Hopkin (b.1950), a recent winner on the TV talent show *Opportunity Knocks*, and the decent but dull Badfinger, led by the tragic and now largely forgotten figure of Peter Ham (1947–1975). And then there was the widely reported internecine conflict caused by the presence in the studio of Lennon's newly acquired cosmic soulmate Yoko Ono (b.1933), not to mention the band's much publicized period of inner reflection with the dubious guru Maharishi Mahesh Yogi (1918–2008). Never had *Private Eye* magazine's imaginary 'popular singing group' Spiggy Topes and the Turds been blessed with so much embarrassing material to satirize.

In the final days, things had reached such a state that the last two albums, *Abbey Road* and *Let It Be* were released in what was effectively counter-chronological order. Even then, the songwriting still shone through, although it could be said that it was mainly Harrison's contributions *Something* and *Here Comes The Sun* that saved the quality control on *Abbey Road*. But *Let It Be* miraculously came up trumps with the noble and contemplative title track, plus the controversial production by Phil Spector (b.1940) of *The Long And Winding Road,* loathed by some (including McCartney) but seen by others as one of the most inspirational swan songs any band ever released.

It was perhaps fitting that this Rolls Royce of pop groups should announce their final exit in the early spring of 1970, the dawn of the decade when rock and pop would at last go their separate ways. All four members went on to enjoy solo successes, Lennon and Harrison retaining the most credibility with rock audiences. As expected, McCartney's career has proved the most lucrative commercially. His 1997 knighthood has made him part of an ennobled rock triumvirate with Sir Cliff Richard and Sir Mick Jagger, McCartney being widely perceived nowadays as closer in spirit to the former than the latter. His career with the group Wings was long and productive, although the 1972 hit *Mary Had A Little Lamb* brought McCartney and his new team perilously close to exhausting what little patience remained within audiences of high school age and above.

Lennon struck gold almost immediately with the nihilistic title track of his 1971 album *Imagine*, some believing the lyrics to be describing a post-hippie utopia. *How Do You Sleep?*, an anti-McCartney rant from the same album, drew widespread approval from his former partner's disenchanted followers. His marriage to Yoko Ono proved to be for keeps, the sincere love song *Woman* providing a touching posthumous No.1 following Lennon's violent death at the hands of a crazed fan in December 1980.

Harrison's post-Beatle career soon made the headlines with the plagiarism scandal and ensuing legal drama surrounding the hit single *My Sweet Lord*. With hindsight, the song's melodic, rhythmic and harmonic resemblance to the US hit *He's So Fine* by the Chiffons, composed in 1962 by Ronnie Mack (not to be confused with the leader of Ronnie Mack and the Black Slacks) seems even more obvious than that of *Sweet Little Sixteen* to *Surfin' USA*, although it took many years of courtroom wrangling before this was officially acknowledged.

Harrison's status as a solo artist was established immediately after the demise of the Beatles with the 1970 triple album *All Things Must Pass*, still seen by many as his masterpiece. He was also the driving force behind the *Concert for Bangladesh* that took place at New York's Madison Square Gardens on 1 August 1971. A significant precursor to such charitable rock extravaganzas as Bob Geldof's *Live Aid*, the event also provided a valuable insight into the current state of relations among the former Beatles. Harrison's invitation for McCartney to take part was turned down flat. Lennon accepted, but then walked out over Harrison's stipulation that Yoko was not to appear on stage. Needless to say, the ever-affable Ringo readily agreed to perform. Other artists who said yes included Eric Clapton, Bob Dylan, Leon Russell and Ravi Shankar.

Always respected but not always highly productive in his later solo career, Harrison went on to enjoy occasional outings as a celebrity guest performer and was a founding member of 'rock oldies' outfit the Traveling Wilburys, together with Jeff Lynne, Tom Petty, Roy Orbison and Bob Dylan. His death from cancer at the age of 58 robbed popular music worldwide of one of its most valued elder statesmen.

The oft-quoted comment that Ringo would continue to prosper by 'just being Ringo' proved accurate. After a modest catalog of hit singles in the early 70s, he reinvented himself as narrator on the massively successful children's TV series *Thomas The Tank Engine,* an oeuvre that some hold in higher esteem than many of McCartney's post-70 offerings.

The bright and breezy synthesis of Rock & Roll, R&B and post-50s pop that made the Beatles such an instant success was just part of a whole Merseyside culture that embraced numerous other exponents. Several enjoyed national success in their own right, Billy J. Kramer and the Dakotas (a Liverpool singer with a Manchester backing band, brought together by Epstein), the Searchers and Gerry and the Pacemakers all achieving UK chart hits. Of these, *Ferry 'Cross The Mersey* by Gerry and the Pacemakers became an anthem of the times, as did *You'll Never Walk Alone,* which the band lifted from the musical *Carousel* in 1963 and has been communally sung on the soccer terraces of Liverpool ever since. No Merseyside band apart from the Beatles was destined for lasting stardom, although several still remain on the road, meeting a limited but regular demand from people who were there at the time and others who wish they had been.

Elsewhere in the country, British music continued to dominate the scene as new talents entered the business. Brian Poole and the Tremeloes (sic), who secured the Decca contract the Beatles had missed, enjoyed a long line of hits from 1963 with their straightforward brand of unpretentious pop. After Poole's retirement, the band made the decision to go it alone from 1967, starting with *Here Comes My Baby* followed by *Silence Is Golden,* originally a US B-side for the Four Seasons. The first song was penned by the London born singer/songwriter Cat Stevens (b.1948, real name: Stephen Demetre Georgiou, later known as Yusuf Islam). A quirky but often compelling talent, Stevens enjoyed a run of successful singles and albums through the late 60s and early 70s. Particularly memorable were the gossamer musical textures of the 1970 hit *Lady D'Arbanville*, a spectral portrayal of Stevens' then girlfriend, the actress Patti D'Arbanville (b.1951). His religious conversion in 1977 precipitated a withdrawal from the music scene, although he has been involved in a number of relatively low profile projects from the mid-80s onwards. For the Tremeloes, the hits dried up after 1971, but regular gigs on the 60s nostalgia circuit kept them afloat for many years to come.

One of the more sophisticated bands of the era was the Zombies, who entered the UK charts with *She's Not There* in the summer of 1964. Reaching US No.2 later the same year, this was to be their only major international hit, although the *Odyssey and Oracle* album from 1968 still enjoys a cult following. Rod Argent (b.1945), the band's keyboard player and co-writer of *She's Not There,* found a second wave of popularity with his self-named prog-rock band in the 70s.

From Northern Ireland came Them, who had Top Ten hits with *Baby Please Don't Go* and *Here Comes The Night* in 1965. Lead singer Van Morrison (b.1945) left in 1966, entering the US charts with *Brown Eyed Girl* two years later. Morrison's long career as a singer/songwriter continues to attract favorable reviews.

A band often referred to as 'the groups' group' was the Hollies. Amid their two dozen 60s hits lies the charming curiosity of *Carrie Anne,*

possibly the first pop record in which the spot usually reserved for the guitar solo is hijacked by Caribbean steel drums. Unlike many of their contemporaries, the Hollies enjoyed a second wind in the 70s, their stylish account of the Albert Hammond song *The Air That I Breathe* reaching UK No.2 in 1974. Born in London in 1944 but raised in Gibraltar before moving to the States, Hammond is a bilingual (English/Spanish) singer/songwriter. He seemed to spend the early 70s on the brink of wider recognition, especially following the chart success of his joyous celebration of misspent youth *Free Electric Band*. Hammond's best known song, *It Never Rains in Southern California* is globally celebrated for the unforgettable rhyming couplet 'It never rains in California, but gurl don't they warn ya'.

Although there was no identifiable genre that might be termed the 'Thames sound', London would soon offer a powerful response to events in Liverpool. In summer 1964, the UK No.1 slot was occupied by a gritty R&B derived song titled *You Really Got Me*. The band was the Kinks and their leader and principal songwriter Ray Davies (b.1944) was different from anything pop music had turned out so far. Despite the song's no-frills approach and urgent beat, Davies delivered the vocal line with a refinement bordering on urbanity. Although his upbringing in the North London district of Muswell Hill had enjoyed only modest prosperity, Davies from the outset came over as the sophisticated man-about-town.

As much a scriptwriter as a composer, he would often present a song 'in character', the upper class idler in the 1966 No.1 *Sunny Afternoon* being one of his most enduring creations. A memorable feature of *You Really Got Me* was the guitar solo, one of the wildest of the era. Few were surprised when rumors started to spread that the guitarist was an incognito Jimmy Page, rather than the band's 'official' lead guitarist, Dave Davies, younger brother of Ray. The follow-up single, *All Day And All Of The Night,* contained a similarly raw and uncompromising flurry of licks, suggesting that either Page had joined the Kinks' permanent payroll, or that the 17-year-old Dave Davies was a remarkably quick learner.

The Kinks were destined to survive well beyond the decade, although the burly transvestite *Lola* from 1970 was to be the last Davies character to enter the national consciousness. But their 60s work ranks amongst the most imaginative of its time, *Waterloo Sunset* from 1967 positively tasting of London at twilight, its everyman figures of Terry and Julie living and breathing forever.

While the Kinks introduced literary characterization into the established boundaries of rock and pop, another London band was taking instrumental virtuosity and musical form to unprecedented heights...

THE WHO

One of the later products of London's R&B venues, notably the Marquee, the quartet of Roger Daltrey (b.1944) (lead vocal), Pete Townshend (b.1945) (guitar), John Entwistle (1944–2002) (bass) and Keith Moon (1946–1978) (drums) became the most prominent and enduring musical force to be associated with the original 60s incarnation of the Mod movement. Apart from the later arrival of Moon, the line-up had been stable since 1962, when the band participated in the death throes of skiffle as the Detours. The name was first changed to the Who soon after, although they later became the High Numbers for a short time at the suggestion of manager Peter Meaden. It was as the High Numbers that they cut their first single, the Slim Harpo-derived *I'm The Face*. Even though Meaden is said to have attempted a chart-fiddle by purchasing 500 copies himself, the single failed to break and Meaden made his exit. The vacancy was filled by the highly regarded team of Kit Lambert and Chris Stamp, both of whom were film directors, originally in search of a group to appear in a movie.

It was around this time that Moon came on the scene and created the first chapter in the long-running saga of 'Moon Mythology' by joining the band on stage after a gig to inform them that their existing drummer Dougie Sandon was 'crap'. The story goes that Moon was wearing an orange suit at the time, and proceeded to demolish the band's drum kit while advising them that he could do Sandon's job better. An informal audition revealed that Moon, a pupil of Screaming Lord Sutch's drummer Carlo Little (1938–2005, real name: Carl O'Neil Little), appeared to have a valid point and was duly hired. A percussionist of outstanding strength and precision, Moon soon became established as the archetypal hotel-trashing rock millionaire. His death in 1978 from an overdose of prescription drugs to curb his alcohol intake robbed the business of a true larger than life character, whose 'Rolls Royce in the swimming pool' lifestyle became at least as famous as his world-class talent as a musician.

This inevitably leads to the hazardous existence of Townshend's guitars, which also stems from an incident in the early days. An accidental collision between his guitar neck and the low ceiling at the Marquee reportedly caused an incandescent Towshend to smash the instrument on stage, while the easily encouraged Moon enthusiastically hastened the demise of his current percussion apparatus. Although many still take a dim view of these profligate and subsequently much imitated antics, it proved an effective means of the Who grabbing the headlines at a time when the richest pickings were becoming the exclusive domain of the Beatles and the Stones.

But no lasting career can be built on gimmicks alone, even the horror movie stage paraphernalia of Screamin' Jay Hawkins (1929–2000) being nothing more than extravagant packaging for a genuine vocal talent. Ironically, there can be little doubt that Hawkins was one of the chief inspirations behind Screaming Lord Sutch, who uniquely managed to forge a successful early career from a combination of Hawkins-like visuals and conspicuous lack of any discernible vocal talent. Although Sutch never lost contact with the music industry, his activities from the mid-60s onwards became increasingly centered on flamboyant fringe politics, culminating in the nationally celebrated Official Monster Raving Loony Party. Unsurprisingly, the MRLP has never been within striking distance of election victory, although it seems clear that they hastened the decline of the short-lived Social Democratic Party by polling more votes in the 1990 Bootle by-election than the SDP candidate. In the light of this unequivocal endorsement, Sutch gleefully contacted SDP leader Dr. David Owen, a former foreign secretary in James Callaghan's Labour government during the late 70s, offering to form a coalition. From the Who's first chart successes in 1965 with *I Can't Explain* and *Anyway Anyhow Anywhere,* it was clear that Townshend, who provided virtually all their original material from the outset, was a songwriter of exceptional skill and imagination. Equally apparent were the band's individual and combined instrumental abilities, an area in which they were soon perceived to be ahead of the Beatles and at least on a par with the Stones. Both these qualities reached an early highpoint with their third success, *My Generation* from November 1965, in which Entwistle's featured bass part was one of the most virtuosic on any hit record of the time. This song also became the band's permanent stage anthem and a defining statement of the era, the line 'Hope I die before I get old' being rock music's first major rent-a-quote.

Their debut album, also titled *My Generation,* is considered by many to have been an only partially successful rush-release in the wake of the title track's success, but the constant flow of hit singles found Townshend's work reaching new heights. The tunes remained bright and catchy, *My Generation* being the most musically 'dark' of their early hits, but Townshend's subject matter became increasingly adventurous. *I'm A Boy* from September 1966 gave a disturbing account of a 'mixed-up' childhood, originally to have formed part of an early Towshend rock opera titled *Quads*, while *Pictures Of Lily* less than a year later told candidly of the physical and emotional needs of male adolescence. The heroine of the song was apparently the actress and royal mistress Lillie Langtry (1853–1929, née Emilie Charlotte Le Breton), the obvious clue coming in the line 'She's been dead since 1929'. Interestingly, one of the female characters Townshend created in *I'm a Boy* bears the unusual Anglo-French feminine name of Jean Marie. In 1881, Lillie Langtry, by now married to the Irish landowner Edward Langtry, gave birth to a daughter whom she named using the French feminine form Jeanne Marie. The child's biological father is widely believed to have been Prince Louis of Battenberg (1854–1921).

The second album, *A Quick One* from 1966, represented a significant advance insofar as the title track *A Quick One While He's Away* was a nine-minute 'mini opera', paving the way for such ambitious Townshend ventures as *Tommy* (1969) and *Quadrophenia* (1973). The whole concept of the rock opera will forever be steeped in controversy, the question of whether or not the use of 'classical' forms in rock music is either viable or even desirable being a recurring topic of debate for the remainder of the 60s and more so during the 70s. But the very scale of *A Quick One* showed that the days of the album as a collection of singles, B-sides and fillers were numbered. In fact, the Who would be one of the last major rock bands whose initial success had been founded largely on the singles chart.

Even at the outset, the extended album track was by no means unique to Townshend, although other examples came mainly from the States. In 1967, the Velvet Underground devoted 18 minutes of *White Light/White Heat* to the depraved scenario of *Sister Ray,* while in the same year an equally large segment of *Da Capo* by Love was taken up by the sprawling jam *Revelation.* The following year, US psychedelic rock pioneers Iron Butterfly released their magnum opus *In-A-Gadda-Da-Vida*, complete with its much discussed 17 minute title track. Less extravagant but still significant due to its scale was Bob Dylan's exquisite *Sad Eyed Lady Of The Lowlands,* a conventionally structured song whose elaborate imagery occupied the last 10'45" of *Blonde On Blonde* in 1966. Perhaps most significant of all, the Doors concluded their self-titled 1967 debut album with almost 12 minutes of *The End,* complete with a hypnotic quasi-Indian guitar fill and a watered-down version of the spoken Oedipal scene that, when performed unexpurgated, had lost the band an early resident gig.

The days when all that teenagers had to worry about was the occasional motorcycle fatality seemed long gone. As long as there were teenagers, the boy-meets-girl narrative would inevitably survive, but this was clearly no longer the sole topic on offer from their musical icons.

As the 60s drew to a close, the Who consolidated their status as a major international force. Their appearance at Monterey in 1967 made a lasting mark on the US psyche, partly due to their decision to take the stage apart before a puzzled audience composed largely of peace-loving flower children. By the time they got to Woodstock in 1969, their legend was such that the crowd would probably have been disappointed not to have witnessed a scene of destruction.

On the home front, the *Tommy* album from 1969 provided the core material for innumerable live shows, movies, orchestrations and both professional and amateur productions, *Pinball Wizard* becoming their best-known song since *My Generation.* After the definitive *Live At*

Leeds in 1970, the next decade found them fully established as one of that elite class of 'stadium' bands, whose earning power was such that most buildings with roofs no longer had enough floor space to cover the costs. But after *Who's Next* from 1971, home of the magnificent *Don't Get Fooled Again,* their recorded output often became competent rather than inspired, *Quadophenia* from 1973 being arguably their last important release.

Past glories ensured their crowd-pulling capacity remained undiminished, Kenny Jones (b.1948), formerly of the Faces, replacing the much lamented Moon. The live album *Who's Last* from 1984 may have suggested the end was nigh, although a reunion for *Live Aid* in 1985 paved the way for more of the same. The death of Entwistle while about to embark on a US tour with the Who in 2002 was at the time perceived as the final paragraph of the closing chapter, his sudden exit following a heart attack at the Las Vegas Hard Rock Hotel, in the company of a known groupie, being a poignant yet undeniably fitting coda to the story of one of rock's truly great teams.

But the Who survived. For the much heralded world tour of 2006-7, Entwistle's place was taken by Welsh born bass player Pino Palladino (b.1957), the drum stool occupied by Zak Starkey (b.1965), son of Ringo Starr.

As British music enjoyed its brief 60s heyday of world dominance, America was finding its own new directions. Soul music, a fresh amalgam of jazz, gospel, blues and rock created almost exclusively by black artists, had grown from the start of the decade. The Detroit based Tamla Motown label owned by Berry Gordy Jr. (b.1929) emerged as a dominant force, its distinctive studio sound enhancing numerous hit records. Meanwhile, white producer Phil Spector had pioneered the near-symphonic 'wall of sound' technique, his roster of female vocal groups providing the first commercial outlet for a creative talent that led to future collaborations with artists as diverse as the Beatles, Leonard Cohen and the Ramones.

Country music retained its following both at home and abroad, with new and enigmatic figures such as Johnny Cash (1932–2003) taking the place of the sober placidity of Jim Reeves (1923–1964). A bridge between country and pop was created by former Sam Phillips protégé Roy Orbison (1936–1988), whose British success was such that his 1963 UK tour saw him billed above the Beatles.

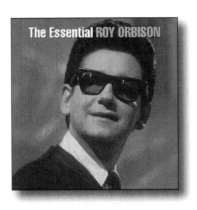

As all these lineages continued to follow their separate courses, America was set to join forces with Britain in shaping the foundations of what was to become the vintage years of rock...

— 6 —

Early Maturity – America from 1967

Ever since the days of *Blackboard Jungle,* rock's ethos had been anti-school and, by extension, dismissive of the mainstream Western culture it taught. Apart from novelty singer Herbert Khaury's decision to dub himself 'Tiny Tim', references to English literature in popular music were far from common, while appreciation of the visual arts had rarely ventured beyond the 1959 reworking of the Nat 'King' Cole standard *Mona Lisa* by Conway Twitty (1933–1993, real name: Harold Lloyd Jenkins). Of the 50s and early 60s musicians involved in the nefarious practice of reading books, only those who wrote protest songs were likely to admit it.

In 1965, a New York band formerly known as both the Warlocks (an early collective title also used by the Grateful Dead) and the Falling Spikes adopted a name taken from Michael Leigh's then largely unknown 1963 study of taboo sexual practices in contemporary America. The Velvet Underground, as the Warlocks/Falling Spikes became, broke further new ground by their association with the fashionable experimental artist Andy Warhol (Warhola) (1928–1987), whose 'banana on a plain white background' design for their debut album still remains the most recognizable 60s LP cover apart from *Sergeant Pepper.* Fronted by the charismatic and slightly camp figure of Lou Reed (b.1942), the band further emphasized their fascination with S&M in the song *Venus in Furs,* a celebration of the 1870 novel by Leopold von Sacher Masoch.

A band like no other of the time, the Velvet Underground was built around Reed's songwriting and the instrumental skills of John Cale (b.1942). Both enjoyed solo success from the 70s onwards, Cale as a pioneering figure in rock's *avant garde,* Reed as a thinking man's chart act with *Walk On The Wild Side* from the *Transformer* album of 1972. Guitarist Sterling Morrison (1942–1995) and drummer Maureen 'Mo' Tucker (b.1944) vanished following the break-up of the band at the start of the 70s, although both re-emerged for a brief reunion in 1993.

Also on the first album, produced by Warhol, was the German actress and model Nico (1938–1988, real name Christa Päffgen), the full album title being *The Velvet Underground and Nico.* Despite her limited musical experience, Nico proved a shrewd addition on Warhol's part. Billed on the album as 'chanteuse', while other members of the band merely did 'vocals', Nico's rich Teutonic contralto created an underground cabaret atmosphere which did much to enhance the band's already arty image. In her subsequent solo career, Nico became a cult icon of 'gothic weird', her albums *The Marble Index* (1969) and *Drama Of Exile* (1981) being particularly powerful testimonies to the enduring appeal of one of rock music's most remarkable one-offs.

Despite its inconsistency of both content and sound quality, *The Velvet Underground and Nico* was to be arguably their finest recorded offering. Uncompromising lyrics, such as *Heroin* and *Waiting For The*

Man, gave graphic accounts of the harsh realities of drug culture (a long way from the somewhat irresponsible 'marmalade skies' imagery being projected by the Beatles and others), while *Sunday Morning* showed Reed's capacity to create simple yet genuinely inspired three-minute pop songs.

By the time of the follow-up *White Light/White Heat,* Nico had departed to pursue solo ventures and the remaining members were relying increasingly on the support of a dwindling fringe audience. Three decades down the line, *Sister Ray* remains an arduous and not particularly rewarding listen.

With Cale out of the team after *White Light/White Heat,* two more 'official' albums would follow before the customary post-split deluge of live material and out-takes. Even in the final years, the band would occasionally hit the spot, Reed's *Sweet Jane* from the valedictory *Loaded* (1970) being one of his best known pre-*Transformer* songs.

One of rock's most powerful 'what if…' questions is that of how things might have been if Verve had released *The Velvet Underground And Nico* just before rather than just after a vital new album on the Elektra label, featuring a band from the opposite side of the nation…

THE DOORS

As a jazz-tinged drum fill from John Densmore announced the unforget-table opening riff to *Break On Through,* waiting in the wings was a voice that, possibly more than any other, would define the era. A Florida born UCLA film student who had come to music through a series of chance meetings, Jim Morrison (1943–1971) was rock's next major literary figure after Bob Dylan. In some ways, the two personalities displayed opposing attributes. If Dylan had made his mark despite limited stage charisma, unprepossessing looks and a less than alluring vocal quality, Morrison drew his audience by having all three qualities in abundance. This is not to suggest that Morrison was an outstanding singer in the technical sense, although both the pitch and the diction on his recorded performances are far better than many give him credit for. These qualities are especially notable since the received wisdom is that he was rarely sober in the studio, at least not until producer Paul Rothchild (1935–1995) took things in hand. But Morrison's brooding all-American baritone could convey a mood without rising above a murmur, his capacity to build up to a controlled scream being one he would use frequently, but only when necessary.

It was not necessary on *Break On Through,* the first track on the first album having made its point subtly but unmistakeably in just over two minutes. This was one of several tracks from *The Doors* (released January 1967) that became a permanent part of the band's live set. With organist Ray Manzarek (b.1939), guitarist Robby Krieger (b.1946) and Densmore (b.1944) on drums, the band's keyboard centered arrangements provided a distinctive yet unobtrusive backdrop for Morrison's magnetic personality. Unusually, the band never had a permanent bass player, the lower register in live performances provided by Manzarek's 'left hand only' second keyboard.

Also on the debut album was the full six minute version of the band's most famous song *Light My Fire,* complete with Krieger's intricate and original guitar break. Omitted from the single edit in favor of Manzarek's organ solo, this was early evidence of the abilities of one of the era's most underrated instrumentalists. Perhaps uniquely for his time, Krieger was a rock guitarist also skilled in flamenco, as revealed in the intro to *Spanish Caravan* from *Waiting For The Sun* (1968), in which over-dubbed flamenco guitars build up to an extended quote from *Asturias* by the Spanish composer and pianist, Isaac Albéniz (1860–1909). Coincidentally, a truly inspired cover of *Light My Fire* became a UK hit for the blind Puerto Rican guitarist José Feliciano (b.1945) in autumn 1968. Different from and yet always respectful of the original, Feliciano's version featured an all-time great acoustic solo on a nylon-strung guitar of the flamenco type.

But amid the mild eroticism of *Light My Fire,* the delicate sensuality of *The Crystal Ship* and the bad-boy R&B of the Willie Dixon classic *Back Door Man,* the track that made *The Doors* such a historic release was that most theatrical of rock anthems *The End.* To describe it as a song does not really tell the story, its true genre being more an experimental performance piece that seemingly starts as a lament for the end of a relationship but then grows into a labyrinthine exploration of the singer/narrator's darkest thoughts and memories. The imagery is often obscure and interpretations vary. Some understand the 'blue bus' that is 'calling us' as being merely a reference to a particular LA service that took fun-loving teens to the beach and would therefore be well-known to Morrison's local audience. Others read deep mythological meanings into the line, a favorite being that it refers to the vessel transporting the souls of the dead across the River Styx. It certainly seems unlikely that Morrison would need to portentously ask 'Driver, where you takin' us?' if they were only heading for the nearest sand and sun.

But there is no doubt what is being alluded to in the Oedipal scene. Morrison's tortured relationship with his own parents had already resulted in his public claim that they were dead, when in fact both would outlive their estranged son. On the studio recording, the last two words of the line starting 'Mother, I want to…' emerged as a strategically placed Morrison scream, although Elektra eventually released the song unexpurgated on various live compilations after Morrison's death. But the song was conspicuously absent from the otherwise representative 1970 double album *Absolutely Live.* This album also included, for the first time, the complete *Celebration Of The Lizard,* an extended sequence of music and spoken text exploring the character of Morrison's much discussed alter ego, the *Lizard King.*

Until the arrival of the Doors, heavyweight literary analysis in rock would mostly have been considered both inappropriate and unforgivably pretentious, even though many future undergraduates and postgraduates majored in Dylan. But with the Doors, such investigations are often desirable and sometimes essential. Even the band's name was a reference to *The Doors of Perception* by Aldous Huxley (1894–1963), a 1954 narrative account of the author's experience with the ancient Mexican hallucinogenic drug mescaline, extracted from the peyote cactus. Huxley's title was itself a quote from William Blake (1757–1827): 'If the doors of perception were cleansed everything will appear to man as it is, infinite'.

Second albums are often problematic and are made all the more so when the first has broken major new ground and enjoyed both critical and commercial success. Despite the merits of subsequent releases, *The Doors* remained an album with no true sequel, even though its successor *Strange Days* contained some strong material. Most notable was *When The Music's Over,* which became a rousing live number, partly derived from a two-chord motif used in *Soul Kitchen* on the first album. Standards were starting to slip on *Waiting For The Sun,* the opening *Hello, I Love You* being an unexceptional pop song that was a little too close in rhythmic and harmonic content to the Kinks' *All Day And All Of The Night.* Ironically, this weak and unrepresentative track became the Doors' only UK Top 20 hit. Not for the singles market, but a vastly superior creation, was *The Unknown Soldier,* a vivid anti-war sermon in which Morrison was symbolically 'shot' during live shows.

The fourth album *Soft Parade* showed visible cracks, with songwriting credits now going to individual band members, rather than simply 'The Doors'. A significant curiosity on this album was Krieger's *Touch Me,* a commercially motivated slice of cabaret fodder, complete with brass and strings, of the type the ageing Elvis Presley might have used. When Morrison performed the song on TV, he was undeniably rather good at charming the gray men and their wives, leading to alarming retrospective thoughts as to what other dark qualities might have emerged had he lived longer.

Much face was saved with *Morrison Hotel* (1970), the decision to release a straight rock album reminding audiences of the band's capacity to deliver the basics. *LA Woman* (1971) took the concept a little further, both the title track and *Riders On The Storm* being late testimonies to the vocal charisma of a performer whose life was shortly to end from heart failure in a Paris hotel.

Numerous compilations and reissues followed. The only significant posthumous release was *An American Prayer* from 1978, in which spoken footage of Morrison reciting his poetry is juxtaposed with original Doors music and new material provided by the surviving members. Attempts to keep the band afloat minus Morrison resulted in two dreadful albums from 1971/2 and are best forgotten. Two decades later, few Doors enthusiasts had a good word to say about the Oliver Stone movie from 1991, with Val Kilmer in the role of Morrison.

A figure of near messianic status, James Douglas Morrison left too deep a mark, too many classic recordings and too much usable film and TV footage for any actor to step into his shoes without coming a poor second to the genuine article.

The environment in which the Doors flourished gradually spawned a whole subgenre that existed under the umbrella title of West Coast Rock. Many of the bands were short-lived, and unwieldy collective names were *de rigueur*. A particular favorite was the West Coast Pop Art Experimental Band, which at least gave an idea of what they were about. Pacific Gas And Electric, Quicksilver Messenger Service and It's A Beautiful Day gave no such clues as to their creative mission, but were nonetheless highly regarded in their time. A later arrival was the LA band Spirit, whose *Twelve Dreams Of Dr. Sardonicus* from 1970 is a particularly significant release from near the end of a golden era.

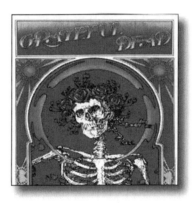

But the band that came to personify West Coast Rock was without doubt the Grateful Dead, whose acid-soaked second album *Anthem Of The Sun* remains a vivid and enduring capture of the loose and kaleidoscopic improvisations that characterized their early live sets. Based in San Francisco, whose burgeoning hippie culture made the district of Haight-Ashbury a promised land for everyone who ever lit a joss-stick, the Grateful Dead had, like the Velvet Underground, enjoyed a brief early incarnation as the Warlocks.

With guitarist and singer Jerry Garcia (1942–1995) at the helm, the band were in for the long haul, even though the uncompromising nature of their early work gradually gave way to a gentle and flawlessly executed brand of country-rock. This latter side of their creativity was

86

definitively represented in the 1971 album *American Beauty.* When they released *Built To Last* in 1989, the title seemed to say it all, their music having aged and/or matured with their audience.

Also from San Francisco came the Jefferson Airplane, whose international hit *White Rabbit,* complete with *Alice In Wonderland* images, became one of many blatant drug celebrations that remarkably few censors saw fit to ban. Originally fronted by *White Rabbit* creator Grace Slick (b.1939, with the almost equally marketable name of Grace Wing), the band found a second wind in the 70s and 80s as Jefferson Starship and eventually just Starship. Their early recorded legacy contained such unforgettable titles as *After Bathing At Baxter's* and the incomparable *Surrealistic Pillow.*

The band whose female lead claimed pole position over all the competition was Big Brother And The Holding Company. Perhaps not a conventional beauty, but a stage performer who exuded unbridled sexuality, Janis Joplin (1943–1970) was blessed with one of those rasping blues voices that could put an expressive edge on even the gentlest of falsetto whispers. Built around the voice and personality of Joplin and driven by the twin lead guitars of Sam Andrew (b.1941) and James Gurley (b.1939), Big Brother had a limited resource of original material but could create convincing and original remakes of what was already out there. On their part-live 1968 masterpiece *Cheap Thrills* (originally to be called *Sex, Drugs And Cheap Thrills* but vetoed by CBS), Gershwin's *Summertime* receives an all-new harmonic treatment, while *Piece Of My Heart,* previously a gospel influenced soul hit for Erma Franklin (1938–2002, sister of Aretha) emerges as a driving rock arrangement with a gritty guitar solo from Andrew.

The album also features the comic strip pop art cover design by Robert Crumb (b.1943), one of the finest of the era. Joplin's death from an overdose in a Hollywood motel room seemed an almost inevitable outcome of her hedonistic lifestyle, a premium quality talent who maybe knew all along where she was going.

As San Francisco basked in its global status as a hippie heaven, a musician from LA was building a remarkable career that from day one represented the very antithesis of flower-power and love-ins...

FRANK ZAPPA

Born – Baltimore, 21 December 1940
Died – Los Angeles, 4 December 1993

Frank Vincent Zappa (not 'Francis', as he would patiently point out in interviews) was one of the most original and productive minds in any field of twentieth century music. Raised in California, his teenage years in the 50s were marked by an interest in the European avant-garde, America's 'do-wop' vocal groups and a fascination with explosives, the oft-quoted claim that he could make gunpowder at the age of six being a favorite rock myth that has yet to be discredited. Another Zappa legend he was always happy to confirm is that his sixteenth (or possibly fifteenth) birthday celebrations included permission from his parents to telephone the composer Edgard Varèse (1883–1965), famous for his pioneering experiments in electronic music and multi-track technology. Sadly, Varèse was not at home, but his work remained the main inspiration behind *The Return Of The Son Of Monster Magnet* on *Freak Out,* Zappa's 1966 debut album as leader of the Mothers of Invention.

A sprawling double LP, sometimes credited as the inaugural release of its type, *Freak Out* by the Mothers of Invention with Zappa at the helm was first issued on the Verve label, as were the official releases of the Velvet Underground. Within a short time, the band's collective title was routinely being shortened to 'Frank Zappa and the Mothers', an abridged form later immortalized in Deep Purple's *Smoke on the Water*. Significantly, *Freak Out* pre-dates both *The Doors* and *The Velvet Underground And Nico.* Starting with 3'27" of *Hungry Freaks, Daddy* the album sets out Zappa's jaundiced view of middle America, while making it equally clear the band was in no way part of the hippie culture.

Almost every track appears to be aimed at a target, the manufactured pop song in *Wowie Zowie*, affluent teenage society in *You're Probably Wondering Why I'm Here* and the shadowy figures of the establishment in *Who Are The Brain Police?*, enigmatically described by Zappa as a 'religious song'. Even innocent young love gets short shrift in *I Ain't Got No Heart*. It was a heavy agenda for a time when America was still besotted with those loveable Liverpool moptops, although Zappa's ability to present his views in catchy three-minute packages, complete with his own intricate and polished guitar fills, made *Freak Out* a less draining experience than might have been feared. It even included the timeless *Go Cry On Somebody Else's Shoulder*, the first and arguably the best in a long line of 'do wop' parodies that would culminate in the entire content of *Cruisin' With Ruben And The Jets* in 1968. *Freak Out* also introduced the recurring figure of Suzy Creamcheese, a composite 60s teenager who, perhaps not unreasonably, has decided not to book Zappa and the Mothers for her high school dance.

The follow-up, *Absolutely Free* (1967) took the concept much further, some shameful goings-on in small town America depicted in *Brown Shoes Don't Make It*, moving segue into *America Drinks And Goes Home*, where Zappa takes on the role of a club singer and compere being ignored by his glass-clinking audience. Despite its complex and episodic musical content, *Brown Shoes Don't Make It* became a regular feature of the Mothers' live sets and remained in Zappa's repertoire for much of his career.

A labyrinthine artist whose work may be seen as an abundant yet rigorously controlled stream of consciousness, Zappa gradually broke away from the first incarnation of the Mothers with such extended concepts as *Lumpy Gravy* (1967) and *Uncle Meat* (1968). Many regard *Hot Rats* (1970) as his most accessible creation, the fun instrumental *Peaches (En Regalia)* leading into a spirited account of *Willie The Pimp* by guest vocalist Captain Beefheart. A high school contemporary of Zappa, Beefheart would make regular appearances alongside Zappa's band, his own uncompromising *Trout Mask Replica* from 1969 being a Zappa production.

By the 70s, Zappa's orchestral writing commanded much of his attention, even though a hectic touring schedule and constant flow of rock releases remained largely uninterrupted. One of Zappa's last recordings was *The Yellow Shark* from 1993, in which a recent collection of chamber works is performed live by the Ensemble Modern. Most of the program is conducted by the Ensemble Modern's Peter Rundel, the cancer-stricken Zappa having been too weak to remain on the podium for the full innings. An orchestral release of particular significance is *The Perfect Stranger* (1984), in which the Ensemble InterContemporain is conducted by

Pierre Boulez (b.1925). Already a senior figure at the highest level of contemporary music, Boulez was by now far too established in his field to be seriously accused of selling his artistic integrity in order to acquire the kudos of working with a rock star.

A final aspect of Zappa's output is his role in the development of the guitar as featured solo instrument. As the 70s progressed, his solos got longer, culminating almost inevitably in *Shut Up 'N' Play Yer Guitar* from 1984, a huge retrospective in which mainly live footage of Zappa in full flight is spliced together, interspersed with random snatches of studio chatter. Regarded by the current generation of guitarists as a seminal figure, whose instrumental skills flourished in the post-Hendrix era, the mature Zappa would frequently go on the road surrounded by younger aspiring virtuosi, including such latter-day heroes as Steve Vai (see Chapter 14).

Composer, conductor, satirist and senior guitar deity, Zappa also became involved in the politics of Eastern Europe and addressed Congress on the subject of censorship in 1985. In a life that spanned just less than 53 years, he covered more ground than most would in a century.

While Zappa's guitar pyrotechnics are perhaps best seen as a late flowering add-on to his core creativity, others soon built their reputations on fretboard acrobatics alone. But a contemporary of Zappa who is still topping the serious polls three decades after his premature death was to use his prodigious instrumental talent as a tool for shaping the future of rock with an innate and eclectic musicality on an unprecedented scale...

Hendrix, his contemporaries and his legacy

As the 60s entered its latter phase, the figure of the rock guitar hero steadily grew in stature, paving the way for what was to become the stereotypical 70s 'axe warrior'. From its origins in blues and jazz, the improvised instrumental solo within a vocal arrangement had been a feature of Rock & Roll from the very start. Although both the piano and the saxophone had their place in the Rock & Roll soundscape, the guitar always seemed to be the instrument that got noticed. In some cases, just one finely crafted guitar break would ensure the immortality of an otherwise forgotten performer, the masterful contribution from Danny Cedrone on *Rock Around The Clock* being one of the most obvious examples.

In a record industry still dominated by the three minute single, guitar breaks captured on vinyl during the early to mid-60s rarely stretched beyond a few seconds. In fact, some of the most imaginative players of the era, including Keith Richards and Pete Townshend, were perceived more as riff-makers *par excellence* than finger-crunching soloists. In the case of the Beatles and their myriad imitators, the guitar was used as little more than the principal backdrop to the band's vocal and songwriting skills, a formula that would re-emerge in the 90s with such Beatles-influenced bands as Oasis (see Chapter 14).

But as the LP became the favored format for the rock audience, guitar maestros who were already wowing the audience at live gigs were offered a wider canvas on which to display their wares to the folks at home. Typically, the guitar hero would be a handsome and charismatic figure, whose crowd pulling power was at least equal to that of the lead vocalist. In some cases, such as Alvin Lee (b.1944, real name: Graham Barnes) of Ten Years After, the guitar hero and lead vocalist was one and the same person. Each guitar hero had his own personal brand of stagecraft and showmanship, the ritual smashing of instruments and amps being a common but by no means universal practice.

The use of gender-specific terminology in the above paragraphs is intentional since, despite the emergence from the 70s onwards of such highly regarded figures as bottleneck virtuoso Bonnie Raitt (b.1949), the arrival of rock music's first truly iconic 'guitar heroine' remains eagerly awaited to this day. This is curious, since female representation in almost every other area of guitar playing had been established even before the 60s. From Peggy Seeger onwards, the new generation of female folk singers had accompanied themselves on guitar, Joan Baez and Julie Felix (both b.1941) being just two of the many solo artists whose instrumental skills were seen to match those of their male counterparts. Later, widely acclaimed singer/songwriters such as Joni Mitchell (b.1943) developed this tradition in a more individual context. Ironically, the type of instrument favored by most female exponents was a steel-strung acoustic, arguably the most physically demanding of all species of contemporary guitar.

By the 60s, women had even made their mark in what was then still the male dominated world of the classical guitar. Luise Walker (1910–1998) was internationally recognized as both a performer and composer, as was Maria Luisa Anido (1907–1996), whose name is now kept in the public eye by the Netherlands based Anido Duo, comprising guitarist Arlette Reulens and guitarist/composer Annette Kruisbrink. Most significant of all was Ida Presti (1924–1967), whose tragic death from an internal hemorrhage just a week before her 43rd birthday, robbed the twentieth century guitar of one of its greatest talents. The recorded legacy of the Presti-Lagoya Duo, together with a relatively small number of solo recordings by Presti, show her to have been a guitarist equal to any of her time and superior to most. And yet even Presti, for whatever reason, never enjoyed the wordwide celebrity status of Andrés Segovia (1893–1987) or his male heirs apparent Julian Bream (b.1933) and John Williams (b.1941), both of whom were to play direct and indirect cameo roles in the development of rock music during the 70s and 80s. But while the upper reaches of the classical music scene retained nothing more than the traditional male bias, instrumental aspects of rock music in the 60s were an almost exclusively masculine domain, even though the increasingly common sighting of a female rock vocalist fronting an all-male band was a significant force and had already produced one of the greatest rock singers of all time in Janis Joplin.

Although many enthusiasts from both sides of the divide might hotly disagree, there can be little doubt that the appeal of the guitar hero was essentially similar to that of the virtuoso instrumentalists who had grabbed the headlines in classical music since the nineteenth century. As the understated craftsmanship of Haydn, Mozart and early Beethoven was gradually superseded by ever more extravagant sonatas, symphonies and blockbuster concertos, that exclusive breed of concertgoers who Segovia grandly termed the 'philharmonic public' would don their evening dress expecting to see a wild-eyed larger-than-life figure grappling with the superhuman tasks set by the composer. If successful, the performance would be an exhilarating experience for all concerned, although it could be said that the capacity of music to touch the deeper emotions was the first casualty in the battle that took place on stage. In this respect, the role of the rock guitar hero is neither more nor less than that of the concerto soloist, except that the guitar hero is responsible for setting his own challenges and, on the best nights, can raise the bar higher than it has ever been before.

But like in all areas of the performing arts, the most refined exponents can use their prodigious skill both to amaze their audience and to communicate on a higher level...

JIMI HENDRIX

Born – Seattle, 27 November 1942
Died – London, 18 September 1970

During a turbulent early childhood that involved bitter disputes between his parents, Johnny Allen Hendrix was formally renamed James Marshall Hendrix shortly before his fourth birthday in 1946. A self-taught musician whose early proficiency allowed him to work with such semi-pro bands as the Rocking Kings and the Tomcats while still in his teens, Hendrix was one of several 60s figures who played the guitar left-handed, a distinction he shared with Paul McCartney. His brief period in the US army during 1961/2 appears to have been one of mixed fortunes, some sources claiming that he lied about his age to get in and then faked an injury to get out. For the next four years, he worked as a full-time pro on the R&B and soul circuit, backing such high-ranking names as Jackie Wilson (1934–1984) and the Isley Brothers. In 1966, he formed his own band and named them the Blue Flames, apparently unaware that the same name was being used in London by the group backing Georgie Fame. Coincidentally, the drummer Hendrix would sign up after arriving in London a year or so later was John 'Mitch' Mitchell (1946–2008), a one-time employee of Georgie Fame.

A number of appearances in Greenwich Village brought Hendrix to the attention of such influential figures as Mike Bloomfield (1943–1981) and Columbia producer John Hammond, already known to audiences as the man who discovered Bob Dylan. It was, however, the British bass player Bryan 'Chas' Chandler (1938–1996), appearing on the farewell US tour by the Animals, who was to prove the most valuable early contact. With plans to venture into production following the impending demise of the Animals, Chandler approached Hendrix with a view to recording a version of *Hey Joe,* a song sometimes described as traditional, sometimes attributed to Billy Roberts (William Moses Roberts Jr.). Recording the song in London and releasing it as a single on the Polydor label, Hendrix took on a series of British and European gigs, backed by the Jimi Hendrix

Experience, comprising Mitchell and guitarist turned bass player Noel Redding (1945–2003). Reaching No.6 in the UK charts at the start of 1967, *Hey Joe* established Hendrix as a thrusting, dynamic guitarist whose vocal skills, although limited in both range and power, created an appealingly laid-back contrast to his uncompromising instrumental style. After *Hey Joe* came the essential Hendrix anthem *Purple Haze,* released as a single on the newly launched Track label. The band was now seen as a major new force on the London scene with the potential to take on the world. By the time they made their headline appearance at the 1967 Monterey Pop Festival, the albums *Are You Experienced?* and its sequel *Axis: Bold As Love* were heading for the UK Top Five. Significantly, the third single was a lyrical and nostalgic ballad titled *The Wind Cries Mary,* in which Hendrix' often overlooked capacity to produce some of the most exquisite and poetic lyrics of the era features prominently.

Much of 1968 was spent in the USA, where members of the Experience and a wide range of guest musicians recorded the magnum opus *Electric Ladyland,* whose classic period cover shot showed a harem of naked young women protecting their modesty with strategically placed LP covers from earlier Hendrix releases. Needless to say, the establishment wagged a disapproving finger, thus generating some welcome, although by no means essential, publicity for what many still consider to be the finest rock album of all time. The ever-growing demand for new Hendrix vinyl was also kept at bay by a definitive early compilation titled *Smash Hits,* this seemingly premature release being justified in part by the fact the several singles, including *Hey Joe,* did not appear on any existing studio album.

Spread over two LPs, *Electric Ladyland* offered a spacious yet disciplined set that spawned *Voodoo Chile* in two sharply contrasting versions. The first, a fifteen-minute blues jam, featured such celebrity guests as keyboard player Steve Winwood (b.1948) of Traffic, later to form the short-lived 'supergroup' Blind Faith. The track appeared to have been recorded 'live in the studio' before a small but appreciative audience of 'hangers on', although most Hendrix scholars maintain the chatter and applause was added some time after the original session. In the tighter hard-rock setting titled *Voodoo Chile (Slight Return)*, which would become a posthumous UK No.1 single, Hendrix brought the album to a close with a dazzling display of symphonic guitar lines before a backdrop of shaman-like imagery and tribal rhythms. An explosion of naked creativity, *Voodoo Chile* brought together the blues conventions, from which Hendrix' guitar and vocal styles were initially derived, and the dark Afro-Caribbean folklore that remained an often unseen force behind the development of the blues as a recognized musical form.

Forever the perfectionist, Hendrix publicly stated his disappointment with the final outcome of *Electric Ladyland,* the '3D' sound he had created in the studio having somehow been lost in the pressing process. He would doubtless have been incandescent had he lived to discover that an early CD reissue on Polydor of *Electric Ladyland* had the tracks in the wrong order, the reprise *Still Raining, Still Dreaming* appearing several slots before *Rainy Day, Dream Away* from which it is so obviously derived. The mistake appears to have stemmed from the fact that the four sides on the original Polydor release (marked A,B,C and D rather than the more usual 1,2,3 and 4) were organized, apparently to facilitate the use of 'stackable' record decks, with one LP housing sides A and D, the other sides B and C.

Complete with that stunning cover of *All Along The Watchtower* and the dream-like soundscape of *Moon Turn The Tides...Gently, Gently Away,* the release of *Electric Ladyland* represents the apogee of an unparalleled artistic career that was to end so wretchedly just two years later. Needless to say, no album is without its downside, the cheesy pop song *Little Miss Strange,* for which Redding took the lead vocal and the songwriting credits, distinguishing itself only insofar as it was even more embarrassing than *She's So Fine,* the token 'Noel song' from *Axis: Bold As Love.* The Beatles' practice of including a daft song for Ringo to sing at least raised a smile, but it is difficult to imagine why such a privilege should be granted to Redding who, quite frankly, was lucky to be where he was in the first place. *Electric Ladyland* marked the last major studio offering from the Hendrix-Redding-Mitchell alliance, although Mitchell remained aboard for later live performances, including the legendary set at the Woodstock Festival in 1969.

But although Hendrix' powers had undoubtedly hit an early peak in *Electric Ladyland,* there is little evidence to support the view that he was by now a spent force. In the 1970 live album *Band of Gypsys,* for which he had recruited Billy Cox (bass) and Buddy Miles (drums), the performance remains entirely convincing, the epic *Machine Gun* containing some of his most celebrated guitar wizardry. Even his controversial appearance at the Isle of Wight Festival in 1970 remains a far more fitting swansong than many gave it credit for at the time. In the 'official' studio releases that came shortly after his death, his songwriting capacity is clearly far from used-up, the poignantly prophetic *Angel* from *Cry of Love* (1971) being one of his most haunting creations.

Hendrix' death following an overdose of barbiturates led to three decades of largely speculative analysis from those who knew him and those who did not. The 1990s saw a bitter legal dispute between Monika Dannemann (1946–1996), who was with Hendrix at the time of death, and another former girlfriend Kathy Etchingham. Towards the end of her life, Dannemann published a controversial but undeniably beautiful book containing her personal account of events, surrounded by her own Hendrix-inspired artwork. Days after losing the protracted libel case to Etchingham, Dannemann was found dead in a fume-filled Mercedes near her cottage in Seaford, East Sussex.

With his business affairs left in the same chaotic state as his private life, record companies large and small seized the opportunity to release archive material before anyone representing Hendrix could hold back the tide. Even EMI's budget UK offshoot Music For Pleasure came up with an offering titled *The Birth Of Success,* in which mainly live footage found the pre-67 Hendrix performing R&B and Motown hits, apparently in the company of Curtis Knight (1929–1999) and others. Although Knight's involvement with Hendrix' pre-Chandler career still remains the subject of considerable controversy, his book *Jimi* (1974) became a valuable early narrative, predating the definitive Hendrix biography *Electric Gypsy* by Harry Shapiro and Caesar Glebbeek.

In fact, the MFP album turned out to be one of the better examples among the numerous opportunistic releases of bootleg quality. Other such enterprises featured voice PAs capable of Dalek-like distortion and even tapes played at the wrong speed, resulting in one of rock music's most revered figures doing a passable imitation of Alvin and the Chipmunks. In addition to the recognized 'work in progress' that was nearing completion at the time of death, the posthumous material of most interest to collectors with less than unlimited budgets and shelf space falls into two categories. Firstly, there were the experimental recordings with avant garde jazz keyboard player Mike Ephron, believed to be from c.1964 and released on a number of different labels under various titles. Crude and low-tech, the Ephron recordings nonetheless show an early manifestation of the enquiring mind that, within the next few years, would shape the future of rock music for decades to come. Secondly, due largely to the outrage they caused at the time, are the notorious 'Douglas albums', in which the enterprising producer Alan Douglas took studio footage and replaced the original musicians, other than Hendrix, with a new team of his own session players. Released on Polydor under such titles as *Crash Landing* and *Midnight Lightning*, the Douglas concoctions are of considerable curiosity value as the albums Hendrix fans most love to hate, Douglas completing his role as the Demon King by sometimes claiming joint songwriting credits with a departed hero who could no longer protect his intellectual property. The contrast between this and the absolute integrity of Hendrix' own work as a producer could scarcely be greater. In 1969, he transformed *Sunrise,* debut album of his erstwhile support band Eire Apparent, into a potent first release, appearing as 'guest guitarist' for much of the proceedings. During the same year, he was a vital yet almost imperceptible presence behind the mixing desk for New York Rock & Rollers Cat Mother And The All-Night Newsboys on their timeless underground classic *The Street Giveth And The Street Taketh Away.*

James Marshall Hendrix would have celebrated his sixtieth birthday on 27 November 2002. In August of that year, readers of *Total Guitar* magazine, many of whom would be the sons and daughters of parents who grew up in the Hendrix era, voted him 'the greatest guitarist ever'.

Despite Hendrix' undisputed supremacy, he is best viewed as 'first among equals' at a time that must now surely be seen as the first golden age of rock guitar. The 70s revealed a whole army of guitar greats from both sides of the Atlantic, this aspect of Frank Zappa's multi-faceted talent being essentially a post-60s flowering.

But within his own lifetime, many notable Hendrix peers hailed from his adoptive home of England. Mostly learning their craft during the R&B boom, Britain's time-served master musicians were set to flourish in an era when success no longer necessarily depended on a string of hit singles, even though it still helped. Various names mentioned in earlier chapters and who will re-emerge further down the line belong in this category. But there was one Brit who, more than any other, was seen as a counterpart and even a rival to Hendrix...

ERIC CLAPTON

Born – Ripley, Surrey, 30 March 1945

Despite being saddled with a name that evokes a comic-strip English workman whose hobby is breeding ferrets, Eric Clapton's creative inclinations first led him to enter Kingston Art School as a student of stained glass design, dropping out to pursue his musical ambitions in 1963. After brief stints with such obscure outfits as Casey Jones And The Engineers, he was recruited by the Yardbirds in October of that year to replace the largely forgotten figure of Tony Topham. Clapton appeared on the Yardbirds singles *I Wish You Would* and *Good Morning Little Schoolgirl,* and was also present on the highly regarded live album with Sonny Boy Williamson. But he left at the time of the band's first big hit *For Your Love,* allegedly on the grounds that their work was becoming too commercial for his tastes. Often portrayed as a blues purist, this 'back to basics' philosophy has been a recurring theme in Clapton's career. The spartan and frequently overrated *Unplugged* sessions of the 1990s found the greying and bespectacled Clapton performing gloomy old songs and looking for all the world like a disillusioned polytechnic lecturer whose application for early retirement had just been rejected.

But despite this initial unwillingness to capitalize on his prodigious talent, Clapton was already gaining a following in his own right. The ironic nickname *Slowhand* that much later became an album title dated back to his time with the Yardbirds. There was even a graffiti campaign in the London area proclaiming 'Clapton is God', which no doubt proved equally embarrassing to both named parties. By this time, Clapton had found his true formative niche as lead guitarist with John Mayall's Bluesbreakers, a post which he held until the launch of Cream in July 1966.

Responding to an invitation from drum legend Pete 'Ginger' Baker (b.1939), Clapton agreed to collaborate on condition that the bass player would be the Scotsman Jack Bruce (b.1943) who, like Baker, had worked with Alexis Korner and had subsequently become a founder member of the Graham Bond Organization. Bruce agreed and the doyen of British 'supergroups' was born. Despite starting out as a blues-based outfit, Cream would soon embrace the changing spirit of the times, the psychedelic cover of their second album *Disraeli Gears* containing a disc that featured just one straight blues cover amid the increasingly marketable products of the songwriting partnership of Jack Bruce and lyricist Pete Brown.

Produced by the Italian-American Felix Pappalardi (1939–1983) who later formed the Cream-inspired American band Mountain, *Disraeli Gears* played host to the mild-mannered hit tune *Strange Brew* and the band's best-known song *Sunshine Of Your Love*. A Bruce/Brown/Clapton creation that aspiring teenage ensembles still cover to this day, *Sunshine Of Your* Love comes complete with the celebrated *Blue Moon* guitar solo in which Clapton, either by accident or design, quotes the opening phrase of the Rodgers and Hart standard from 1934. The embarrassment, however, is the concluding *Mother's Lament*, in which the band members adopt joke Cockney accents for an excruciating rendition of the laborious music hall song in which an unfortunate infant meets his fate after being washed down the plughole at bath time. Had it not been for the remunerative royalty checks dropping through the letter box, Clapton must surely have been regretting his departure from the Yardbirds, let alone the Bluesbreakers.

As Cream's star continued to rise, their live performances became increasingly extravagant affairs, with audiences egging them on to take ever more extended solos. There can be little doubt, however, that this was the environment that yielded some of Clapton's finest moments, the live version of *Crossroads* seen by many as containing the greatest solo of his entire career and the monumental version of *I'm So Glad* developing into nothing less than a gladiatorial contest of skill and stamina between Clapton and Bruce. Herein lies a discernible difference between the creative approaches of Clapton and Hendrix who, in stark contrast to

Clapton, produced his best work alongside musicians whose function was to provide a reliable but relatively unobtrusive accompaniment. This said, some commentators rightly draw attention to the subtle improvised dialogues that often developed between Hendrix and Mitchell.

Following the demise of Cream in 1968, Clapton and Baker formed the ill-starred Blind Faith alongside Traffic frontman Steve Winwood and bass player Ric Grech (1946–1990), poached from the respected British mainstream rockers Family. Hampered from the outset by the conflicting career ambitions of each individual member, Blind Faith gave their first performance to an estimated 100,000 people in London's Hyde Park and managed to stay afloat for a lucrative US tour before throwing in the towel, Clapton reportedly being the first to realize the project was doomed. Their self-titled debut album, notorious for its waist-upwards cover shot of a naked prepubescent girl, was their only studio legacy and is a more convincing set than many give it credit for.

Going it alone for the first time, Clapton released a pleasant if unarresting self-titled solo album in 1970, his light and expressive lead vocals proving surprisingly effective in his own *Let It Rain* and the cover version of *After Midnight* by J.J. Cale (b.1938, no relation to John Cale of the Velvet Underground). Even though the album was ostensibly a solo offering, the cover showed a group photo of some seventeen people, all of whom are formally identified and most of whom have made a musical contribution. Perhaps most significant was the husband and wife team of Delaney and Bonnie (Bramlett), whose ever-changing musical co-operative known simply as the Friends was to provide several of the key personnel on a slightly later album set to become Clapton's equivalent of *Electric Ladyland*.

Incredible though it seems in retrospect, *Layla and Other Assorted Love Songs* was not perceived as a resounding success at the outset. Using the less than inspired collective title of Derek And The Dominos (sic), Clapton and his associates created an all-new sound texture centered around the vibrant contrast between his own lead guitar style and that of Duane Allman (1946–1971). The atmosphere was that of an all-star jam session, its multi-layered tapestry breathing new life into such ancient warhorses as *Key To The Highway* and *Nobody Knows You When You're Down And Out*. The formula did not work every time: the ill-advised attempt at Hendrix' *Little Wing* emerged as one of the clumsiest cover versions ever released by a team of recognized players. But in the title track, for which he shared the writing credits with drummer and pianist Jim Gordon, Clapton struck gold.

Layla and Other Assorted Love Songs

With Allman's slide guitar soaring above one of the most compelling riffs ever created, *Layla* was a song that would remain a dominant force in rock music throughout the 70s, 80s and 90s. Originally spanning seven minutes, the radio-friendly single version was an early fade rather than a pruned edit. The extended piano solo disappeared altogether, but the main core of both the song and the performance left unaltered.

It is one of the cruellest episodes in rock history that, when *Layla* became a worldwide hit in 1972, Allman had already died in a motorcycle accident. By this time, Clapton was reportedly addicted to heroin. His morale cannot have been improved after the model Patti(e) Boyd (b.1944), then wife of George Harrison and generally believed to be the subject of the song, had allegedly spurned his early advances, even though the couple eventually married in 1979.

In the period following *Layla,* Clapton appeared to go quiet for a while before a remarkably successful flirtation with reggae, scoring an immediate hit with the Bob Marley song *I Shot The Sheriff* from the 1974 album *461 Ocean Boulevard.* For the rest of the 70s, Clapton remained largely faithful to his blues roots, the live album *E.C. Was Here* (1975) delighting those who rued the day he parted company with Mayall. By the 80s, Clapton had consolidated his role as an elder statesman of British rock, appearing at large-scale media gatherings alongside such ubiquitous celebs as Phil Collins.

Tragedy then struck twice within a frighteningly short period of time. On 27 August 1990, Texan blues guitar virtuoso Stevie Ray Vaughan died in a helicopter crash near Troy, Wisconsin after a concert alongside

Clapton and others at the Alpine Valley Music Theater. According to some reports, Vaughan's seat on the helicopter had originally been intended for Clapton.

Then, on 20 March 1991, Clapton's four-year-old son Conor died in a fall from the window of the New York apartment of the child's mother Lori Del Santo. To his eternal credit, Clapton's musical tribute to Conor *Tears In Heaven* emerged as a sincere, moving and disarmingly unmawkish ballad, its presence on *Unplugged* (1992) successfully diverting attention from a dreadful acoustic arrangement of *Layla*.

A premier league talent whose long career has been marked by the most extreme highs and lows, Eric Clapton's patrician status in rock music was recognized with a CBE in the *New Year's Honours List* for 2004, the same award going to Ray Davies of the Kinks.

As the 70s approached, other guitarists made their debuts on the world stage. Despite the commanding presence of Hendrix, Alvin Lee made his mark at Woodstock, as did the dashing young Mexican Carlos Santana (b.1947). Fronting a band that bore his own surname, Santana introduced a new and vibrant synthesis of cutting edge rock and the complex rhythms of his own Latin American culture. Ranging from the exuberant to the lyrical, Santana's textures became associated with and yet remained essentially distinct from that worthy but at times sterile 70s incarnation of the hybrid known as jazz-rock.

Back in England, the final chapter of the blues era featured the first and finest incarnation of Fleetwood Mac, centered on the reclusive figure of Peter Green (b.1946, real name: Peter Allen Greenbaum), who had successfully replaced Clapton in John Mayall's team. Although not the most thrilling guitarist technically, Green was a steady and refined player whose immortality was assured in the 1968 hit instrumental *Albatross*. An ethereal and heavily reverbed sound painting on a two-chord ostinato, *Albatross* was far from representative of the band's live sets and earlier recordings. But its classic status as a one-off miniature masterpiece is beyond question. A small clutch of lesser hit singles followed in its wake before Green entered a long period of self-imposed exile from the music business. Unconfirmed tales of psychological problems were rife, the favorite being an episode in which Green allegedly assaulted his own accountant, who was merely attempting to hand him a sizeable royalty check. Green was finally tempted out of retirement during the 90s as the figurehead of what became Peter Green's Splinter Group, a controversial and speculative venture playing to a guaranteed audience of mature enthusiasts paying homage to a deservedly respected musician.

But waiting in the wings was one James Patrick Page, a slightly-built former London session man whose formidable guitar sound would come to define one of rock music's most enduring sub-genres...

— 8 —

"Heavy Metal Thunder"

When the title of this chapter and many others like it first appeared as the second line of the second verse in the 1968 Steppenwolf biker anthem *Born To Be Wild,* it was perceived as nothing more than just another meteorological metaphor. But within a few years, it had become nothing less than a two-word epithet, 'thunder' having silently dropped, that represented the formal separation of rock music from the hippie culture in which it had flourished.

Although hippies still exist in the twenty-first century, as do mods and teddy boys, the philosophy they represented was either peacefully laid to rest at Woodstock or, as some would insist, viciously slain with the violent death of 18-year-old Meredith Hunter during the Rolling Stones' set at the Altamont Raceway Park, Northern California, in December 1969. Reports vary considerably, but what is known is that Alan David Passaro (1948–1985) was tried for the stabbing of Hunter and acquitted on the grounds of self-defense. What is not known is whether or not Passaro and the other individuals in charge of 'security' were fully-fledged members of the Hells Angels motorcycle club, or merely aspiring members eager to display their pugilistic skills. One piece of supporting evidence for the view that Passaro & co. were not the genuine article is the fact that the Grateful Dead, who were also due to appear at Altamont, had reportedly hired the Hells Angels to provide crowd-control on several previous occasions and been perfectly happy with the firm but non-confrontational presence they offered. Contemporary accounts suggest the Dead had been given no say in the arrangements at Altamont.

Given the exceptional nature of events at Altamont, the temptation to favor the Woodstock scenario is strong, the oft-quoted statistic that two deaths and two births took place on site during a gathering of half a million people summing up that frequently invoked sense of harmony and balance. But it was not all caring and sharing with flowers in your hair. Traffic queues were as long as twenty miles and, once you got there, sanitation was hopelessly inadequate. And then came the rain. By the time Indian sitar maestro Ravi Shankar (b.1920) presented his legendary set, the crowd took in the exotic vibe while ankle deep in mud.

Rock music had become a global industry, in which investors large and small could earn millions or lose the shirts off their backs. Woodstock alone had shown the sheer magnitude of the rock audience, but much of that audience was becoming increasingly non-radical. More than ever before, they saw music as representing not so much an alternative lifestyle but a temporary escape from the routine daily life they would return to after the show. They craved a rollercoaster experience in sound and vision that dominated the senses, blocking out everything other than itself. For every college student who 'gave it up for music and the *Free Electric Band'*, there were thousands more who planned to finish their course and start applying for jobs. Music was to them what golf was to their fathers: a rewarding and addictive diversion that came complete with its own social life. Going to a concert was a social event at which the paying audience expected to experience an emotional high from everything they heard and saw. Heavy Metal met those requirements and continues to do so in the next millennium.

Hippies in the 70s found a haven in bands such as Gong, whose sartorial penchant for kaftans and woolly hats was reflected in such gentle and spiritual offerings as *The Pothead Pixies* from the 1973 album *Flying Teapot*. Fronted by the gnome-like figure of Daevid Allen (b.1938), Gong was one of many respected but uncommercial UK-based bands to benefit from the munificence of Virgin Records, a theme to be developed in later chapters.

But who were Steppenwolf and where did they come from? One of the richest ironies in rock history is that the creators of one of its defining songs left the stage virtually unnoticed and even managed to maintain an unprecedented degree of anonymity during their heyday. Three decades down the line, only a few widely read enthusiasts could name a single member of the band and even many of them would admit defeat if we made it any member other than lead singer John Kay (b.1944, real name: Joachim Fritz Krauledat). More obscure still is the writer of the song, which is usually credited to one Mars Bonfire, a nom de plume used by Dennis Edmonton (formerly Dennis McCrohan), brother of the band's drummer Jerry Edmonton (1946–1993, real name: Jerry McCrohan – both brothers had adopted the non-Celtic surname before the launch of Steppenwolf). Formed in their native Toronto under the rather less imposing name of Sparrow, the band borrowed their Teutonic collective title from the Hermann Hesse novel after moving to California in 1967. Perceived as an outstanding live band, their recorded output was highly regarded but not always plentiful. After *Born To Be Wild,* they scored one more major hit single (US only) with *Magic Carpet Ride.* They disbanded in 1971-2, although the name was revived by Kay and an otherwise new line-up for a tour in 1990.

With both the term and the genre established in the lexicon, the stage was set for Heavy Metal's most representative exponents...

LED ZEPPELIN

A leading session guitarist whose clientele included the Who, Tom Jones and Joe Cocker, the revered figure of Jimmy Page (b.1944) is yet another former member of the Yardbirds. Initially turning down an offer to replace Eric Clapton in 1964, Page eventually joined the band two years later as bass player, following the departure of Paul Samwell-Smith. By this time, the lead guitarist was Jeff Beck (b.1944), whose sabbatical due to illness resulted in Page being effectively promoted. When Beck returned, the band briefly adopted a twin lead guitar format until Beck officially handed over to Page. By this time, the whole band was disintegrating and Page, despite being a relative newcomer, inherited both the name and a tour of Scandinavia. Faced with a contract but no band, Page sought the assistance of session bass player John Paul Jones (b.1946, real name: John Baldwin) and manager Peter Grant (1935–1995). Completing what started as a makeshift team were the relatively unknown drummer John Bonham (1948–1980) and vocalist Robert Plant (b.1948), who had previously worked together in the now largely forgotten Band of Joy.

After successfully touring Scandinavia as the New Yardbirds, the band cut their first album using just 30 hours' studio time and did their first live gigs as Led Zeppelin. The origin of the name is the topic of many a spontaneous anecdote, the most usual version being that Keith Moon of the Who had predicted that the band's career would plummet like a lead balloon, then developing the image by coining the term 'lead Zeppelin'. Or was the unforgettable collective title of US band Iron Butterfly (formed 1966) possibly an unacknowledged factor? A truly bizarre postscript took place on 21 February 1970, when Led Zeppelin appeared in Copenhagen as the Nobs, reason being that Eva von Zeppelin, a descendant of the aviation innovator, had allegedly threatened the band with legal action for unauthorized use of the family name.

The self-titled first album took British rock and blues into a new era, juxtaposing the Willie Dixon classic *You Shook Me* with the band's own hi-tech blues lament *Dazed And Confused,* said to have been indirectly derived from an earlier song by the singer and jingle-writer Jake Holmes. Driven by a relentless 4/4 from Bonham and Jones, the partnership of Page and Plant remains unsurpassed in its dynamic force. With his Les Paul hung low, Page was the quintessential unassuming figure who took on a whole new expressive persona as the lights were turned up. The gods had been uncommonly generous when creating Plant, blessing him with one of the greatest ever white blues voices, plus classic Anglo-Saxon features and a lion's mane of flowing golden locks. To say that every English-speaking adolescent male in 1970 dreamed of playing guitar like

Page and looking like Plant cannot be far from the truth. But despite their lasting stardom and seemingly unlimited personal charisma, the band were always known for their self-parodying humor, Plant remarking in a later interview that the spoof rock movie *This is Spinal Tap* (1984) was 'like a Led Zeppelin documentary'.

In 1969, *Led Zeppelin II* met all expectations, the barnstorming *Whole Lotta Love* becoming their best-known song before *Stairway To Heaven*. The opening riff to *Whole Lotta Love* soon became known to practically every TV owner in the United Kingdom as the new theme music for the BBC flagship *Top Of The Pops,* performed in an all-new brass arrangement by CCS (Collective Consciousness Society). A fleetingly popular studio-based 'big band' put together by Alexis Korner (see Chapter 4), CCS enjoyed several chart successes on the commercially motivated RAK label masterminded by Mickie Most. Paradoxically, the members of Led Zeppelin were determined never to release a UK single and, unlike many who had sworn the same oath, never did. Not, that is, until the original version of *Whole Lotta Love* spent all of two weeks in the UK charts, peaking at No.21, in September 1997. Although this and later tracks were released in the US as 45s at the time of creation, the 'albums first' point had been well and truly made, with other bands following suit over the next few years. A further philosophical statement came in 1971, when the band toured the UK revisiting their former venues at the original fee, on condition that ticket prices were also the same as before. Although condemned by some as a gimmick, this gesture was invariably appreciated by the fans who were able to get in the building.

Led Zeppelin III enjoyed a relatively mixed reception in 1970, a softer artistic line featuring Page's gentle acoustic backdrop on the ballad *Tangerine* being a convincing diversion from the main agenda but not quite what the fans had come to expect. Emerging from a period spent in the seclusion of a now famous Welsh country cottage at Bron-Yr-Aur (apparently misspelled in the title of *Bron-Y-Aur Stomp* from *Led Zeppelin III*), the album represented a more spiritual phase in the band's history and yet still contained enough pyrotechnics to satisfy all but the seriously addicted.

By the untitled fourth album, usually referred to as *Four Symbols* due to the rune-like figures (see above) on the inner sleeve, said to represent the individual members of the band, the acoustic side of Led Zeppelin was fully established. The opening bars of *Stairway To Heaven* became so popular with fledgling guitarists that music shops threatened to ban customers from playing it, a practice later observed in the 1992 movie *Wayne's World.* Although much parodied, *Stairway* nonetheless remains one of the key moments in the history of rock music, an eight-minute composition in which quasi-traditional folk melodies and pagan imagery culminate in an unaccompanied coda from Plant, preceded by one of the truly essential heavy metal guitar breaks from Page. Music on this level can withstand any satirical attack, the surviving band members having reportedly been delighted when the painter, singer and professional Australian Rolf Harris (b.1930) finally made *Stairway* a UK hit single (No.7) in 1993.

Houses Of The Holy (1973) and the extravagantly packaged double album *Physical Graffiti* (1975) concluded the vintage years, the exotic and elaborately orchestrated *Kashmir* from the latter being arguably the last Led Zeppelin track to earn classic status. The 1976 movie *The Song Remains The Same* provides valuable footage of Led Zeppelin at the height of their success.

The death of Plant's son from a mystery stomach complaint, two separate car crashes injuring Bonham, Plant and Plant's wife and then the death of Bonham following a drinking binge at Page's house all led to dark rumors that the band was cursed. Page's alleged fascination with the occult writings of Aleister Crowley (1875–1947, real name: Edward Alexander Crowley), famous for his unreadable 'autohagiography' and the maxim 'Do as thou wilt shall be the whole of the law', did little to help the situation. A 1985 Live Aid reunion with Phil Collins on drums showed it was time to move on. Solo projects from Page and Plant, and their respective liaisons with the Honeydrippers and the Firm (the latter fronted by Paul Rodgers, formerly of Free and Bad Company) met with relatively modest commercial success and mixed critical response. A one-off reunion with Jason Bonham, son of the late John, on drums was arranged in 1988 to celebrate the 40th anniversary of Atlantic Records, the label from which the band had benefited and vice versa. Rumors of further reunions, together with occasional appearances together by Page and Plant, have continued ever since. The much heralded 1997 release of the *BBC Sessions* (recorded in 1969 and 1971) was surely not before time.

We might not immediately recall that the bass player with Steppenwolf was one Rushton Morave, but the names of Plant, Page, Jones and Bonham will forever be known to anyone who grew up in the formative years of Heavy Metal.

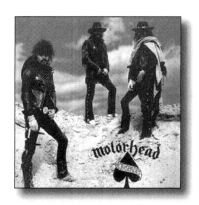

With Led Zeppelin leading the field, a whole generation of Heavy Metal bands consolidated, and sometimes concluded, their collective careers during the late 60s and early 70s. A second wave of new acts emerged in the mid-70s. Foremost among these was the British trio Motörhead, fronted by the ageless figure of Ian Kilminster (b.1945), known since the 60s as Lemmy. Few Heavy Metal icons could claim a more apposite early CV. A former Hendrix roadie, Lemmy had been associated with such obscure psychedelic bands as Opal Butterfly before hitting the underground bigtime with Hawkwind in 1971. He was sacked by Hawkwind in 1975, on the somewhat flimsy grounds that he had been busted for drugs during a Canadian tour. Recruiting drummer Lucas Fox and former Pink Fairies guitarist Larry Wallis (later to become a producer for the influential Stiff Records – see Chapter 11), Lemmy launched Motörhead as what was generally perceived as a fundamentalist Heavy Metal trio, even though he reportedly preferred the term Rock & Roll. His own dual contribution was a pounding plectrum driven bass style and a lead vocal that could strip paint at fifty yards.

More than a quarter of a century down the line, Motörhead has become a national and international institution, the central figure of Lemmy remaining at the helm throughout a tortuous history of line-up changes. Interestingly, much of the band's early support was drawn from the late 70s punk audience, thus creating an unlikely yet seemingly secure bridge between the Mohican coiffured angry young boys and the rock music establishment they claimed to despise.

A perennial problem in tracing the development of Heavy Metal is that of determining which bands belong in the category. Black Sabbath should almost certainly be included, whereas the extensive recorded legacy of Deep Purple is arguably better listed under the broader heading of Hard Rock.

But should the same apply to the Canadian trio Rush, extrovert 70s Australian rockers AC/DC or the British band Uriah Heep, whose 1970 debut album prompted the legendary critical response "…if this group makes it, I'll have to commit suicide"? Despite this somewhat discouraging reception, Heep managed to hold down contracts with Vertigo Records and then Bronze Records lasting well into the 70s. Even though they have disappeared from most rock histories, the band remains active to this day, releasing mainly live albums in recent years. The fate of the critic is unknown.

For the past quarter of a century, all aspects of Heavy Metal and its related categories are faithfully chronicled in the pages of the inimitable *Kerrang!* magazine (first published in June 1981), complete with its email *Noiseletter*. Sadly, no such specifically targeted journal of equivalent quality seems to have been around during the formative years of the 60s and 70s. Nor does any contemporary document appear to definitively answer the question of when the genre that was to become Heavy Metal first appeared.

It has been said, with some justification, that the seeds were planted in such hit singles as *You Really Got Me* by the Kinks (note the alleged Jimmy Page connection) and its sequel *All Day And All Of The Night,* even though few would seriously describe Ray Davies and his team as a Heavy Metal band. One founding figure whose contribution can easily be overlooked is Alice Cooper (b.1948, real name: Vincent Damon Furnier), whose early ventures the Earwigs and the Spiders were active as long ago as 1966. Although he later came to represent the darker side of the often undervalued 70s genre of Glam Rock, Cooper was essentially a Heavy Metal pioneer, complete with the occult stage props that would later be adopted by Black Sabbath and many more. Although often ridiculed in retrospect, a situation not helped by the decision of lead singer Ozzie Osbourne (b.1948, real name: John Michael Osbourne) to subject his entire family to the public humiliation of twenty-first century "reality" TV, Sabbath remained a potent force in their time, guitarist Tony Iommi (b.1948) being one of the most underrated axe warriors of the era. In contrast to his fuse-blowing electric riffs, Iommi was one of the first players to sample the parallel universe of the classical guitar, initially to create neo-gothic interludes between tracks of Sabbath albums.

In doing so, Iommi and others laid the foundations of what became a defining force in 70s rock…

9

The Excellence and Excesses of Symphonic Rock and the Psychedelic Survivors

In October 1969, an album reached the stores that could scarcely be ignored. The gory red and purple cover painting, depicting a close-up of a human face apparently screaming in terror, was guaranteed to grab the attention of even the most casual browser. The absence of any printed text meant the potential purchaser had to examine the spine in order to establish he was holding an LP with the arresting, if somewhat pretentious, title *In the Court of the Crimson King – An Observation by King Crimson.*

An all-British product that would leave its mark throughout the next decade, the album was released on the soon-to-be pivotal Island

Records. Performed by a team of largely unknown musicians from the south of England, it opened with what became the band's stage anthem, *21st Century Schizoid Man*. Evoking the doom-laden atmosphere of a cult sci-fi movie, the imposing and heavily overdubbed saxophone motif gave way to a robotic vocal line, electronically distorted to a degree that the bleak, Orwellian lyrics were only partly discernible. A central instrumental episode subtitled *Mirrors* provided a further showcase for the skills of the saxophonist and subtly revealed the almost spectral presence of an equally adept lead guitarist. The sax player was Ian MacDonald and the guitarist Robert Fripp (both b.1946), the latter being the only name that would remain a permanent fixture in a band that seemed genetically programmed to transform its personnel, and often its entire aesthetic, between one album and the next. If Fripp was not already synonymous with King Crimson in 1969, he would soon become so by virtue of the fact that no-one else stayed long enough to share the honors.

After *Schizoid Man* came the soft-focus ballad *I Talk to the Wind*, in which MacDonald was again featured prominently, providing multiple layers of flutes and clarinets. The arrangement also highlighted the restrained and accomplished style of drummer Michael Giles (b.1942), whose decision to leave following the first US tour (although he still appears on the second album) removed a key component in the band's early soundscape.

But it was the closing track on Side One that fully defined the main precedent established by this agenda-setting coda to the 60s. Announcing its arrival by means of a rumbling crescendo on the timpani, *Epitaph* was centered on the forceful and richly enunciated vocals of Greg Lake (b.1947), supported by a huge battalion of orchestral strings. For the similarly conceived title track that ended Side Two, the already dense texture was further augmented by massed human voices.

But there was no orchestra and no choir, that huge expanse of sound emanating from just one instrument, the largely forgotten electro-mechanical beast known as the Mellotron. Housing several banks of pre-recorded tape strips, this temperamental but groundbreaking piece of kit was a direct precursor to the myriad string synthesizers that would reach full maturity in the 70s. It was also using sampling techniques at least ten years before the term entered the general lexicon.

As the new decade unfolded, these sounds became increasingly commonplace, with rock launching its orchestrated campaign to be acknowledged as a serious creative form. But in the context of 1969, *In the Court of the Crimson King* represented an important early manifestation of an accident-prone yet ultimately fruitful dialogue between two areas of music that had previously been regarded as mutually exclusive. Symphonic rock had arrived, with King Crimson among the first major exponents.

Although the band's turbulent future odyssey was to yield further significant releases, that first album would prove to be the highpoint in their period as doyens of symphonic rock. It also secured Fripp's well-earned status as a cult guitar hero, his unassuming, bespectacled countenance and penchant for performing seated (soon to be adopted by Steve Hackett of Genesis) denying him the iconic prominence of his Heavy Metal brethren.

The album's 1970 successor, *In the Wake of Poseidon,* was fairly criticized for being highly derivative of what had gone before, although there were mitigating circumstances deriving from the abrupt exits of several key figures both before and during the recording. With the release of *Lizard* later the same year, the band entered an intermediate phase of producing rather quirky shorter songs that defied categorization, although the symphonic leanings remained present in a title track occupying the whole of Side Two. One of several guest musicians on *Lizard* was vocalist Jon Anderson, already destined for symphonic rock stardom as a founder member of Yes, a band that provided a symbolic farewell to the 60s as one of the last headline acts of the era to serve an apprenticeship at the Marquee Club.

Lizard, like every subsequent Crimson release (except the bootleg-quality live set *Earthbound* from 1972), certainly had its moments of inspiration, most notably in the delicate acoustic lyricism of *Lady of the Dancing Water* that closed Side One. But it was not until early 1973, when Fripp reformed the band with a world-class rhythm section comprising bass player John Wetton and drummer Bill Bruford (both b.1949), that full quality control was re-established. By this time, the band had developed a curious but by no means unsuccessful formula of powerful driving rock with jazz leanings, mixed in with gentler vocal tracks (Wetton doubling as lead singer) and contrasting acoustic lines from violinist David Cross (b.1949) and oddball percussionist Jamie Muir, whose contribution to the much praised *Larks' Tongues in Aspic* (1973) included what was possibly rock music's first application of the African thumb piano. The band also expanded their taste for the live instrumental improvisations first heard on *Earthbound,* with album tracks often simply adopting the name of the location where they were recorded. *Asbury Park* from the valedictory live album *USA* (1975) remains a particularly tight and inspired example. Throughout the Fripp/Wetton/Bruford era, this line of unstructured creativity yielded far more consistent results than might have been expected. The restful free form dreamscape of *Trio* from *Starless and Bible Black* (1974) remains one of the most sublime moments in the band's entire history.

Incredibly, King Crimson were still with us at the turn of the millennium, the line-up at the time of writing being the ever-present Fripp, plus Adrian Belew (b.1949, real name: Robert Steven Belew) (guitar, lead vocals), Pat Mastelotto (b.1955) (drums) and Trey Gunn (b.1960, not to be confused with Tracii Guns – see Chapter 14) on touch guitar, a ten-string 'tapped' instrument related to the Chapman Stick (see also Chapter 14). Belew, who can justly claim to be the longest-serving member apart from Fripp himself, has been associated with Crimson since the *Discipline* album of 1981. This highly regarded release had marked Fripp's revival of the name six years after *USA*, on which the supposed finality of the band's 1974-5 split had been marked by a reverential RIP at the foot of the credits.

Back in 1970, one of the more significant of the *Poseidon* departures was that of Greg Lake, who sought greater fame and fortune in a triumvirate that was effectively the first symphonic rock supergroup, albeit one that John Peel famously described as representing the 'sillier side' of the genre...

EMERSON, LAKE AND PALMER

Although history now credits King Crimson as the first global standard-bearers of symphonic rock, there can be little doubt that smaller scale precedents existed in such late 60s chart successes as *Nights in White Satin* by the Moody Blues and the Bach-influenced *A Whiter Shade of Pale* by the keyboard-centered and enigmatically named British quintet Procol Harum. This imposing motto is usually translated as 'beyond these things', although it has been suggested on more than one occasion that the correct Latin form is *Procul His*. Rising from the ashes of highly-regarded R&B ensemble the Paramounts and featuring the gritty baritone of principal keyboard man Gary Brooker (b.1945), the band also set a small but significant precedent in affording lyricist Keith Reid (b.1946) the status of *de facto* band member. King Crimson lyricist and muse Peter Sinfield (b.1943) would soon enjoy a similarly elevated position on the credits for *In the Court of the Crimson King*, where his role is grandly summarized as 'words and illumination'. Whether this second role merely meant he was in charge of the lighting rig or something altogether more profound is not divulged. Although such Procol Harum albums as *A Salty Dog* (1969) found favor with the rock audience, the band remains principally associated with quality hit singles, the UK No.1 ranking of *A Whiter Shade of Pale* in spring 1967 being closely followed by the equally enduring *Homburg* (UK No.6 in the autumn of the same year).

On a larger and more album-centered scale were the ambitious musical concepts that characterized the Nice. Built around the nucleus of Keith Emerson (b.1944) (keyboards) and Lee Jackson (b.1943) (bass), who had previously worked together in blues band the T-Bones, the Nice first came together in 1967 as backing band for the soul singer P.P. Arnold (b.1945, real name: Patricia Ann Cole). With Emerson and Jackson in the company of David O'List (guitar/vocals) and Brian 'Blinky' Davison (drums), the band received enthusiastic receptions for their warm-up sets at Arnold's concerts, the international success of Arnold's single *The First Cut is the Deepest* always ensuring they played to a sizeable crowd. Her best-known hit *Angel of the Morning* followed a year later, by which time the Nice had released their debut album *Thoughts of Emerlist Davjack* on the Immediate label, which also handled the UK arm of Arnold's catalog. It was in June 1968 that the band ensured its place in rock history by burning the Stars and Stripes during a performance of *America* from *West Side Story,* a stunt that prompted national headlines and an instant ban from the Albert Hall. The situation was either assisted or exacerbated, depending on your level of cynicism, by an advertising campaign that showed children with the adult faces of John Kennedy, Robert Kennedy and Martin Luther King. This raised the band's international profile immeasurably, with the composer of *America*, Leonard Bernstein (1918–1990), taking legal steps to ban the release of the track in the USA.

From this point onwards, the Nice moved inexorably in the direction of symphonic rock, a journey that culminated in the *Five Bridges Suite,* released on Tony Stratton-Smith's recently launched Charisma label in 1970. Recorded live at the Fairfield Halls, Croydon, in October 1969, Emerson and Jackson's creative collaboration with conductor Joseph Eger found the band, reduced to a trio since the early departure of O'List, performing alongside the Sinfonia of London under the baton of Eger.

Originally commissioned by the Newcastle Arts Festival, the *Five Bridges Suite* contains strong evidence of Emerson's capacity as a composer to handle such arcane classical forms as the fugue. But hearing it again almost four decades down the line, there can be little doubt that *Five Bridges* has become a period piece of the type unlikely to benefit from a twenty-first century revival, the stilted delivery of Jackson's lyrics proving grimly reminiscent of the commercial actor/singers we still find in the cast of the stage musicals of Tim Rice and Andrew Lloyd Webber. But the very nature of the *Five Bridges* concept places the Nice alongside King Crimson as founding fathers of symphonic rock.

Contemporaneous with *Five Bridges* was the equally ambitious *Concerto for Group and Orchestra* by Jon Lord (b.1941), keyboard player with Deep Purple. Recorded live at the Albert Hall with an apparently under-rehearsed Royal Philharmonic Orchestra conducted by the English composer Malcolm Arnold (1921–2006, knighted 1993), *Concerto for Group and Orchestra* proved to be the band's first and only true encounter with symphonic rock until the work's revival in 2000. With the definitive line-up of Lord, alongside Ian Gillan (b.1945) (vocals), Ritchie Blackmore (b.1945) (guitar), Roger Glover (b.1945) (bass) and Ian Paice (b.1948) (drums), the band emerged in the early 70s as one of the finest purveyors of premium grade hard rock, as distinct from Heavy Metal. They also became exemplary exponents of that much-misused format, the live album. In so many cases, a live disc would be released merely to keep the fans happy (and the cashflow regular) until the next studio offering was complete. With the imposing double LP *Made in Japan* (1972), home of the definitive version of that essential rock anthem *Smoke on the Water,* Deep Purple unleashed scorching performances that easily surpassed their own existing studio versions. The later sequel, *Made in Europe* (1976) offered more of the same, the opening account of the title track from *Burn* (1974) being one of those exhilarating moments in rock through which no sentient human being could possibly remain seated. If *Made in Europe* failed to attain the legendary status of its predecessor, it was perhaps because the band's sometimes relatively lackluster studio offerings had noticeably improved in the meantime.

By now, Gillan had been replaced by David Coverdale (b.1951) and Glover by Glenn Hughes (b.1952). Blackmore would shortly be replaced by tragic guitar prodigy Tommy Bolin (1951–1976). The ensuing solo project Ritchie Blackmore's Rainbow offered a softer focus rock that disappointed many Purple fans. The band also suffered adolescent ridicule in the UK due to a logo that resembled that of the pre-school TV show *Rainbow,* featuring a guy dressed as a teddy bear named Bungle.

Blackmore's Rainbow   Bungle's Rainbow

After a successful 80s/90s run with various reincarnations of Deep Purple, Blackmore found an unexpected new direction in 1997 with Blackmore's Night, a mainly acoustic quasi-renaissance ensemble whose inspired brand of musical theater has attracted many, including those who never cared much for Deep Purple or any other rock band.

To perceive Emerson, Lake and Palmer as an amalgamation of King Crimson and the Nice would be a distortion of the truth, Emerson's influence within his former band being far more pivotal than Lake's could possibly have been under the established coalition of Fripp, MacDonald and Giles. In any case, King Crimson minus Lake remained a going concern for years to come, whereas the Nice had effectively disintegrated by the time of Emerson's departure.

The third man in the new venture was Carl Palmer (b.1950), a drummer of prodigious skill who had first gained recognition at the age of sixteen as a member of Chris Farlowe's Thunderbirds. Later working with the Crazy World of Arthur Brown and Atomic Rooster, Palmer was recruited by Emerson and Lake after a reported plan for them to link up with Jimi Hendrix and Mitch Mitchell failed to take root. What might have emerged from this proposed interstellar alliance has been the subject of endless speculation, although many Hendrix fans are quietly relieved it never happened.

Releasing their self-titled debut album in 1970, the trio already known as ELP gained immediate approval from the growing legions of symphonic rock devotees. With Lake's instrumental contribution limited primarily to bass guitar, his refined acoustic guitar fills enjoying only occasional outings, the ELP soundscape was always focused on the ever-growing bank of keyboards operated by Emerson. Visually, Emerson was also first among equals, his stage acrobatics and knife-throwing routines (usually aimed at his own equipment) having been carried over from his time with the Nice. *Tarkus,* released in 1971, took the concepts of the first album several stages further, the title track being a continuous extended creation, divided into individually titled sections, as was the custom of the time. It was one of these 'movements', titled *Manticore,* that later provided the name of the band's own record label.

But it was the third album, also from 1971, that fully defined the ELP aesthetic in the minds of both their supporters and their detractors.

Recorded live before a seemingly ecstatic audience, *Pictures at an Exhibition* was an offering to which no-one could be indifferent. Taking just a few selected movements from the suite for piano by Modeste Mussorgsky (1839–1981), later orchestrated by Ravel and others, ELP recreated the originals in their own image. They added lyrics to *Promenade* and the *Great Gate of Kiev,* not to mention a *Blues Variation* to an already unrecognizable setting of *The Old Castle.* With the benefit of hindsight, the album can only be described as painfully pretentious, its one saving grace being Lake's gentle acoustic song *The Sage,* the only item on the agenda (apart from an added episode in the *Baba Yaga* sequence and Kim Fowley's *Nutrocker,* which appears as an encore) in which the hapless Mussorgsky had no hand. In a typically informed and succinct thumbnail guide to what he chose to term 'art rock', broadcast in the late 70s on the BBC classical station Radio 3, John Peel played the closing moments of ELP's *Great Gate of Kiev* and the thunderous ovation that followed, admitting to his listeners that he left the first ELP concert 'in tears in the face of applause like that'. But although many empathized with Peel at the time, and doubtless many more have come to do so since, the influence of ELP on both sides of the Atlantic remained huge throughout the first half of the 70s. This said, the task of finding someone who admits to having been an ELP fan is rather like finding someone who admits to having been one of the eager British electorate that voted *en masse* for Margaret Thatcher in 1979. Following two more studio releases, ELP reached further heights of excess with the 1974 live triple *Welcome Back, My Friends, To The Show That Never Ends, Ladies and Gentlemen…*

But it soon became clear that the show was about to end, the last release of any significance being the ominously titled *Works Vol.1* from 1977, a double LP of which three out of the four sides were devoted to solo offerings from each band member. All attempts to revive ELP, including a 1992 reunion, have proved short-lived, although the brief liaison of *Emerson, Lake and (Cozy) Powell* yielded one successful album and a few live dates in the mid 80s.

An extreme product of an extreme era, ELP are all too easy to attack from a twenty-first century perspective. But there is also the parallel danger of perceiving the aesthetics of the time as a catch-all excuse for a recorded legacy that, at its most extravagant, hits the highest of all possible readings on the cringe scale. To take just one of many counter-examples, *The Six Wives of Henry VIII* (1973) by Rick Wakeman (b.1949) has worn remarkably well, the strength of Wakeman's themes and the rich but uncluttered arrangements providing a quality period piece for which few allowances need be made. As keyboard player with Yes, Wakeman was seen by many as one of Emerson's few serious competitors, the late 60s and early 70s explosion of guitar virtuosity having yielded only a handful of corresponding keyboard glitterati. His often regal but less aggressive stage persona tended to make Wakeman appear second best, although few would question that history has shown his work in the more favorable light. As was inevitably the case with a band whose creations regularly covered a whole side of an album, ELP were never destined to make regular assaults on the singles chart, their only major hit being an uncharacteristically straightforward reworking of Copland's *Fanfare for the Common Man* from *Works Vol.1* (UK No.13, 1977). And let it not be forgotten that Greg Lake hit the UK No.2 spot in 1975 with *I Believe In Father Christmas.* But the emphasis on albums to the near exclusion of the single was a policy ELP would naturally share with the majority of

131

exponents of symphonic rock. There was, however, one notable exception whose early success rested on a string of hit singles in the final months of the 60s…

JETHRO TULL

When the wild Dickensian figure of Ian Anderson (b.1947) appeared on *Top of the Pops* in 1969, miming the words and flute lines from *Living in the Past,* it was not unreasonably assumed that he was Jethro Tull and that the other performers wielding unplugged electric guitars and hitting silent drums were merely his backing band.

In fact, the name of Jethro Tull (1674–1741), high profile English agriculturalist and inventor of the mechanical seed drill, had only recently been adopted as the collective title for a band fronted by Anderson and featuring the newly recruited and appropriately named lead guitarist Martin Barre (b.1946, sometimes credited as Martin Lancelot Barre). A replacement for founder member Mick Abrahams (b.1943), whose own band Blodwyn Pig would, like Tull, prove to be one of rock's most long-lived acts, Barre soon achieved legendary status for his extended solo on the title track of the 1971 Tull album *Aqualung*. He was joining an established team, comprising Anderson plus Glenn Cornick (b.1947)

(bass) and Clive Bunker (b.1946) (drums). Keyboard player John Evan(s) (b.1948) was an associate member during the early years and had joined full-time by 1971, the very existence of Jethro Tull having first emerged from the Blackpool based John Evan Band. Over the next few years, Cornick and Bunker were replaced by Jeffrey Hammond (b.1946, sometimes credited as Jeffrey Hammond-Hammond) and Barriemore Barlow (b.1949), a line-up that saw few further changes before the late 70s. Even before 1970, Anderson was firmly established as the band's dominant creative force and principal songwriter.

What TOTP's teenage studio audience made of him is difficult to imagine. The program had played host to some pretty bizarre presentations in recent years, most notably the pyromaniac routines of Arthur Brown. But like many a fine showman, Brown gave every impression that, having removed and extinguished his flaming headdress, he would leave the building as a regular sort of guy who had just completed an honest day's toil. But Anderson was different, the demented bug-eyed vagrant who played demonic flute lines while balanced precariously on one leg being just that little bit too convincing to be dismissed as a mere stage act. This said, the kids still bought his records, *Living in the Past* reaching UK No.3 and two further Top Ten successes to follow within the year.

Of these, it was *The Witch's Promise* that most accurately defined the band's long-term identity. The urban contemporary jazz leanings of *Living in the Past* and the mainstream hard rock of *Sweet Dream* were quality representations of Tull as they were in 1969 and would remain up to and including *Aqualung.* But the pagan rural imagery and Shakespearean overtones of *The Witch's Promise* introduced an element that distinguished Tull from all other major exponents of symphonic rock and would later enjoy free rein on such classic albums as *Minstrel in the Gallery* (1975), *Song from the Wood* (1977) and *Heavy Horses* (1978).

By the time of these landmark releases, Anderson's public persona had matured into that of a benevolent country squire and champion of traditional industries. On the cover of *Heavy Horses,* the tweed-jacketed Anderson is seen leading a pair of magnificent shire horses, the lavishly orchestrated title track being a poignant and sincere eulogy to these noble working beasts. With the possible exception of the ageing biker he depicts in *Too Old to Rock & Roll, Too Young to Die* (1976), every character Anderson creates for himself seems wholly believable, in the case of *Aqualung* rather chillingly so.

Preceded by *This Was* (1968), *Stand Up* (1969) and *Benefit* (1970), the second of which remains particularly highly regarded, *Aqualung* was the defining release of Tull as a major international force. Although comprising eleven individual songs, the album is divided into two halves (two sides on the original LP) subtitled *Aqualung* and *My God*, the character known as *Aqualung* being portrayed as a depraved and unsavory down-and-out far beyond the scary but ultimately harmless character seen on TOTP. The relationship between *Aqualung* and his deity is disturbingly expressed in a pseudo-biblical printed text, starting with the words 'In the beginning, man created God...'

In terms of musical content, *Aqualung* was essentially a high caliber rock album with only modest symphonic leanings, although it did mark a further guest appearance by David (later Dee) Palmer (b.1937), whose string and brass arrangements can be traced back to the first album and were to remain a feature of Tull releases throughout the 70s. Otherwise, the prominence of Anderson's trademark flute and quasi-renaissance acoustic guitar style were the only aspects of the instrumentation to venture beyond the traditional rock format.

It was the next release, *Thick as a Brick* (1972), that marked Anderson's first tentative exploration of a wider canvas. Comprising an extended setting of a sprawling poem, the album contains just two continuous tracks, clocking in at 22'45" and 21'05". Despite the melodic inventiveness of Anderson's principal theme, *Thick as a Brick* will forever be seen as one of his most opaque releases, the development of the theme lacking the diversity needed to sustain such a lengthy innings. An elaborate but unfunny cover design, that witlessly parodies a provincial English newspaper, does little to help the cause. The sequel, *A Passion Play* (1973), attempts a similarly ambitious musical format with equally disappointing results.

But there can be few doubts that both these albums provide a lasting monument to the sheer professionalism of Anderson's work. Heroic failures though they may have been in artistic terms, the performance from all concerned remains of the highest order. Whilst other large-scale releases of the era, including the agenda-setting *Tubular Bells* by Mike Oldfield, contained obvious, although by no means fatal, technical blemishes, both *Thick as a Brick* and *A Passion Play* still stand up to the closest scrutiny. Early and unrepresentative blips in the huge output of an exceptional talent, these albums are nonetheless worthy of respect, if not affection.

In *War Child* (1974), Anderson was well and truly back on message. A concept album only in the broadest sense, *War Child* was a collection of tightly structured songs of which only one, *Back Door Angels,* exceeded the five-minute barrier. A thumbnail miniaturist of the highest order, Anderson was in his element, the doom-laden images of the title track merging seamlessly into such charming lightweights as *Bungle in the Jungle,* a hit single in the USA that received airplay but never charted on home territory. *War Child* also introduced more extensive use of Palmer's input, his powerful orchestrations now playing a key role that reached a high point in *Heavy Horses.*

With *War Child,* the band entered a period of unparalleled creativity that continued for the remainder of the 70s and well into the 80s, Tull being one of those select bands who appeared untouched by the cataclysmic events of the Punk era. The rate of production had slowed by the mid 80s, the superb *Crest of a Knave* (1987) seen by many as the final product of a long vintage era.

Still active in the twenty-first century, Ian Anderson must surely be seen as one of rock's truly great musicians.

Drawing much of his inspiration from Britain's rural past made Anderson something of an exception at a time when, in the world of music, electric was giving way to electronic. Cumbersome Hammond organs, complete with revolving Leslie speakers, were being replaced by all manner of streamlined and increasingly user-friendly keyboard instruments with a seemingly unlimited range of sounds and effects. Across the Western World, music stores were piled high with secondhand tape loop echo units that had been traded in for the latest solid state marvel.

It was in this environment that the sci-fi imagery of bands such as Pink Floyd enjoyed a second flowering. The ultimate psychedelic survivors, these stalwarts of comic strip space travel had delighted their followers with random galactic gurglings ever since *Interstellar Overdrive* occupied a rambling ten minutes of their debut album, titled for far from obvious reasons *The Piper at the Gates of Dawn* (1967). Under the leadership of the allegedly brilliant Syd Barrett (1946–2006, real name: Roger Keith Barrett), the Floyd had cut two classic singles with *Arnold Layne* and *See Emily Play,* the childhood dreamscapes and kaleidoscopic instrumentation of the latter making it one of the masterpieces of British psychedelia. Supported by the competent rather than commanding talents of Roger Waters (b.1943) (bass), Richard Wright (1943–2008) (keyboards) and Nick Mason (b.1944) (drums), later to be joined by guitarist David Gilmour (b.1946), Barrett can justly claim credit in these two songs for two of the most memorable UK hits of 1967.

But his work was never consistent, attempts to be psychedelically humorous in such album tracks as *The Gnome, Scarecrow* and *Bike* proving embarrassingly silly. Following Barrett's reportedly LSD-induced departure, the Floyd found themselves a comfortable niche weaving loose electronic tapestries around rudimentary songs and instrumentals that placed minimal demands on both the emotions and the intellect. So it was that such simple fare as *Set the Controls for the Heart of the Sun* and *Careful With That Axe, Eugene* became required listening for sulky teenagers and students at low ranking universities, eager to distance themselves from the three-minute single with the minimum mental exertion. The Floyd's supremacy in this lucrative sector reached its zenith with the multi-million seller *The Dark Side of the Moon* (1973), worshipped by many but seen by others as the most overrated rock album of all time. Ironically, the title appears to have been secondhand, *Dark Side of the Moon* by British duo Medicine Head having been released on John Peel's ill-fated Dandelion label in 1972. Comprising John Fiddler (guitar/vocals) and Peter Hope-Evans (harmonica/jew's-harp), Medicine Head's subsequent move to Polydor yielded three memorable UK hit singles: *One And One Is One* (UK No.3, 1973), *Rising Sun* (No.11, 1973) and *Slip and Slide* (No.22, 1974).

As the 70s wore on, the Floyd's cash-generating powers remained assured, *The Wall* (1979) yielding a No.1 hit single and an easy acoustic guitar riff that could even be managed by those incapable of negotiating the opening bars of *Stairway to Heaven.* But as tank-topped adolescents carefully stored their Floyd LPs alongside Mum and Dad's cherished library of the Carpenters and James Last, a shy 19-year-old was taking the first cautious steps towards realizing a dream that would make him famous and his backer seriously rich...

MIKE OLDFIELD

Born – Reading, England, 15 May 1953

Performing since the age of 14 in the folk duo Sallyangie with his older sister, Sally Oldfield (b.1950), this quietly studious young Englishman was the very antithesis of the Strat-burning rock star. The duo's Transatlantic album *Children of the Sun* (1968) had been favorably received in folk circles but made little impact on the wider world. After forming a short-lived band Barefeet (or Barefoot) with brother Terry (b.1949), Oldfield was invited to join Kevin Ayers and the Whole World, first as bass player and later as lead guitarist. By the time the Whole World folded in 1971, Oldfield was already doing the rounds of the record companies in the hope of finding an outlet for an ambitious fifty minute composition on which he would personally overdub almost all the instruments. No takers were found until some months later, when he finally struck a deal with a then largely unknown entrepreneur named Richard Branson (b.1950, knighted 1999). Branson, at 22, was less than three years Oldfield's senior.

What happened next is one of the most widely told success stories in the history of rock music, Oldfield's *Tubular Bells* becoming the first release on Virgin Records and its phenomenal success paving the way for the global business empire Branson created over the following decades. Applying minimalist techniques before the term became standard currency outside its own specialized field, *Tubular Bells* is essentially a patchwork of diverse themes, in which dense layers of mesmeric sound drift into folk inspired melodic passages. Despite the heavy application of what were then still perceived as cutting edge studio techniques, Oldfield's use of electronic sound is relatively sparing, his decision to allow a solo

Spanish guitar the final word at the end of Side One being a subtle yet telling reference to his own acoustic roots. Like the Ninth Symphony of Beethoven, *Tubular Bells* was a monumental work of the imagination that had no direct precedent. Inevitably, it left Oldfield with the problem of building on his success with a credible follow-up. This he did with *Hergest Ridge* (1974), although both the press and the public gave the album considerably less acclaim than it deserved. Similar to *Tubular Bells* insofar as it was another continuous studio creation based on multi-layered overdubs, *Hergest Ridge* was a considerably more unified composition in which both sides were derived from the same basic theme. It also lacked the episodic quality of *Tubular Bells,* resulting in a sense of structured thematic development rather than a sequence of conjoined ideas.

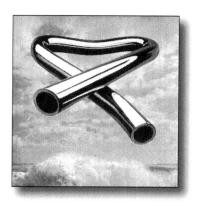

After this commercially successful but much maligned release, Oldfield found critical favor again in 1975 with *Ommadawn.* The final part of what could be seen as a three-album triptych, *Ommadawn* finds Oldfield sharing the workload with such diverse musical characters as a team of African drummers and a Northumbrian piper identified only as Herbie. These newly added textures greatly expanded Oldfield's expressive range, the dodgy vocal performance in the closing 'horse song' (later released on single as *On Horseback*) being instantly forgiven amid the splendor of what had gone before.

By now a national institution who was soon to become the first rock musician after Paul McCartney to have an entry in the hallowed pages of *Who's Who,* Oldfield continued to release albums at irregular intervals throughout the 70s, 80s and 90s, *Incantations* from 1978 further developing the *Tubular Bells* formula and featuring an outstanding contribution by guest vocalist Maddy Prior of Steeleye Span (see Chapter 10). He also made surprisingly frequent appearances in the singles' chart, *Moonlight Shadow* with Scottish singer Maggie Reilly (b.1956) (UK No.4, 1983) providing what was widely seen as a poignant tribute to the memory of John Lennon. The fact that he never achieved quite the same iconic status in the USA is maybe due to Oldfield being perceived at the time as a quintessentially British artist, whose idiomatic language is perhaps appreciated most readily by a domestic audience. This said, the use of material from *Tubular Bells* in the 1973 William Friedkin movie *The Exorcist* undoubtedly brought his work to the attention of a wider US audience and earned him a Grammy Award in 1975.

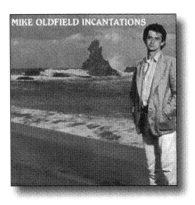

As for Richard Branson, his high-profile lifestyle and multifarious business activities have attracted the attention of gossip columnists and serious journalists alike, a recent biography by the much feared investigative writer Tom Bower placing him alongside such colorful Bower subjects as Mohammed al Fayed, Tiny Rowland and Robert Maxwell.

But let it not be forgotten that, under Branson's stewardship, Virgin Records effectively played what John Peel termed 'Arts Council' to a whole generation of worthy but uncommercial musicians on the fringes of rock. Some, including the austere yet compelling German synthesizer trio Tangerine Dream, were to prove a shrewd long-term investment, with *Phaedra* (1974), *Rubycon* (1975) and the live edit *Ricochet* (1975) all entering the UK album charts. The band's remarkable appeal may be illustrated by the legendary concert at Rheims Cathedral in December 1974, where a reported 6000 fans arrived in the hope of gaining access to a 2000 seat venue.

Other Virgin signings, such as the Marxist avant-garde collective Henry Cow, were surely never destined to even recoup their overheads. But Henry Cow's small recorded legacy, recognizable by the recurring 'woven sock' cover motif, is greatly prized by a devoted minority and surely would never have happened without Virgin Records and the extraordinary success of *Tubular Bells*.

Although it took a little time for the US market to fully embrace Oldfield's early work, other symphonic rock acts found their richest pickings in that part of the world. Buried deep within the cover to *Thick as a Brick,* a mock LP review bemoans the fact that the popularity of Jethro Tull with the American audience had made live UK appearances a rarity. Strange, then, that symphonic rock should remain an essentially

Anglo-European genre, the buoyant US music scene finding its own directions to be discussed in later chapters.

Nevertheless, Vanilla Fudge certainly touched on the symphonic via the somewhat curious route of reworking older chart hits in a vaguely Spectoresque soundscape, after first slowing them down to a processional pace. Best remembered is their 1967 revival of *You Keep Me Hanging On*, originally an up tempo hit for the Supremes. Songs by the Beatles were also a favorite hunting ground, with *Ticket to Ride* and *Eleanor Rigby* undergoing similar treatment. When described in words, the Fudge approach to music inevitably threatens to be insufferably ponderous and grandiose, although the cover versions listed above have stood the test of time with disarming conviction. If nothing else, they certainly meet the critical requirement that a valid cover should in some way introduce new thinking, rather than merely replicate the original. Built around the long-running partnership of Tim Bogert (b.1944) (bass/vocals) and Carmine Appice (b.1946) (drums), with Mark Stein (b.1947) (keyboards) and Vince Martell (b.1945) (guitar), the Fudge disbanded in 1970, but relaunched themselves in 1984 for the largely unloved *Mystery* album. Live appearances seem to have continued at least into the 90s, resulting in a complex back catalog of recordings drawn from often undated and undocumented performances. During the 70s, Bogert and Appice briefly joined forces with English guitarist Jeff Beck to form Beck, Bogert and

Appice, an alliance that yielded a rarely seen but highly rated self-titled studio album in 1973.

In Britain and Europe, though, the influence of symphonic rock was far more profound, a trickle-down effect having the capacity to breathe new vitality into hard-gigging mainstream rock bands such as Wishbone Ash. Fronted by the twin lead guitars of Andy Powell and David 'Ted' Turner (both b.1950), the absence of a charismatic lead vocalist would forever deny this otherwise highly skilled outfit star billing. Amid such routine rock numbers as *Lady Whisky,* symphonic leanings were apparent in the imposing *Phoenix* that closed the band's self-titled debut album in 1970. A helmeted mythical warrior on the cover of *Argus* (1973) heralded further moves in that direction, heroic numbers such as *The King Will Come* and *Throw Down the Sword* becoming the songs everyone demanded to hear at live gigs. Despite not having gained full access to rock's historic pantheon, Wishbone Ash remained on the road at the turn of the millennium, Powell in the company of an all-new team making several successful UK tours in the late 90s.

A strong and distinctive vocal style was most certainly a feature of Yes, although it has to be said that the strangulated falsetto of Jo(h)n Anderson (b.1944) was always an acquired taste. With Rick Wakeman (keyboards) and Steve Howe (b.1947) (guitar), one of the most accomplished instrumental pairings of all time, alongside

Chris Squire (b.1948) (bass) and future King Crimson drummer Bill Bruford, Anderson's elfin stage presence also provided a visual focus at live shows. Early releases, including *The Yes Album* (1971) and *Fragile* (1972) provide a retrospective tale of mixed fortunes, with such classic performances as Howe's acoustic solo *Mood for a Day* hidden amongst some best forgotten relics like the profoundly unamusing *Cans and Brahms*. But within a year of releasing *Fragile,* the band came up with what many see as the essential symphonic rock album. Comprising just three extended tracks, *Close to the Edge* (1972) is a release of timeless brilliance, the majestic orchestral soundscape of the 19-minute title track and the delicate acoustic textures of *And You And I* finally giving way to the dashing rock rhythms of *Siberian Khatru,* home to one of the most compelling guitar riffs ever recorded.

Although *Close to the Edge* was a near impossible act to follow, the band's status was further consolidated by a concentrated period of creativity that produced *Yessongs* (1973), *Tales from Topographic Oceans* (1973) and *Relayer* (1974). It was during this time that both Wakeman and Bruford made their exits. Their replacements, Patrick Moraz (b.1948) and Alan White (b.1949), proved highly skilled in their respective fields, but there can be little doubt that their arrival came at the end of the vintage years. Even so, the band continued to enjoy public acclaim for the remainder of the 70s, the 1976 album *Going for the One* yielding the hit single *Wondrous Stories* (UK No.7, 1977). By this time, Wakeman had been tempted to rejoin the band, his post-Yes solo ventures having included the soundtrack to the 1976 Winter Olympics movie *White Rock.* But by now the New Wave was approaching and Yes, like so many heroes of the early 70s, would find themselves both unable and most likely unwilling to embrace the radical change of aesthetic. Attempted revivals have been frequent, the support of a dedicated but ageing audience being always guaranteed.

But there was one major provider of symphonic rock that managed to both weather the storm and then positively prosper in the barren years of the 80s...

GENESIS

Formed c.1967 around the darkly charismatic Peter Gabriel (b.1950), this seemingly indestructible English ensemble was essentially a product of the exclusive Charterhouse public school. The original line-up is generally believed to have included Tony Banks (b.1950) (keyboards), Anthony Phillips (b.1951) (guitar) and Mike Rutherford (b.1950) (bass). The identity of the original drummer has been a matter of speculation. Some sources credit John Silver, while others suggest it was Gabriel himself. At the time of writing, the odds-on favorite is one Chris Stewart, a self-confessed 'musical incompetent' who later found fame and fortune writing a series of highly readable books about restoring a derelict Spanish farmhouse. Silver, it seems, was Stewart's successor, his own brief tenure being terminated with the arrival of John Mayhew.

Under the guidance of pop entrepreneur and Charterhouse old boy Jonathan King (b.1944), the band cut an initially ignored Decca album *From Genesis to Revelation* (1969, reissued in 1974 as *In the Beginning*). A move to the Charisma label, under the stewardship of Tony Stratton-Smith, resulted in *Trespass* (1970). More enthusiastically welcomed than its predecessor, this album played host to *The Knife,* one of their finest early songs and the one for which the audience clamor on

Genesis Live (1973). Following the ensuing promotional tour, Mayhew and Phillips left, to be replaced by Phil Collins (b.1951) and, after a reported six-month search, Steve Hackett (b.1950). The classic Genesis line-up was now in place, although no-one could possibly have predicted what the future would hold, particularly with regard to the role of Collins, a former child actor and alleged knitwear model whose chirpy Cockney image was far removed from the patrician aloofness of Gabriel and the near anonymity of the other band members. This would serve him well in later years.

Seen by many as one of the finest Genesis albums, *Nursery Cryme* (1971) played host to *The Musical Box,* a disturbing 10-minute narrative of traumatic childhood fantasies, set in an English country house. It was this track that generated the arresting cover painting, depicting a little girl in Victorian dress wielding a croquet mallet on a lawn strewn with severed heads. Since the Doors unleashed *The End* and the Velvet Underground entertained us with *Sister Ray,* few holds had been barred in rock lyrics. But never had such goings-on been placed in such a genteel setting.

But here was the calling card of Peter Gabriel's Genesis, an English rock band from the upper-middle classes with a penchant for the quaint and the theatrical. But it was not all violence and lust, *The Musical Box* being followed by *For Absent Friends,* a gentle Betjemanesque vignette of two elderly widows attending church. *Foxtrot* (1972) was a less

147

distinguished offering in terms of lyrical content, the emphasis being more on musical development. *Supper's Ready,* which occupied most of Side Two, was the band's most extended composition to date, Steve Hackett's acoustic solo *Horizons* providing an effective instrumental preamble based loosely on the *Prelude* from *Cello Suite No.1 BWV 1007* by J.S. Bach. Perceived at the time as one of the era's less astounding instrumentalists, Hackett later re-invented himself as a fully-fledged classical guitarist, his eighteen-movement *Midsummer Night's Dream,* performed and recorded with the Royal Philharmonic Orchestra in 1997, showing an incredible technical and artistic transformation of the type many have attempted but few have successfully achieved.

With *Selling England by the Pound* (1973), the content was starting to wear thin. An attempt to mention as many British supermarkets as possible in the closing *Aisle of Plenty* proved neither funny nor particularly clever. Only in the gentle English eccentricity of *I Know What I Like (In Your Wardrobe),* which later emerged as the only Genesis hit single of the Gabriel era (UK No.21, 1974), was the strange and compelling world of *Nursery Cryme* even distantly visible. Ironically, the other track on the album that carries its age with dignity is *More Fool Me,* an acoustic ballad that marked what was then a rare appearance of Collins as lead vocalist, a distinction it shares with *For Absent Friends*. But it was the next album that would be the real one-off...

The Lamb Lies Down on Broadway (1974) was an extravagant concept double LP, in which Gabriel acted out the role of Rael, a spraygun-toting urban delinquent who finds himself drawn into a white-knuckle odyssey of the mind and body. Although Genesis, like the Doors, had traditionally credited the compositions to the whole band, Mike Rutherford stated in a BBC interview with the jazz critic Derek Jewell that this album had been 'largely Pete's brainchild.' From the majesty of the opening title track, through the sumptuous textures of *The Carpet Crawlers,* to the dramatic culmination of the closing *It,* a track that prompted the usually reserved Jewell to comment 'Wasn't that tremendous?', *The Lamb Lies Down on Broadway* was unlike anything Genesis, or any other band, had ever attempted. Criticized by advocates of the post-Gabriel Genesis as pretentious and impenetrable, it provided the final crowning glory on a reign of mixed fortunes for those who still see Genesis minus Gabriel as Hamlet without the Prince.

Gabriel's subsequent departure was greeted with shock at the time, although in retrospect it was perhaps inevitable. Having unleashed his *magnum opus* on a stunned but, at the time, highly appreciative fanbase, his work with the band was surely at an end. Later years have seen him enjoy several high profile successes, interspersed with periods of apparent inactivity, but many of those who were there at the time hold the view that Genesis without Gabriel is incomplete and *vice versa.*

The image of a jubilant Phil Collins leaping from the drum stool and grabbing the microphone before Gabriel was out of the building is one that delights Collins' many detractors. However, Genesis historians assure us that there was a lengthy period of auditions before the other members of the band finally accepted Collins as the new lead vocalist. From that moment onwards, Genesis became a fundamentally different band, *A Trick of the Tail* (1976) containing an expertly presented agenda of neatly crafted pop songs for grown-ups. Many long-term fans were outraged by what they saw and heard, but most reviews were favorable and the album soon found its way into the sparse record collections of dilettante listeners who could not have cared less about the fate of Rael. Collins was soon relishing his new-found fame, launching himself as a solo artist and media personality before the corpse of Gabriel's Genesis was cold in its grave. A string of hits followed, Collins' cover of *You Can't Hurry Love* reaching the UK No.1 spot in the winter of 1982-3 and a similarly workmanlike restatement of *A Groovy Kind of Love* doing the same in autumn 1988. Both songs had acquired classic status during the 60s as hits for the Supremes and Wayne Fontana respectively.

A highly skilled showbiz professional whose credentials were perhaps established before he even joined the band, Collins' capacity to reinvent himself as whatever the TV viewing public wanted him to be should surprise no-one. How the other members of Genesis, one of the most creative and original British bands of the early 70s, managed to transform themselves in the same chameleon-like manner is a question that has puzzled many for more than a quarter of a century.

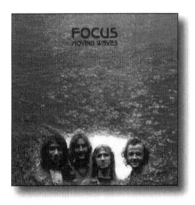

Although symphonic rock remained a predominantly British genre, there was significant input from mainland Europe. Most prominent amongst the continental faction was the Dutch band Focus, fronted by the often uneasy alliance between flutist, keyboard player and principal composer Thijs van Leer (b.1948) and the prodigiously talented guitar virtuoso Jan Akkerman (b.1946). Originally a trio, comprising Van Leer with Martin Dresden (bass) and Hans Cleuver (drums), the band first worked together on the cabaret circuit before being hired for the 1969 Dutch production of *Hair*. Akkerman joined during the recording of the first album, *In and Out of Focus* (1971). This first release enjoyed a lukewarm critical reception, with disposable pop songs such as *Black Beauty* and *Sugar Island*, despite the latter's underlying political message, blinding most of the rock audience to such strong instrumentals as *Anonymus* and Akkerman's triumphant *House of the King*. A few years down the line, this last item became universally known in households across Britain as the theme music for Yorkshire Television's family science show *Don't Ask Me*, featuring the apparently insane but in fact highly informative Dr. Magnus Pyke (1908–1992). Ironically, the medieval musical language and choice of the flute as lead instrument in *House of the King* led many viewers to wrongly assume they were listening to Jethro Tull.

Akkerman left after the first album to rejoin drummer Pierre van der Linden, with whom he had played in the Dutch bands Brainbox and the Hunters. Van Leer followed Akkerman, the arrival of bass player Cyril Havermans completing the definitive Focus line-up that delivered the ground-breaking *Moving Waves* (1971). Starting with the quirky instrumental *Hocus Pocus,* in which Akkerman played frenetic and technically stunning guitar lines while Van Leer yodelled, Side One played host to the haunting flute solo *Janis* and Akkerman's stylish classical guitar miniature *Le Clochard*. The whole of Side Two was occupied by the colossal *Eruption*, a mainly Van Leer composition, in which thematic material from the opera *Orfeo* by Claudio Monteverdi (1567–1643) was juxtaposed with a range of thrusting rock guitar motifs and quasi-romantic piano episodes. Akkerman contributed a fluid account of the Santanaesque instrumental *Tommy* by Dutch saxophonist Tom Barlage, plus a spectacular electric guitar cadenza titled simply *The Bridge*. Like *Tubular Bells* and *Close to the Edge, Eruption* represented symphonic rock at its highest level.

Sadly, *Moving Waves* was to be the pinnacle of a short collective innings that left a back catalog of just eight albums, including the aficionados-only live set *Focus at the Rainbow* (1973) and the obligatory posthumous out-takes anthology *Ship of Memories* (1976). There are hidden gems to be found in most of the other releases, the catchy instrumental *Sylvia,* which became the band's biggest international hit, lurking amid an otherwise disappointing agenda on the double album *Focus 3* (1972). With *Hamburger Concerto* (1974), most notably in Akkerman's composition *Birth,* the band finally came close to reclaiming the heights of *Moving Waves,* although daft subtitles such as *Rare, Medium* and *Well Done* left fans wondering if the band even wanted to be taken seriously again. Likewise the stupidly named *Mother Focus* (1975), on which is hiding an early studio version of the gentle *No Hang Ups* by Paul Stoppelman, a piece which remained in Akkerman's solo set long after the demise of Focus. By this time, both Havermans and Van der Linden were gone, their places being taken by Bert Ruiter and Colin Allen, the latter formerly of Stone the Crows.

It was after this album that Akkerman also made good his escape, the band's new lead guitarist being Belgian jazz-rock luminary Philip Catherine (b.1942). His stay would prove brief but eventful, *Focus Con Proby* (1977) launching the new line-up in the company of, believe it or not, trouser-splitting 60s heartthrob P.J. Proby (b.1938, real name: James Marcus Smith). Although not essential listening, the album is by no means the disaster many predicted, both the vocal performance and the soaring guitar lines on the opening *Wingless* showing the idea had at least some basis in reality. Also of significance is Catherine's exhilarating instrumental *Sneezing Bull,* a piece that he brought to Focus and would take away with him afterwards. But the time had now come for everyone to move on. One of the most frustrating bands in the history of rock, Focus surely touched greatness with *Moving Waves,* but were reduced to sporadic flashes of brilliance for the remainder of their short life.

An area known and appreciated only by the most serious devotees is Akkerman's extensive solo output, a production line that was up and running both before and during the Focus years. In 1972, Harvest Records released an LP titled *Profile,* on which Akkerman presents a selection of classical guitar solos, renaissance lute solos and all-electric group items, supported by a range of guest musicians including some names from Focus. The absence of any information to the contrary suggests the album is a 1972 recording, possibly made between engagements with Focus. However, later interviews with Akkerman have confirmed that the material had been 'in the can' since the late 60s, the decision by Harvest to release it when they did being an obvious and reasonable response to the new-found prominence of Akkerman as an internationally renowned master of his instrument. What makes the dates significant is that they show Akkerman to have been exploring the world of classical and renaissance music long before it became the done thing amongst rock musicians. The most revealing tracks are the anonymous *Kemp's Jig* (renaissance lute) and Diabelli's *Andante Sostenuto* (classical guitar), both of which reveal a direct line from Akkerman to the English classical guitarist and lutenist, Julian Bream. In *Kemp's Jig,* Akkerman includes an intricate ornamental figure not shown on the original sixteenth century tablature but present on Bream's 1962 recording for RCA. In the Diabelli, Akkerman performs the piece in the key of E major, the original key having been C major. This can only point to him using the version contained in the Diabelli/Bream *Sonata in A,* for which Bream took what he considered to be the stronger movements from two separate Diabelli sonatas in order to create a new 'composite' work. This involved transposing some of the movements into keys related to A major, of which E major is the dominant. At the time Akkerman made his recording, Bream had released the composite sonata on RCA but did not publish the score until some years later. Bream's version of *Andante Sostenuto* includes several further modifications to the original, all of which also appear on the Akkerman recording.

It would be pleasing at this point to reveal that Akkerman had been a Bream student all along and that the performances on *Profile* were the result of intensive coaching from the maestro. In fact, the two never worked together, Akkerman's extensive knowledge of the Bream repertoire being the result of a close and meticulous study of Bream's prodigious recorded output, an oeuvre that, by the early 90s, had spawned a back catalog of 28 full-length CDs on RCA alone. What has surely been established from this brief investigation is that Jan Akkerman was a pioneering figure in the breaking down of barriers between rock and classical music.

This phase of his career reached its zenith with *Tabernakel* (1973), in which Akkerman fields a program of lute solos by John Dowland (1563–1626), Anthony Holborne (c.1550–1602) and others alongside some ambitious new collaborations with the composer and conductor George Flynn. Finest of all is *Javeh* for guitar and orchestra, in which Akkerman's solo classical guitar shimmers amid Flynn's intoxicating string arrangement. In 1997, Akkerman ended a long absence from British soil by appearing at the Wirral International Guitar Festival. When a fan asked him to sign a well-worn copy of *Tabernakel,* he described the 24-year-old disc as '…the one I'm proud of.'

Following the demise of Focus, Thijs van Leer went commercial, but did so with dignity, expanding on his connection with the composer and arranger Rogier van Otterloo (1941–1988) with a long line of superbly presented light classical albums. Akkerman went on to greatly expand his solo output, building a positively labyrinthine catalog of releases on numerous different labels. His involvement with classical music appeared to have already run its course, although Dowland's *Come Heavy Sleep* reworked for metal-strung guitar appears on the album *Live at the Priory* (1997), recorded during the *Wirral Festival.*

A baroque lute album from the early 80s is rumored to exist, but most of Akkerman's energies have been directed towards his lifelong interest in jazz. A 1978 live album, recorded at the Montreux Jazz Festival, is among the first of many outstanding releases in this genre.

Still on the road in the twenty-first century, Jan Akkerman is a key figure amongst the outstanding artists who have built bridges between the established conventions of music and the new, less structured language of rock…

10

Hybrid Forms and the
Rise of the Singer/Songwriter

Even at its most basic, rock music is a mixed genre of traditional languages that are not only international but intercontinental, with Africa and America providing the cultural foundations while Europe offered further creative input and played a vital nurturing role from the early 60s onwards. A chronology of the parallel historic lines of rock and pop, from their early postwar origins to the present day, would be an easy tale to tell, if only it had been that simple.

But like all improvised forms, rock music is an art that naturally absorbs and reflects the multifarious popular cultures that flourish around it. The earliest hyphenated genre to be officially recognized, folk-rock, was fully active from the early 60s and has been partially examined in previous chapters. Although folk-rock was an essentially American form at its mid-60s inception, many of its American exponents had, by the start of the 70s, reinvented themselves as pioneers of what was to become recognized as country-rock. It was thus primarily the British exponents of folk-rock who carried the baton through the 70s and beyond. At the forefront, there were two principal bands: Fairport Convention and Steeleye Span. In terms of both instrumentation and the resultant sound textures, Fairport and Steeleye were similar but by no means indistinguishable, the fiddle virtuosity of Dave Swarbrick (b.1941) and the subtle electric guitar fills of Richard Thompson (b.1949) being as specific to Fairport as the angelic lead vocals of Maddy Prior (b.1947) were to Steeleye. There were also differences of musical identity, Fairport having on board Sandy Denny (1947–1978) who, although less than Prior's equal in vocal terms, was a songwriter whose huge potential possibly never reached full fruition in her tragically short life. Denny's exquisite ballad *Who Knows Where the Time Goes,* recorded on the Fairport album *Unhalfbricking* (1969), remains one of the truly sublime moments of British folk-rock. One of Fairport's most ambitious undertakings was the album *Babbacombe Lee* (1971), a continuous narrative set to music telling the shocking tale of John 'Babbacombe' Lee (1864–1941?), a convicted murderer who had always protested his innocence and, in 1885, cheated the gallows after the mechanism failed no fewer than three times.

Steeleye were always perceived as the more traditionally based, the two LP series *Folk Songs of Old England (1968)* by Prior and fellow band member Tim Hart (b.1948) being a representative anthology that could almost be used as a reference source. In 2003/4, bass player Ashley 'Tyger' Hutchings (b.1945), who founded Steeleye in 1969 having also been a founder member of Fairport, undertook a major tour of UK folk venues, celebrating the 100th anniversary of the first traditional song to be noted down by Cecil Sharp (1859–1924). Working alongside the young singer/guitarist Emily Slade and squeezebox maestro Simon Care, Hutchings performed songs taken from Sharp's collection and then donned the trademark panama hat, seen in so many period photos of Sharp, while reading from the diary of this iconic figure. Quaint and quintessentially English, the sheer sincerity of Hutchings' performances left them almost immune to any charges of folksy sentimentality. From the early 70s onwards, Fairport and Steeleye were fully accepted by the mainstream rock audience, both bands enjoying full coverage in the specialist press and receiving detailed entries in the principal rock encyclopedias. Steeleye even enjoyed a surprise Christmas hit with *Gaudete* (UK No.14, 1973), possibly an unprecedented case of a chart single being performed both *a cappella* and in Latin. Three years earlier, Pentangle had entered the lower reaches of the UK singles' chart with the ethereal acoustic modern jazz of *Light Flight,* a commercial breakthrough undoubtedly assisted by the adoption of the song as theme music to the BBC drama series *Take Three Girls.*

Described at the time, not without justification, as a 'folk-rock supergroup', Pentangle harnessed the combined guitar virtuosity of Bert Jansch (b.1943) and John Renbourn (b.1944) to the captivating vocals of Jacqui McShee, whose technical excellence was considered by many to be second only to that of Prior. With Danny Thompson (double bass) and Terry Cox (drums), Pentangle's collective career lasted just four years, although various combinations of band members have worked together since. Duo appearances by McShee and Renbourn in 2002/3 were well received, and an all-new line-up bearing the name Jacqui McShee's

Pentangle has in recent years offered a further revival of a unique and fondly remembered sound.

Mainstream commercial success was never destined to visit the Incredible String Band, although they have remained on the road, with extended sabbaticals and innumerable changes of personnel, for an impressive four decades. Even the guiding partnership of Mike Heron (b.1942) and Robin Williamson (b.1943) was officially annulled in 1974, only to be revived several times over. It remained active as recently as 2003. Both have enjoyed parallel solo careers, Williamson's collaborations with John Renbourn and others winning particular critical acclaim. A master of the Celtic harp, Williamson is now a noted authority on the bardic tradition, his work in this field collected in his book *The Craneskin Bag* (Cannongate Publishing 1989).

Although British folk-rock rarely matched the mainstream artists in terms of record sales, its enduring popularity as a live attraction spawned many new bands and solo acts from the mid-70s onwards. Particularly prominent among these was the Albion Band, founded by, once again, Ashley Hutchings. By the time Hutchings temporarily mothballed the band after touring in Autumn 2002, it had provided a vital training ground for numerous younger artists before they embarked on a solo career, notable recent members including the singer/songwriter Kellie While and master fiddler Joe Broughton. One fansite lists an astonishing forty-two names of one-time Albion members, charting the involvement of each individual on an Excel Spreadsheet. Hutchings' latter-day nickname 'The Guv'nor' is well deserved.

One artist whose work remains notoriously difficult to categorize is the English guitarist and occasional singer Gordon Giltrap (b.1948). His preference for metal-strung acoustic guitars and open-string tunings has led him, not unreasonably, to be placed alongside such names as Jansch, Renbourn and Davy Graham (1940–2008), creator of the ubiquitous acoustic guitar instrumental *Anji*. Although something of a shadowy figure in recent years, Graham's influence in the 60s may be illustrated by the decision of Paul Simon to include his own 'straight' acoustic version of *Anji* on the *Sounds of Silence* album.

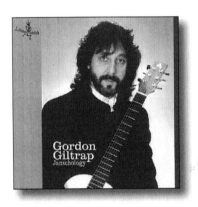

But despite having served much of his apprenticeship on the fringes of the folk circuit, Giltrap's extensive back catalog contains hardly any traditional material, his self-titled debut release on Transatlantic in 1968 being the work of a solo singer/songwriter whose instrumental excellence would gradually eclipse his early aspirations as a vocalist and lyricist. Securing a small and dedicated following through the early 70s, Giltrap gained national prominence after an appearance on the *Old Grey Whistle Test* presided over, as ever, by 'Whispering' Bob Harris. By now, Giltrap's output was almost entirely instrumental, his choice for *Whistle Test* being the string-breaking acoustic solo *Lucifer's Cage*.

A technical *tour de force* that has appeared in several different arrangements over the years, *Lucifer's Cage* made its vinyl debut on Giltrap's second album, *Portrait* (1969). The mid-70s proved a vintage era for Giltrap, a steady run of quality albums and critically acclaimed live shows culminating in *Visionary* (1976), an ambitious instrumental homage to the poetry of William Blake. By now, Giltrap was working alongside Rod Edwards (keyboards), John G. Perry (bass) and Simon Philips (drums). For *Visionary,* a team of eight additional musicians, plus a small string orchestra, was brought into the studio. This provided an impressive showcase for Giltrap's extraordinary skill – his mastery of baroque style left hand ornamentation remains second to none. He had also evolved a unique and amazingly effective right hand technique, in which a conventionally held flatpick is supplemented by the nail of the *fourth* finger. Whatever Giltrap was creating on *Visionary,* it was a long way from folk or folk-rock, the admittedly cumbersome term 'acoustic symphonic rock' perhaps being nearer the mark. Over the next few years, television continued to further Giltrap's career. The decision of the BBC to use *Heartsong* from *Perilous Journey* (1977) as theme music for the travel show *Holiday* resulted in an unexpected assault on the singles chart in January 1978. Working in recent years primarily as a solo artist minus band, Giltrap remains one of the most respected and hard-gigging guitarists on the UK scene. A collaboration with the award-winning jazz guitarist Martin Taylor (b.1956) resulted in the outstanding CD *A Matter of Time* (1991) for which Giltrap provided most of the material, and a more recent collaboration with the classical guitarist Raymond Burley (b.1948) yielded the equally impressive release *Double Vision* (2004).

But as folk-rock became increasingly centered on its British identity, other hybrid forms remained very much the products of America's musical heritage…

From the earliest flowerings of Rock & Roll, jazz was gradually displaced to an almost patrician role in popular culture. Needless to say, jazz and its multifarious subcategories continued to develop throughout the 50s and 60s, with such key figures as Dizzy Gillespie (1917–1993) and Miles Davis (1926–1991) producing some of their most influential work during those two decades. But apart from such one-off international hits as *Take Five* by the Dave Brubeck Quartet, which was being played throughout the Western World in autumn 1961, contemporary jazz would only rarely show its face in a scene dominated by the latter phases of 50s Rock & Roll and the first manifestations of pre-Beatle pop.

A straightforward but wonderfully imaginative composition by Brubeck's saxophonist Paul Desmond (1924–1977), *Take Five* has remained Brubeck's signature tune long after Desmond's departure. A particularly powerful reworking is the live version from 1971, in which Gerry Mulligan (1927–1996) provides a superbly gritty lead solo on baritone sax and Brubeck responds with one of his most explosive piano breaks. At the turn of the millennium, the now octogenarian Brubeck was still on the road playing to packed houses, ending his set with yet another take on *Take Five,* in which the piano introduction could hardly be heard over the tumultuous applause. The early 60s incarnation of the Brubeck Quartet enjoyed further chart success with *It's a Raggy Waltz* and *Unsquare Dance* in the spring of 1962, although neither fully achieved the classic status of their predecessor. Both were Brubeck compositions, the latter, with its seven-in-the-bar opening motif, being a subtle yet unmistakeable sequel to the 3+2 rhythms of *Take Five*. Although the success of *Take Five* elevated the then 40-year-old Brubeck from the status of respected jazz pianist to international star, the jazz world was to remain, in the eyes of the 60s generation, the exclusive preserve of mature audiences, the word 'mature' in this context meaning 'over 25'. Paradoxically, the other jazz acts to enjoy fleeting chart success in the early 60s were such retro trad jazz outfits as Acker Bilk and his Paramount Jazz Band and the knockaround light cabaret act Kenny Ball and his Jazzmen. Bilk (b.1929, real name: Bernard Stanley Bilk) remains forever associated with the gentle clarinet solo *Stranger on the Shore* (UK No.2, 1961), a sentimental yet sincere composition that he has since described as 'my pension'. Ironically, the UK copyright on the recording of *Stranger on the Shore* is shortly due to expire under existing legislation. At the time of writing, a campaign is underway led by the British Phonographic Industry (BPI) to extend the UK copyright period beyond its current 50 years, possibly to the 95 years that now applies under US law.

But the growth in the 40s and 50s of such acquired tastes as Bebop and its various derivatives had caused the current state of jazz to be seen by many of the general public as an increasingly esoteric genre, appreciated only by a dwindling band of diehard fanatics. The accessible work of

Brubeck and others was, in itself, sufficient to illustrate the unjustness of this perception, although there can be little doubt that large parts of the 60s were wilderness years for this most developed and refined area of popular culture. But as the decade progressed and rock music achieved its own levels of sophistication, the way was clear for a new dialogue with its direct ancestor.

Despite being a key source of the instrumental brilliance that dominated the 70s rock scene, with the clinical virtuosity of John McLaughlin (b.1942) and others seen by many as the most pure manifestations of the contemporary guitarist's art, the origins of jazz-rock may be traced back to several channels of development in the mid-to-late 60s. In Britain, the R&B culture had clear jazz links, with such leading practitioners as Graham Bond (see Chapter 4), former saxophonist with the Don Rendell Quintet, serving their apprenticeship in that field. It is also worth noting that keyboard players such as Georgie Fame undoubtedly gained inspiration from the American-led jazz organ style, spearheaded by the flamboyant figure of Jimmy Smith (1925–2005) who, at the age of 75, brought the Hammond organ into the twenty-first century with the 2001 release of *Dot Com Blues*.

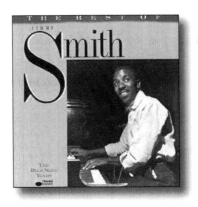

It cannot be overlooked that Smith's instrument had, in the 1970s, become a figure of widespread ridicule. This was especially true in the UK, where almost every social club and downmarket restaurant seemed to have a tobacco-stained C3 or L100, on which a middle-aged semi-pro in a velvet lounge jacket would pump out such chart horrors as *Tie a Yellow Ribbon (Round the Old Oak Tree)*. But for Smith and his contemporaries, the Hammond organ was an instrument of huge creative potential, its survival to the present day perhaps being due in part to the eventual replacement of the men in velvet jackets with the even greater embarrassment of karaoke. In other words, the Hammond made good its escape just before its reputation was beyond salvation.

Students of American jazz-rock often perceive the early years as being represented by the brass-driven big band arrangements adopted by such late 60s bands as Blood, Sweat and Tears and Chicago. A further figure who invariably enters the frame is Paul Butterfield (1942–1987) who, as frontman of the Paul Butterfield Blues Band, was responsible for such influential releases as the memorably titled 1968 album *Resurrection of Pigboy Crabshaw.*

But it was the arrival on the scene of McLaughlin and a whole generation of master instrumentalists that gave jazz-rock its distinctive 70s identity, far removed from the blues, although not always unrelated to the more progressive practitioners of big band jazz. Jazz-rock also had a sibling relationship with the Latin-rock launched at Woodstock by the then possibly unique concept of Santana (see also Chapter 7). Centered around the refined guitar style of Mexican born Carlos Santana, the band wove a vibrant rhythmic tapestry of Latin percussion alongside a conventional drum kit. Although Santana as a band were never textbook purveyors of 70s jazz-rock, their influence on several fully-fledged exponents was discernible. One of the most notable was Al Di Meola (b.1954), whose distinguished stint as guitarist with Return to Forever, fronted by jazz pianist Chick Corea (b.1941), led to an impressive catalog of solo releases. Of these, *Land of the Midnight Sun* and *Elegant Gypsy*, from 1976 and 1977 respectively, are possibly the best remembered.

The relationship between Carlos Santana and jazz-rock was consummated with the 1973 release *Love, Devotion, Surrender.* A one-off joint venture with John McLaughlin, the album appeared at a time when both guitarists were disciples of the guru Sri Chinmoy (1931–2007) and was condemned by some critics as little more than a fly-on-the-wall jam session in which neither performer seemed at his most inspired.

Although Eastern mysticism only occasionally manifested itself in the work of Santana, it was to be a permanent fixture for McLaughlin throughout the 70s and beyond. This first became apparent in both the title and the content of the 1971 solo album *My Goal's Beyond,* a prelude to the launch of the Mahavishnu Orchestra, a somewhat misleading title for a team whose core personnel was no more numerous than that of the average rock band or small jazz combo. In its earliest permanent form, the band comprised McLaughlin in the company of Jerry Goodman (violin), Jan Hammer (b.1948) (keyboards), Rick Laird (b.1940) (bass) and Billy Cobham (b.1944) (drums). A later incarnation of the band included a small string section and performed alongside the London Symphony Orchestra, but this did not come to full fruition until the *Apocalypse* album of 1974. Of the original Mahavishnu line-up, Hammer and Cobham in particular achieved future prominence fronting their own bands. Cobham possibly followed the lead of fellow drum major Tony Williams (1945–1997), whose pioneering jazz fusion band the Tony Williams Lifetime had given an early platform to the already prodigious technical skills of the pre-Mahavishnu McLaughlin. Both Williams and McLaughlin had in turn served under the guiding hand of Miles Davis, McLaughlin first gaining the attention of the jazz audience through his work on the late 60s Davis releases *In a Silent Way* and *Bitches Brew*.

With the 1972 release of *The Inner Mounting Flame* and its 1973 sequel *Birds of Fire,* the Mahavishnu Orchestra became arguably the first band to gain the full support of both the rock and the jazz audiences. Their arrival was perfectly timed. Rock music and its antecedents had by now spent almost two decades applying shock tactics against the establishment. The new decade heralded a craving amongst rock musicians and their followers to be recognized as a serious artistic movement that could compete on equal terms in both technical skill and compositional development. The symphonic rock bands discussed in Chapter 9 were already making their mark. McLaughlin's band, with their impeccable credentials in the rarefied world of contemporary jazz, opened up a whole new front. It is interesting to recall at this point that, with such notable exceptions as Thijs van Leer of Focus, few of symphonic rock's major players had undergone formal classical training. But in John McLaughlin, rock music had acquired a time-served jazz master, whose CV could scarcely have been more impressive.

By the mid-70s, the Mahavishnu Orchestra appeared to be in gradual decline, the more prominent members of the present team, including former Zappa violinist Jean-Luc Ponty (b.1942), now engaged in their own solo projects. Incidentally, let it not be forgotten that Zappa himself was a highly influential figure in the early development of jazz-rock, his importance often being overshadowed by his more prominent activities in unrelated fields. But *The Orange County Lumber Truck,* featured on the 1970 retrospective *Weasels Ripped My Flesh* and various other Zappa releases, is a textbook example of a big band jazz arrangement applied in a rock context. A few years later, the title track of *Zoot Allures* (1976) showed Zappa's capacity to create some of the silkiest jazz-rock textures of the era, a muscle he only occasionally chose to flex.

Despite having reportedly severed links with Chinmoy, McLaughlin maintained his passion for Eastern culture, re-launching his career in 1976 in the company of Indian band Shakti, for which McLaughlin adopted a custom-built acoustic guitar with distinctive crossover drone strings. It was an alliance that would serve McLaughlin well over the next few years. It also, rather unexpectedly, broadened his audience considerably, the gentle and spiritual soundscape of the 1976 album *Shakti with John McLaughlin* becoming an upmarket dinner party favorite, especially with the curry-mad British public.

Although the various incarnations of the Mahavishnu Orchestra were arguably the most prominent exponents of the new jazz-rock of the early 70s, they were never a lone force. Chick Corea's highly regarded Return to Forever entered the frame in 1972, the seemingly obscure collective name of the band being taken from an earlier album. A prolific composer and jazz pianist of formidable ability, Corea, like McLaughlin, was a former Miles Davis protégé. Their paths had crossed when both players appeared on the same two Davis albums at the turn of the decade. After various line-up changes in the early days, the RTF alliance of Corea and Al Di Meola was finally established in 1974. With Corea and Di Meola sharing the lead lines, RTF boasted a world class rhythm section of bass virtuoso Stanley Clarke (b.1951) and drummer Lenny White (b.1949), yet another Miles Davis luminary. Clarke, like Di Meola, would soon branch out with a string of solo releases, his breathtaking capacity to perform quickfire scales using the conventional alternating right hand technique practiced by the majority of bass guitarists elevating his instrument to a level previously considered unattainable. White also released a number of solo albums which, although well received, never enjoyed the prominence of his Mahavishnu counterpart, Billy Cobham.

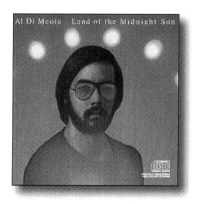

Mahavishnu-related, but with pronounced Latin leanings, the RTF concept proved profoundly influential but ultimately short-lived, the solo careers of each individual member eventually eclipsing the activities of the band as a whole. A reunion of Corea, Di Meola, Clarke and White resulted in a 1983 tour and various re-issues. Ad hoc collaborations continued to take place over the years, Corea's guest spot on Di Meola's *Land of the Midnight Sun* yielding what is perhaps the definitive account of Corea's acoustic composition for guitar and piano, *Short Tales of the Black Forest.*

Di Meola later worked alongside McLaughlin as the jazz audience acquired a taste for the somewhat overblown extravaganzas bearing such commercially driven titles as *Night of the Great Guitars.* Typically, these performances featured three players. Other members of the pool included Larry Coryell (b.1943) and flamenco fusion hero Paco de Lucía (b.1947, real name: Francisco Sánchez Gómez). Mainstream jazz guitarists soon followed the lead, with British maestro Martin Taylor touring in the 80s and 90s alongside such senior American figures as Barney Kessel (1923–2004) and Charlie Byrd (1925–1999).

One world-ranking jazz-rock band that, like RTF, played host to a star bassist and also predated both RTF and the Mahavishnu Orchestra, was Weather Report. Releasing their self-titled debut album on CBS in 1970, this constantly changing team was built around the two-man mature directorate of Josef Zawinul (1932–2007) (keyboards) and Wayne Shorter (b.1933) (saxophone), both of whom had previously served under the ever-present figure of Miles Davis. The bass virtuoso referred to above was Jaco Pastorius (1951–1987, real name: John Francis Pastorius), whose tragic early death in a fight with a nightclub bouncer came after a period of reported manic depression and erratic behaviour. Earlier on that fateful evening, Pastorius had apparently attempted to make an unscheduled guest appearance at a Santana concert, only to be removed from the stage by security guards who had no idea who he was. But during his brief tenure with Weather Report and troubled yet productive solo career, Pastorius became universally recognized as an unsurpassed exponent of the fretless bass. What Stanley Clarke had in sheer technical force, Pastorius matched in his fluidity of tone and melodic invention.

Pastorius made his Weather Report debut on the 1976 album *Black Market,* replacing former bass player Alphonso Johnson (b.1951), himself a replacement for founding bassist Miroslav Vitous (b.1947). To list the other musicians who have worked with Weather Report would provide a wide and varied inventory. A name that catches the eye is one-time Zappa drummer Chester Thompson (b.1948), who would later take over the drum role of Phil Collins in the post-Gabriel Genesis. Significantly, the Weather Report line-up appears never to have included a permanent guitarist, although Ralph Towner (b.1940) made a one-off guest appearance, playing twelve-string guitar, on the 1972 album *I Sing the Body Electric.* The band also broke with jazz rock tradition when Zawinul's catchy instrumental *Birdland,* from the 1977 album *Heavy Weather,* enjoyed worldwide airplay on mainstream stations. It was later adopted, in a characteristically elaborate vocal setting, by 40s revival group Manhattan Transfer, whose intricate harmonies and dynamic stage presentations earned them a well-deserved cult status with the rock audience.

Although members of the Mahavishnu Orchestra and Return to Forever had branched out in their own directions before the end of the 70s, Weather Report soldiered on for much of the next decade. Their final release, *This is This* from 1986, is seen by most fans as an undistinguished swansong, Pastorius by now having been replaced by the able but relatively unknown Victor Bailey.

McLaughlin notwithstanding, 70s jazz-rock was essentially an American genre, although a number of British bands such as Soft Machine and Matching Mole (a Soft Machine spin-off, whose name was derived from translating the original band's name into French) all played their subsidiary roles.

But there was one hyphenated genre in whose development the British had no hand...

Although America has every reason to blame the British for making the Hammond organ an object of ridicule, that all-American genre of Country & Western did a pretty good job of destroying much of its own street-cred. With lantern-jawed manly men dressed like cartoon cowboys and peroxide blonde women whose plaintive vocal style sounded like they might burst into tears at any moment, it is difficult to imagine the world of C&W without a hefty, and not necessarily intentional, dose of showbiz self-parody. Simple and often downright corny diatonic melodies were accompanied by a rudimentary guitar strum, the bass player being required to do little more than alternate the root and fifth, perhaps with a perfunctory scale run when he felt a shift in harmony coming on. And that was before any close analysis of the lyrics, which for the most part seemed to express mawkish devotion to a spouse, a parent or a place of birth. Animals, chiefly horses and dogs, also received their unsolicited share of cringe-making eulogy, often on a level that even the quadruped-obsessed British found hard to stomach.

Strange, then, that this mass market brand of commercial entertainment should spawn such a huge number of world-class instrumentalists, the term 'Nashville session man' being one that is, with good reason, uttered in reverential tones. The reality has to be that, although the world of C&W has never perceived itself as 'high art', the culture and lifestyle it expresses is surely an essential feature of the postcard image of rural America as seen by visiting foreigners and perhaps even by a significant number of city-dwelling Americans. In truth, no-one ever seriously believed that regular twentieth century Americans spend their day-to-day lives wearing Stetson hats and riding around on horseback in search of moral injustices, any more than the average Scotsman sets out for the office wearing a kilt and illustrates every statement with a quote from Robert Burns. But in both cases, the idealized guidebook image is a potentially fruitful starting point for a popular musical genre. This parallel applies equally to the music itself, the harmonic simplicity of the rich culture of Celtic jigs and reels providing an uncluttered platform for the breathtaking skills of its practitioners, especially the generations of master fiddlers. Likewise the three-chord fundamentals of C&W, which could be magically transformed in the hands of a Chet Atkins (1924–2001) or a Merle Travis (1917–1983).

There can be little doubt that, in its earliest manifestations, C&W was a genre where, with notable exceptions, the performer was king (or queen). With a little imagination, the most mediocre of tunes could be brought to life by a suitable dose of instrumental brilliance or, let it be said, a genuinely charismatic singer. Everyone recalls the huge and mainly posthumous success of Jim Reeves (1923–1964), whose first big break had come in 1952 when he stood in for C&W godfather Hank Williams (1923–1953) on the radio show *Louisiana Hayride*. This is the official account, as told in a number of Reeves' interviews, although some versions state that the absentee performer was not Williams, but Sleepy LaBeef (b.1935, real name: Thomas Paulsley LaBeff). If all the given dates are correct, LaBeef must have been at an early stage in his career at the time.

But how many of us can remember who wrote the songs that made Reeves a world star? To take just one example, only the most informed sources acknowledge that his massive international hit *Distant Drums* was penned by the highly respected veteran C&W songwriter Cindy Walker (1918–2006), who put her successful early performing career on hold in order to concentrate on composition. Significantly, Reeves was one of the few C&W artists of his time to reject the customary cowboy gear in favor of a sober suit and tie. Reeves' recordings also moved away from standard C&W instrumentation, the traditional mix of strummed guitars and lone fiddler often being replaced by piano and string orchestra. The man who can take much of the credit for this sound makeover is none other than Chet Atkins who, in his capacity as manager of RCA's Nashville studio, was both the commercial and the artistic brains behind many of Reeves' most successful releases.

All this was undoubtedly the overriding factor in Reeves' continuing worldwide status, although such astute maneuvres as emphasizing his Irish roots by performing *Danny Boy* and parading his Christian faith in a regular sequence of 'religious songs' must also have furthered the cause. Displaying the chameleon-like quality of a true professional, Reeves even enjoyed lasting success amid the political tensions of South Africa, eventually making a movie there and recording in the Afrikaans language. The fact that his untimely death in a light aircraft crash happened to take place on the outskirts of Nashville did much to make permanent Reeves' iconic status. He will be forever remembered as the wholesome, pipe-smoking nice guy of laid-back C&W. His much loved collie dog, named Cheyenne, was buried at his feet in 1969.

It was not until the mid-60s that the songwriter and, in many cases, the singer/songwriter started to play a central role, the brooding figure of Johnny Cash (1932–2003) finally taking the C&W genre beyond the cosy world of farms, dogs and doting little women. Cash's early life was stock C&W, a childhood working alongside his siblings on the impoverished family farm having been illuminated by his mother playing the guitar and singing hymns on the porch after a modest supper. It perhaps should also be noted that, despite the hard-drinking, truck-driving scenario with which Cash's music is inextricably linked, several of his best known songs toed the old party line to a greater extent than many of his admirers would care to admit. His worldwide 70s hit *A Thing Called Love* displayed all the saccharine pseudo-philosophy of Reeves at his most cloyingly sincere, while the painfully unfunny *Boy Named Sue* from 1969 surely represented cowboy humor at its lowest ebb.

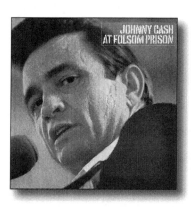

But it was clear almost from the outset that Cash's career would chart a new course. When he signed up with Sun Records in 1954, it was Cash's own song *Hey Porter* that allegedly swung the deal with Sam Phillips.

Written while Cash was returning home from a stint in the Air Force, *Hey Porter* provided Cash with his first major success, the single reportedly selling 100,000 copies in the southern states alone. It was coupled with the ballad *Cry, Cry, Cry,* another Cash composition that was said to have been written more or less overnight at Phillips' request. So even at this early stage, Cash was a pre-60s manifestation of what later became the independent genre of singer/songwriter. By this time, he was working with guitarist Luther Perkins (1928–1968, no relation to Sun Records stablemate, Carl Perkins) and bass player Marshall Grant, under the collective name of Johnny Cash and the Tennessee Two. Touring alongside other Sun Records artists, including Elvis Presley, Cash appeared on the influential *Louisiana Hayride,* where Reeves had also found early success. After scoring a national hit with *Folsom Prison Blues,* Cash had his first million seller in 1956 with *I Walk The Line.* By now, he had been invited to appear in Nashville's legendary Grand Ole Opry, perceived both then and now as the citadel of country music excellence.

In the early 60s, Cash had settled in California and was also spending an increasing amount of time amongst the poets, folksingers and revolutionaries of New York's Greenwich Village. By this time, he had moved from Sun Records to Columbia, where he first made contact with a radical young singer and songwriter named Bob Dylan. In 1964, Cash shared the bill with Dylan at the Newport Folk Festival, a highly publicized expression of unity between two genres that, although they both claimed to represent the culture of 'ordinary people', were widely seen as mutually exclusive. It was in that same year that Cash celebrated his own perceived Cherokee ancestry with the album *Bitter Tears – Ballads of the American Indian,* a radical release at the time.

From this point onwards, Cash became the personification of the new, politically aware country music. His dark, troubled countenance was as far as it could possibly be from such grinning rhinestone entertainers as Slim Whitman (b.1924, real name: Otis Dewey Whitman Jr.), whose surprise 1974 hit *Happy Anniversary* revealed that the market for old-time gooey C&W was still alarmingly buoyant. With his yodelling skills almost as precisely honed as his pencil mustache, Whitman enjoyed an even later flowering in the 1996 sci-fi spoof *Mars Attacks!*, in which his rendition of *Indian Love Call* proves an effective weapon in the face of alien invasion.

By the time Cash's link with Dylan was further reinforced by a guest appearance on the *Nashville Skyline* album in 1969, the first manifestations of what became Country-Rock were already visible from several quarters. Many sources see the founding father as Gram Parsons (1946–1973, real name: Ingram Cecil Connor III), whose brief but much discussed stint with the Byrds yielded the 1968 album *Sweetheart of the Rodeo,* in which the title imagery is obvious.

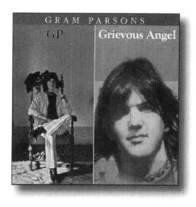

In association with ex-Byrds bass player Chris Hillman (b.1944), now redeployed on guitar, Parsons went on to form the Flying Burrito Brothers, the other founder members being Chris Ethridge (bass) and 'Sneaky' Pete Kleinow (pedal steel guitar). After working with various session drummers, the band finally engaged another former Byrd, Michael Clarke (1944–1993, real name: Michael James Dick), in 1969. Despite numerous changes of personnel, the band survived at least into the late 90s, although many fans disown the later incarnations as being unrepresentative of the original concept. Hillman resurfaced in 1973 as one of the leading triumvirate in the Souther-Hillman-Furay Band, a putative West Coast supergroup that, as tends to be the case with such ventures, was soon playing second fiddle to various members' solo aspirations and is now largely forgotten. By the time of Parsons' death and its bizarre aftermath (his body was illegally removed and cremated at the *Joshua Tree National Monument,* allegedly in accordance with his own final requests), he had already parted company with the FBBs, a legacy of just two highly regarded solo albums on the Reprise label having kept his legend alive into the twenty-first century.

But there was one supergroup working in on the edge of this field that would prove a productive and profoundly influential concept...

CROSBY, STILLS, NASH AND YOUNG

Formed in 1969 as an Anglo-American trio, to which the Canadian Neil Young (b.1945) was added after the first album, these masters of freewheeling vocal harmony allegedly got together at the house of either John Sebastian (leader of quality 60s pop act, the Lovin' Spoonful) or Joni Mitchell, depending on which source you believe. The story goes that the English member, Graham Nash (b.1942), was touring the States with the Hollies, with whom he had enjoyed a string of hit singles that, like those of the Spoonful, were by and large a legacy to be proud of. But it was widely reported at the time that Nash was less than happy with the 1969 album *Hollies Sing Dylan* and, in the light of an inspiring jam session at the Sebastian/Mitchell residence, took little persuading to jump ship.

Following a successful early showing at Woodstock, part of which made it to the movie, the trio's self-titled debut album was released to universal public acclaim. The vocal compatibility of Nash and David (Van Cortland) Crosby (b.1941, yet another former Byrd) harnessed to the songwriting abilities of Stephen Stills (b.1945, formerly of Buffalo Springfield) lived up to all its early promise. The Stills composition *Suite – Judy Blue Eyes* became a permanent anthem, not only for the trio but for the entire sub-genre they came to represent. As would almost immediately be revealed, the subject of the song was the singer Judy Collins (b.1939), whose pristine voice had prompted the cult novelist and songwriter Richard Fariña (1937–1966) to comment: 'If amethysts could sing...they would sound like Judy Collins'. The title of Fariña's 1966 underground novel *Been Down So Long, It Looks Like Up To Me* was later quoted verbatim by Jim Morrison in the song *Been Down So Long* on the *LA Woman* album. Complete with ethnic percussion and a Hispanic voiceover prior to the fadeout, *Suite – Judy Blue Eyes* was an exotic creation far removed from the homespun ethos of C&W, although the country influence was always present both here and in the band's subsequent creations. At the other end of the aesthetic scale was Crosby's exquisite *Guinevere,* in which the quietly contemplative mood generated an almost monastic atmosphere amid the elaborate harmonies of Nash's *Marakesh Express* and the Crosby/Stills composition *Wooden Ships.*

Despite bearing the title *Déjà Vu,* the second album, released on Atlantic in 1970, marked a distinct change of direction towards a less pastoral and more electric soundscape. Particularly disappointing was a leaden account of the Joni Mitchell classic *Woodstock,* which failed to capture the spiritual charm of the one-off hit single by an otherwise obscure Fairport Convention spin-off named Matthews Southern Comfort (UK No.1, 1970). Whether or not this change of direction can be attributed to the arrival of Young (a former colleague of Stills in Buffalo Springfield) will forever be the subject of speculation, and it has to be noted that Young, both as a solo artist and as frontman to Crazy Horse, enjoys an enviable track record as a prolific recording artist and live performer. Vocally, his whining drawl is very much an acquired taste, although it did not stop *Heart of Gold* from the 1972 album *Harvest* becoming a worldwide hit. But for better or worse, many still consider that magnificent first CS&N release as the most pure representation of their gentle yet compelling sound...

In the meantime, Gerry Garcia of the Grateful Dead had made the extraordinary yet shrewd move of taking up the steel guitar and furthering his existing association with the wonderfully named New Riders of the Purple Sage. It was this alliance that led to the outstanding 1970 Grateful Dead release *American Beauty,* in which the tightly structured, acoustically centered songs were a long way indeed from the freeform acid-fuelled improvisations with which the Dead first found fame. Behind the gentle vocal lines, which were more direct in their delivery and considerably less harmonized than those of CS&N, the instrumentation on *American Beauty* came straight from the heart of country music, the bluegrass mandolinist David Grisman (b.1945) guesting on two tracks.

As the decade drew to a close, enough bands were on the starting blocks to make country-rock a recognized category that would shortly have its own section in larger record stores. Some collective titles, such as Country Gazette, featuring bluegrass fiddle hero Byron Berline (b.1944), displayed their creative origins with pride. Others, such as Asleep at the Wheel or Commander Cody and his Lost Planet Airmen, seemed calculated to keep the public guessing. One subtle name whose secret could easily be unveiled with the help of a phone book was Area Code 615, a premier team of Nashville session musicians whose brilliantly imaginative instrumental *Stone Fox Chase* became known to all British rockers as the title music for Whisperin' Bob's *Old Grey Whistle Test*. In 1973, John Fogerty (b.1945), whose rustic leanings had been a recurring theme in the 'swamp rock' hit singles of Creedence Clearwater Revival, both reinvented and replicated himself by overdubbing all the parts on an album titled *Blue Ridge Rangers*. Buffalo Springfield survivors Ritchie Furay (b.1944) and Jim Messina (b.1947), who had completed the band's final album without the support of the other members, regrouped themselves in August 1968 as founding fathers of Poco (briefly known in the early days as Pogo), who in 1976 produced one of the great country-rock classics with the imposing title track from the otherwise undistinguished album *Rose of Cimarron*.

One pioneer of country-rock who, despite a long and productive recording career in his own right, was often seen more as a behind the scenes figure is Mike Nesmith (b.1942). Globally renowned as the troublesome ex-member of prototype TV 'boy band' the Monkees, the one who had the effrontery to suggest they actually played on their own records, the wealth and fame Nesmith had acquired as a Monkee left him in pole position to redirect his considerable talents into launching a solo career with the country orientated album *The Wichita Train Whistle Sings* in 1968.

In fact, Nesmith would probably not have been starved of start-up capital even if the Monkees had never happened. His mother, Bette Nesmith Graham (1924–1980), was the former typist who invented the correcting fluid marketed as *Liquid Paper*. In 1979, the Gillette Corporation purchased the rights to *Liquid Paper* from Mrs. Nesmith Graham, reportedly for a handsome $47.5 million.

Collaborating with patrician pedal steel guitarist Orville 'Red' Rhodes (b.1930), alongside John London (bass) and John Ware (drums), Nesmith formed the First National Band with whom he released *Magnetic South* in 1970, yielding the US hit single *Joanne*. The collective title proved prescient, the FNB going their separate ways during the recording of the 1971 album *Nevada Fighter*. The Second National Band was duly formed, with Nesmith and Rhodes now performing in the company of Michael Cohen (keyboards), Johnny Meeks (bass) and Jack Panelli (drums). This line-up survived for only one album, the ominously titled *Tantamount to Treason* (1971), with Nesmith and Rhodes performing as a duo on *And The Hits Just Keep On Coming* (1972).

Alongside this rollercoaster 70s recording career, Nesmith emerged as a producer and entrepreneur of considerable skill, launching his own Countryside label as a subsidiary of Elektra. With its mandate of providing an outlet for country performers based around Los Angeles, Countryside proved a short-lived venture, its demise reportedly being hastened by the arrival at Elektra of David Geffen (b.1943), following a merger with Geffen's own Asylum label. Geffen is a name that often enters the frame during this transitional phase of rock history. His management company Geffen-Roberts (the other half of the partnership being the relatively low-profile Elliot Roberts) had been involved with Joni Mitchell and others prior to the launch of Asylum in 1971. Nesmith responded to the setback by persuading RCA to release him from his own existing contract, enabling him to launch the Pacific Arts Corporation, for which he produced the ambitious 1975 book and soundtrack package *The Prison*.

One of the new breed of country acts to have benefited from Nesmith's early input was Linda Ronstadt (b.1946), who achieved her first major US hit single in 1967 with the Nesmith song *Different Drum*. Despite her country roots, Ronstadt's global success in the 70s and beyond was essentially the result of a superbly marketed series of easy-listening pop albums, the cover version of the 60s standard *You're No Good* from the 1974 album *Heart Like a Wheel* becoming arguably her best-known international hit. In fact, some Ronstadt discographies are subdivided into Country and Pop categories. A strikingly attractive brunette, Ronstadt has been openly accused by some sectors of the music press for trading more on her looks than her talent, although it could equally be argued that the overt raunchiness of her stage persona paved the way for the current new wave of female country singers, such as Shania Twain and Faith Hill.

Ironically, as Ronstadt acquired fame and fortune by venturing beyond country music, it was the considerably more accomplished Dolly Parton (b.1946) who bucked the 70s trend by selling the media an image that took all the visual excesses of the traditional female country singer to their logical conclusion. A natural wit and high priestess of the quotable soundbite, the peroxide-coiffured Parton would regularly disarm her critics with such self-parodying comments as 'I know I'm not dumb, and I know I'm not blonde'.

Now a mass-media figure of incalculable wealth, the finest jewel in Parton's commercial crown is without doubt the family theme park at Pigeon Forge TN, inevitably named *Dollywood*. But let it not be forgotten that, in addition to being a wonderfully engaging performer and raconteur, Parton remains a songwriter of considerable force, her recurring theme of the eternal love triangle viewed from the standpoint of the weaker female party being most poignantly expressed in the 1973 mid-tempo ballad *Jolene*. A similarly emotional yet schmaltz-free scenario is depicted in her best-known song *I Will Always Love You,* the gentle and touching delivery in Parton's own 1974 recording being cruelly ripped apart in the hysterical over-interpretation that became an international hit in 1992 for Whitney Houston.

On the male side of the equation, the mature figure of Willie Nelson (b.1933) found international fame in the 70s, having already clocked up two decades in and around the music business. With an output that to this day rarely ventures far beyond the conventions of mainstream contemporary C&W, it was Nelson's genial hobo image, plus possibly his decision to move from RCA to Atlantic, that made him acceptable to the post-Woodstock rock audience and even launched a whole generation of analogous performers.

185

Had Nelson opted for a shave, haircut and rhinestone shirt, such picturesque rustic American artists as Waylon Jennings (1937–2002) may never have happened on quite such a grand scale. Jennings took this image to its natural conclusion by singing the title song and then providing the folksy voiceover between fist fights and rural car chases in the internationally successful cult TV series *The Dukes of Hazzard*, a role for which Jennings appeared in the credits as 'The Balladeer'. In 2005, *The Dukes of Hazzard* became the latest 70s classic to be subjected to a critically panned movie remake, the key role of Daisy Duke that was first created by the incomparable Catherine Bach inexplicably being given to a blonde.

It was undoubtedly this newly generated global awareness of the culture and lifestyle of the Southern States that paved the way for Southern Rock, an all new genre that, although displaying a country influence, was essentially independent of country-rock. From its earliest days, it even had its own dedicated record label, an MCA-distributed independent named *Sounds of the South*, brainchild of Al Kooper (b.1944). A producer, keyboard player and guitarist who always had a nose for where the action is, Kooper's CV as a session man already read like a Who's Who of Rock & Roll, with such names as Dylan, Hendrix and the Rolling Stones appearing at the top of a long and illustrious roster. Kooper's most prominent signing was a tragic yet enduring team from

Jacksonville, Florida named Lynyrd Skynyrd. Taking their collective title from one Leonard Skinner, a macho and hard-line gym coach at the high school most of the early band members had attended, Skynyrd ensured their elevated long-term status with the magnificent ten minute *Free Bird* from the cumbersomely titled 1973 debut album *Pronounced Leh-nerd Skin-nerd.*

Details of personnel were always something of a variable, although the core line-up of Ronnie Van Zant (1948–1977) (vocals), Billy Powell (1952–2009) (keyboards), Robert Burns (b.1950) (drums) and the twin lead guitars of Allen Collins (1952–1990) and Gary Rossington (b.1951) that cut the first album is still seen by many as the quintessential Skynyrd. Bass playing duties on the album were shared between Leon Wilkeson (sometimes spelt Wilkerson) (1952–2001) and Ed King (b.1949), both of whom went on to become permanent members of the band, the latter as a third lead guitarist. Even the cover of that first album has earned its place in rock history, the unsmiling 'don't mess with us' photo of the band on the main street of an archetypal southern town summing up the essential Sounds of the South ethos. On the reverse of the gatefold cover was a freshly opened pack of imaginary *Lynyrd Skynyrd Smokes*, its skull and crossbones motif being adopted, apparently without acknowledgement, two decades later by a short-lived real brand named Death Lites, marketed in the UK to a largely unreceptive public of British Marlboro men and women.

The 1974 follow-up album *Second Helping* consolidated the band's reputation and yielded the hit single *Sweet Home Alabama,* its relative brevity making it more suitable for mainstream airplay than the unedited version of *Free Bird.* A rousing celebration of life in the Southern States, *Sweet Home Alabama* devoted its second verse to dismissing the charges contained in Neil Young's *Southern Man,* first released on the *After the Goldrush* album in 1970. A mental image of the clientele in a small town bar gathering around the jukebox to join in the line 'Well I hope Neil Young will remember, a Southern Man don't need him around, anyhow…' was vivid and inspirational. It is to be hoped such scenes still take place to this day. The next batch of Skynyrd releases, including *Nuthin' Fancy* (1975) and *Gimme Back My Bullets* (1976), proved less noteworthy, although their world status as a compelling live act kept the tour dates plentiful and lucrative.

Tragedy struck in October 1977, when a light aircraft carrying the band and part of its road crew crashed in Mississippi, claiming the lives of Van Zant, guitarist Steve Gaines (who had replaced King in 1975), backing singer Cassie Gaines (sister of Steve) and assistant road manager Dean Kilpatrick. The surviving members, amid numerous personnel changes, kept the band afloat through the 80s and 90s, with the dynamic female singer Dale Krantz (to become the wife of Gary Rossington) and Ronnie Van Zant's brothers Donnie and Johnny(!) all taking a turn as lead vocalist. Collins and Rossington branched out with the Collins-Rossington Band in 1979. Their albums *Anytime, Anyplace, Anywhere* (1980) and *This is the Way* (1981) entered the US album charts but had limited impact elsewhere. The band split up two years later. Collins' career effectively ended after he was paralyzed from the waist down after a car accident near Jacksonville in 1986. His death from pneumonia four years later was reportedly the result of reduced lung capacity, caused by his paralysis. Perhaps the most tragic of all Skynyrd members, it has been said that Collins never fully came to terms with the death of his wife

Cathy Johns at the start of the first tour by the Collins-Rossington Band. His memory will be cherished forever, both as a master guitarist and as the co-creator (with Ronnie Van Zant) of *Free Bird*.

One band, whose unique blend of country, blues and contemporary jazz predated and, in the view of many commentators, surpassed the 70s explosion of country-rock was the Allman Brothers. Fronted by slide guitar genius Duane Allman (1946–1971) and his younger brother and keyboard player Greg (b.1947), later to become a husband of Cher, the band played their first gigs in the mid-60s as the Allman Joys before evolving into the studio band Hourglass, whose self-titled debut album was released on the Liberty label in 1968. Despite having relatively little impact at the time, the album was successfully reissued in 1974 in response to the Allmans' global success. By the time of the reissue, Duane was sadly long-gone, the band comprising Greg in the company of Dickie Betts (b.1943) (guitar/vocals), Chuck Leavell (b.1952) (keyboards), Lamar Williams (1949–1983) (bass), Claude 'Butch' Trucks (b.1947) (drums) and Jai Johnny Johanson (b.1944, real name: John Lee Johnson) (congas). The band had also by now lost the original bass player Berry Oakley (1948–1972), whose death in a motorcycle accident in Macon, Georgia, was an eerie rerun of Duane's tragic demise in similar circumstances and in the same district of Macon a year earlier.

With his flowing golden hair and handlebar mustache, Duane Allman's dashing and mature appearance make it all too easy to forget his life ended when he was just 24. By this time, in addition to his work with the band, he had appeared as a session man on numerous successful recordings, including the celebrated cover version of *Hey Jude* by Wilson Pickett (1941–2006). One man responsible for first spotting his artistic excellence and huge earning potential was Rick Hall, whose FAME (*Florence Alabama Music Enterprises*) studio in Muscle Shoals, Alabama, had become synonymous with a carefully nurtured texture of sounds that almost tasted of the Southern States. In the same town was the world renowned Muscle Shoals Sound Studios, whose in-house Muscle Shoals Rhythm Section, known as the Swampers, are referred to in Lynyrd Skynyrd's *Sweet Home Alabama.*

But Duane Allman's most prized session gig resulted from an invitation by Eric Clapton to appear as an adjunct member of Derek and the Dominos on *Layla and Other Assorted Love Songs.* As was discussed in Chapter 7, Allman's performance was such that it is almost impossible to imagine the album hanging together without him. Some commentators have even suggested, with considerable justification, that *Layla* was as much Allman's album as Clapton's.

Although Duane Allman had made his untimely exit before the band released their most celebrated track, Betts' magnificent freewheeling instrumental *Jessica* from *Brothers and Sisters* (1973), he was around when they recorded the equally compelling jazz-tinged instrumental *In Memory of Elizabeth Reed* on *Idlewild South* in 1970. At the time of his death, the band's quintessential studio/live double album *Eat a Peach* was still in preparation. His gentle acoustic guitar piece *Little Martha* became a touching epitaph as the closing track of Side 3.

With numerous outstanding subsequent releases, including some of the finest live albums the 70s produced, the Allman Brothers Band are rightly seen as one of the era's most elite forces. They brought country into rock on a level that harmed neither and enhanced both.

Between the extremes of Parton and Ronstadt came the universally respected figure of Emmylou Harris (b.1947), whose early contact with Gram Parsons and the Flying Burrito Brothers led to her singing on both Parsons' solo albums, her role on the second release, *Grievous Angel,* being particularly prominent. Harris then went on to further Bob Dylan's country connection, first opened up by Cash, with a highly acclaimed guest appearance on the 1976 album *Desire.* But it was Ronstadt's early 70s backing band, comprising Glenn Frey (b.1948) (guitar), Randy Meisner (b.1946) (bass) and Don Henley (b.1947) (drums), that emerged as a world-ranking team that would, for many, represent the very essence of country-rock...

THE EAGLES

Together with Bernie Leadon (b.1947) (guitar, banjo, mandolin), it was Frey, Meisner and Henley who cut the band's self-titled debut release on Geffen's Asylum label in 1972. Despite the quintessentially American nature of everything the band represented, the album was recorded at the Olympic Studios in London, under the guidance of British producer Glyn Johns (b.1942).

Its 1973 sequel *Desperado* was also recorded in London, only this time at the Island Studios. Johns remained in the producer's chair, the reason for the change of venue being, according to a later interview with Leadon, simply that the Olympic Studios were already booked. Both albums enjoyed instant commercial success, yielding such classic songs as *Take It Easy* and *Tequila Sunrise* respectively. The title track of the second album also found fame in its own right, with Ronstadt becoming one of many artists to release a cover version. The third album, *On the Border* (1974), saw the second appearance by Florida slide-guitar maestro Don Felder (b.1947), who subsequently became a permanent member of the team.

With the release of *One of These Nights* in 1975, the Eagles were set to achieve world prominence. Both the title track and *Lyin' Eyes* entered the UK singles chart. The British conquest was consolidated in the same year with a critically acclaimed live appearance alongside the Beach Boys and Elton John at Wembley Stadium. With their gentle falsetto vocal lines and breezy cruising rhythms, the Eagles successfully captured the outer reaches of the large and lucrative easy-listening market while maintaining their credibility with the more discerning rock audiences.This delicate balance of aesthetics became further enriched with the arrival in 1976 of master rock guitarist Joe Walsh (b.1947), replacing Bernie Leadon. First finding fame as lead guitarist with late 60s hard rock trio the James

Gang, it had been Walsh's virtuoso performance on *Funk No. 49* from *The James Gang Rides Again* (1970) that gave the band what many see as their finest hour. Subsequently establishing himself as a solo artist, with *So What* (1974) and its memorably titled 1973 predecessor *The Smoker You Drink, The Player You Get* enjoying critical acclaim on both sides of the Atlantic, Walsh's surprise decision to join the Eagles was greeted by a sceptical press predicting an early departure to concentrate on solo ventures. The pundits were proved wrong, with Walsh playing a starring role on the long-awaited 1976 release *Hotel California,* widely considered to be the band's greatest achievement.

By this time, the band had reached a platform from which the most lucrative engagements were theirs for the asking, with a steady flow of best-selling compilation albums following their dissolution in the early 80s. Walsh's 1978 solo hit *Life's Been Good* successfully lampooned the cash-fuelled rock star lifestyle he and his colleagues had come to represent. In creating this disarming thumbnail self-portrait, Walsh presumably added a further modest stipend to his already considerable wealth...

Although no necessary link exists, the spheres of folk-rock, country-rock and the singer/songwriter often intersect. This is partly because the earliest American singer/songwriters, from Leadbelly, via Woody Guthrie and Pete Seeger, to Bob Dylan were pioneers and products of the folk/protest movement of the 50s and 60s. All were bardic figures who used the acoustic guitar as their preferred, and often only, accompanying instrument. This tradition was maintained by many of the next generation, including Joni Mitchell (b.1943, née Roberta Joan Anderson), Jim Croce (1943–1973) and John Denver (1943–1997, real name: John Henry Deutschendorf). Of these, Mitchell became particularly highly regarded by the rock audience, especially in the UK. Her appearance at the Isle of Wight Festival in 1970 led to high-profile performances at such prestigious London venues as the Albert Hall and Royal Festival

Hall, culminating her sharing the bill in 1974 with Crosby, Stills, Nash and Young at Wembley Stadium.

Croce, who was killed in a 1973 plane crash alongside his guitarist Maury Meuhliesen, left a small but highly prized legacy of recorded material, in which his own well-crafted guitar accompaniments were complemented by the imaginative acoustic lead lines of Meuhliesen. As any Croce enthusiast will rightly insist, the saloon bar humor of his best-known song, *Big, Bad Leroy Brown,* was not fully representative of his *oeuvre*, the wit, transparency and sincerity of such gentle vignettes as *Operator* and *Lover's Cross* indicating a writer with a keen eye and ear for life's most defining episodes.

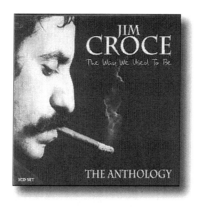

It seems highly probable that Denver's career generated at least as much cash as those of the other two put together, his royalty checks from cover versions of such Denver creations as *Leaving on a Jet Plane* (Peter, Paul and Mary) and *Take Me Home, Country Roads* (Olivia Newton-John, and a US hit for Denver himself) paying many grocery bills before he conquered the world twice over with *Annie's Song*. First came his own vocal interpretation (1974 onwards) and then instrumental cover by celebrity classical flute maestro James Galway (1978).

Commercially minded to the last, Denver climbed aboard the 80s fad for portly opera singers by recording *Perhaps Love (1982)* alongside Placido Domingo. Prior to this, he had risked losing what street cred he ever had by releasing *A Christmas Together* (1979) in the company of the Muppets. But for all his cheesiness, Denver was a talented and hugely successful pro who was not without his admirers in the mainstream of rock. The oft-quoted statement from Grace Slick that starts 'I'm a John Denver freak…' and then goes on to draw a curious parallel between Denver's physical appearance and that of a turkey apparently prompted no complaints from the man himself, although the comparison possibly wounded the self-esteem of many a Thanksgiving fowl.

By the start of the 70s, a more urban breed of singer-songwriter, with little or no connection with the folk/protest movement, was starting to emerge. Significantly, these polished and sophisticated performers would often adopt the piano (never less than a concert grand) as their instrument of self-accompaniment. In England, there was Elton John (b.1947, real name: Reginald Kenneth Dwight, legally changed in 1972 to Elton Hercules John). His long and productive career as an upmarket pop celebrity earned him a CBE in 1996 and a knighthood in 1998.

In the US, there was talented and streetwise New Yorker Carole King (b.1942, real name: Carole Klein), whose award-winning 1971 release *Tapestry* was the crowning glory in a new line of creativity for an artist who, in partnership with her erstwhile husband Gerry Goffin (b.1939), had been a major player on the commercial songwriting circuit since the late 50s. It was an open secret that she was the subject of the hit single *Oh Carol* by her onetime boyfriend Neil Sedaka, the omission of the final 'e' fooling no-one. And yes, King really did write a lesser-known reply single titled *Oh Neil.* But by the time of *Tapestry,* King had put away childish things, the hit single *It's Too Late* remaining a masterpiece of the singer/songwriter's art. The album also featured an inspired reworking of the Goffin/King classic *Will You Still Love Me Tomorrow?,* a mid-tempo teen classic for the Shirelles a decade earlier, now a wistful grown-up ballad in the hands of its co-creator.

It is maybe significant that the character of Courtney Patterson, portrayed by Natalie Wood in the 1973 movie *The Affair,* is a piano-playing singer/songwriter. Although the central aspect of the character is her physical disability (a polio victim who can only get around with the aid of crutches), her choice of profession would clearly have been recognizable to mainstream American audiences at the time the film was released. Interestingly, Patterson is not seen as a bohemian figure, more a creature of sheltered upbringing whose first serious relationship (at the screen age of thirty-two) is with her wealthy father's staid attorney, played by Wood's on-off husband Robert Wagner. Needless to say, *The Affair* was just one of many examples of the music business and the movie industry landing on the same square, a tradition first established by spin-off movies starring Elvis Presley *et al*, closely followed by Cliff Richard, the Beatles and numerous other 50s and 60s icons. By the time *The Affair* was on general release, every rock aficionado had seen *Easy Rider* (1969), with music by the Steppenwolf, Hendrix, the Byrds and others, and *Zabriskie Point* (featuring the music of Pink Floyd, the Grateful Dead etc.).

Unique among singer/songwriters stands the imposing literary figure of Leonard Cohen (b.1934). Although a sizeable number of rock stars have produced poetry, novels and other writings at various stages in their career, Cohen was a published poet almost a decade before his musical career took off. This said, it is often overlooked that Montreal-born Cohen formed a country trio named the Buckskin Boys while still a teenager in the early 50s. But poetry was his first serious activity, a volume titled *Let Us Compare Mythologies* being published while he was still a student at McGill University in 1956. A second collection, *The Spice Box of Earth* (1961), gained wider recognition. Cohen's elevated status in the literary world led to a brief period at New York's Columbia University and a grant that enabled him to travel across Europe. Settling on the Greek island of Hydra, Cohen shared his new home with Marianne Jenson and her son Axel. This episode in his life is generally perceived as the inspiration behind the song *So Long, Marianne* from his Columbia debut album *Songs of Leonard Cohen* in 1968. Before this, he had published his third and most controversial collection of poetry, *Flowers for Hitler* (1964) and two highly acclaimed novels, *The Favorite Game* (1963) and *Beautiful Losers* (1966). Described on its dust jacket as 'a disagreeable religious epic of incomparable beauty', *Beautiful Losers* prompted the Boston Globe to claim 'James Joyce is not dead. He is living in Montreal under the name of Cohen'.

An early champion of Cohen's songs was Judy Collins, who included her own versions of both *Suzanne* and *Dress Rehearsal Rag* on the 1966 album *In My Life*. The first, which later appeared as the opening track on *Songs of Leonard Cohen,* was to become his best-known and most widely admired song, the gentle imagery floating above a smooth and uncluttered melodic line and harmonic progression. Most sources now agree that the subject of the song was not Suzanne Elrod, who became the mother of Cohen's children, but Suzanne Verdal, a dancer who was married to the Montreal sculptor Armand Vaillancourt. This makes sense insofar as Cohen's long-term relationship with Elrod appears only to have started in 1970, long after the song was written, their children Adam and Lorca being born in 1973 and 1974 respectively. Despite the sensual content of the song, Cohen always insisted no physical relationship had ever developed with Verdal, a line later echoed by Verdal herself (now using the name Suzanne Verdal McCallister) in an interview for BBC Radio 4 in June 1998.

The second song Collins chose, with its squalid setting and razor blade imagery, is a classic example of the 'singing suicide note' with which Cohen became inextricably linked. Not recorded by its creator until his third album, *Songs of Love and Hate* (1970), it was the perfect vehicle for his flat and portentous vocal style. If Cohen's work has been the victim of critical stereotyping, the majority of his songs being considerably more amiable than many commentators would have us believe, his public image of a black-suited prophet of doom has served him well over the years. One of his most successful later songs, *First We Take Manhattan* from the 1988 album *I'm Your Man* finds him reciting a bitter, vengeful monologue over a robotic computer-generated backing track. It is all a long way from *Suzanne,* in which 'the sun pours down like honey on Our Lady of the Harbour' (a reference to one of Montreal's best-known Christian monuments), but the words and their delivery have a similarly lasting impact.

In the meantime, an almost comic episode in Cohen's career was the circumstances surrounding *Death of a Ladies' Man* (1977). Produced and lavishly orchestrated by Phil Spector, the project was always destined to be a volatile meeting of minds, the term 'grotesque' being used retrospectively by Cohen on more than one occasion. In an interview published on his own website, Cohen recalls the episode with typically sardonic humor: 'It was a catastrophe. Those are all scratch vocals, and Phil mixed it in secret under armed guard. I had to decide whether I was going to hire my own private army and fight it out on Sunset Boulevard, or let it go. I let it go.'

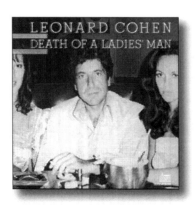

A solitary presence on the fringes of music and contemporary literature, future generations will surely look back on Leonard Cohen as one of the most remarkable, if at times impenetrable, singer/songwriters of our time.

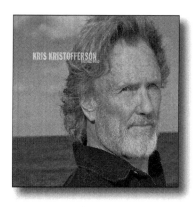

A less high-profile singer/songwriter with early literary ambitions and an academic record that at least equalled that of Cohen was the Texan Kris Kristofferson (b.1936), whose amiable mid-tempo ballad *Me and Bobby McGhee* is one of the most covered strumalong songs of all time, most notably by Roger Miller (1936–1992) and later by Janis Joplin. An academic high-flyer who went to study in England on a Rhodes Scholarship, Kristofferson has regularly been asked if he shared any Oxford memories with fellow Rhodes Scholar and future US president Bill Clinton, Kristofferson's stock reply being 'No, I always inhaled'. Kristofferson's time at Oxford also differs from that of Clinton in that Kristofferson obtained a degree.

Although the 70s will forever be seen as a time of musical integration, rock music still remained largely the white man's domain. Of the hybrid genres examined above, only jazz-rock had a sizeable black representation. Elsewhere, exceptions such as the permanent presence of a black percussionist in the line-up of the Allman Brothers Band were remarkably thin on the ground. Looking at the previous decade, it has even been provocatively suggested that it was only the unparalleled genius of

Jimi Hendrix that persuaded the mainstream rock audience to accept him as an 'honorary white', a curious state of affairs in a genre whose roots lie in that most Afro-American of all musical languages, the blues.

 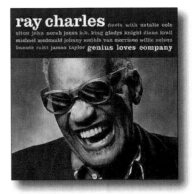

Needless to say, a whole generation of black artists had, since the late 50s, ploughed their own unique furrow in the hugely productive field of soul music. From the foundations laid by such revered figures as Ray Charles (1932–2004) and Sam Cooke (1937–1964), acts such as the Temptations, Marvin Gaye, James Brown and, perhaps most of all, Stevie Wonder enjoyed the support of the more broad-based rock audiences from the mid-60s onwards. From time to time, a specific album would find favor, one such being the enigmatically titled *3+3*, released in 1973 by the Isley Brothers.

A former Motown act (see below), the Isleys' post-1970 work was by now appearing internationally on the less specifically targeted Epic label, a subsidiary of Columbia. A key ingredient in the album's wide appeal was undoubtedly the stylish, rock-inspired guitar lines of the curiously underrated Ernie Isley (b.1952), whose extended solos were often hidden on the *Part 2* B-sides of hit singles such as *That Lady* and *Summer Breeze*. The latter was a lavish cover of an earlier US hit for the white Texan songwriting team of Seals and Crofts, the Isleys' fuzzy and phased guitar providing a disarmingly effective alternative to the acoustic mandolin of Dash Crofts. Originally a vocal trio comprising Ronald,

Rudolph and Kelly (formerly O'Kelly), the Isleys had for more than a decade been recognized as quality purveyors of high octane dance floor classics. As long ago as 1959, they scored a US million seller with the frantic two-chorder *Shout,* later to be covered in the UK by a squawking Glasgow teenager and future Bee Gee wife using the name of Lulu (b.1948, real name: Marie McDonald McLaughlin Lawrie). Eventually to become an enduring and undistinguished cabaret act, Lulu's footnote in rock history was secured following a live performance on her national TV show by the Jimi Hendrix Experience, coyly announced by the mini-skirted hostess as 'Jimi and the boys'.

Following the success of *Shout,* the Isleys went on to enjoy a string of potent and energetic worldwide hits, including what is seen by many as the definitive account of the evergreen *La Bamba* derivative, *Twist and Shout.* The early 70s line-up was augmented by the recruitment of three younger relatives, of which Ernie was one, the other two being Marvin Isley (bass) and brother-in-law Chris Jasper (keyboards). It was this extended family unit that gave the ground breaking new album its title.

The role played in the development of soul music by the Detroit-based Tamla Motown label and its president Berry Gordy Jr. (see also Chapter 5) was central, the crisp and focused sound emanating from Gordy's studios being seemingly impossible to replicate in any other environment. Motown artists were almost exclusively black. A trickle of releases by artists such as the Canadian songwriter R. Dean Taylor (b.1939) and the English singer Kiki Dee (b.1947, real name: Pauline Matthews) were among the few Motown discs to feature white performers. In fact, Taylor's international hit *Indiana Wants Me* from 1970 was released in the US on the Rare Earth label, a Gordy subsidiary specifically intended for white artists, although earlier Taylor singles, including *There's a Ghost in My House* (first released in 1965 but not a major hit until 1974) did appear on Motown. Dee's brief stint with Motown yielded just one album, *Great Expectations* from 1970, and the obscure single *The Day Will Come*. She later found fame as a lightweight pop act on Elton John's Rocket label, scoring a worldwide hit in 1974 with the karaoke standard *I've Got The Music In Me* and duetting with the man himself two years later on the similarly light and lucrative *Don't Go Breaking My Heart*. Her one moment of distinction had come in 1973 with the exquisite post-coital ballad *Amoureuse,* Dee's dark and smoky vocal adding what was inevitably seen in retrospect as an uncharacteristic degree of maturity and gravitas to a potent song and suitably soft-focus arrangement. Running parallel with Motown was the Memphis based Stax label, founded in 1959 by white entrepreneur Jim Stewart (b.1930) and his sister Estelle Axton (1918–2004). Seen as the home of what might broadly be termed Southern Soul, the Stax roster soon boasted such key names as Rufus Thomas (1917–2001), Otis Redding (1941–1967) and inter-racial instrumental groups the Mar-Keys and Booker T. and the MGs.

After Redding's death following a plane crash in Madison, Stax had lost one of their most respected and high-earning artists, the huge posthumous success of *Sitting on the Dock of the Bay* showing a tantalizing glimpse of what might have followed. Redding's first big break at Stax is the stuff of which legends are made, his arrival on their premises as the 21-year-old driver for the then successful but now largely forgotten Johnny Jenkins leading to a 30-minute trial session to use up the pre-booked studio time. The result was Redding's first US hit, a self-penned ballad titled *These Arms of Mine* released on the Stax R&B subsidiary Volt Records. Shortly after Redding's death, what at first appeared to be a routine renegotiation of a distribution deal with Atlantic Records revealed that Atlantic effectively now owned the entire pre-1968 Stax catalog. It was a blow from which the label never fully recovered, although Stewart was able to sell the company to Gulf and Western, reportedly for several million dollars, in May 1968. He then bought it back for an undisclosed sum in July 1970.

The 70s brought a new wave of high-profile Stax artists, including Isaac Hayes (b.1942), whose elaborate creations such as the *Theme from 'Shaft'* earned him the title 'Wagner of Soul'. Hayes later became a cult figure with a whole new generation of millennium kids as the voice of Chef in the anarchic and groundbreaking cartoon series *South Park*. With such artists as Hayes and the Staple Singers providing a new source of revenue, the future of Stax for a time seemed relatively secure, but a further financial crisis led to the label finally folding in January 1976.

From the late 60s onwards, a new force in soul music that had long been waiting in the wings began to assert itself. It has been suggested that, since the end of the 50s, the city of Philadelphia was second only to New York as a center of pop music culture, the Philly-based TV show *American Bandstand* fronted by Dick Clark (b.1929) providing an early platform for everyone from middle-ranking rocker Freddy Cannon to a youthful Simon and Garfunkel, still known in those days as Tom & Jerry. Despite the arrival in the late 50s of the Cameo-Parkway record label, whose roster included Chubby Checker, Bobby Rydell and the Orlons, it was not until the end of the 60s and the launch of Sigma Sound that the city boasted its own fully equipped four-track studio. An enterprise that was to have a profound effect on 70s soul, Sigma Sound was the brainchild of the production and songwriting partnership of Kenny Gamble (b.1943) and Leon Huff (b.1942). By the time they launched the Philadelphia International label in 1973, Gamble and Huff, having by now enlisted the creative input of producer and arranger Thom Bell, were well on the way to establishing the smooth and silky 'Philadelphia Sound' that had first manifested itself in the early hit singles of the precisely choreographed black vocal group the O'Jays. Something that was rarely reported at the time was that, when they scored their first worldwide success with *Backstabbers* in 1972, the O'Jays had been around some fourteen years, their patience being finally rewarded with a further string of hit singles and the highly regarded 1973 album *Ship Ahoy.* Over the next few years, Philadelphia International chalked up worldwide successes for such artists as Harold Melvin and the Bluenotes and Billy Paul, although only the Three Degrees seemed destined to match the lasting prominence of the O'Jays. The label even enjoyed global airplay with its mainly instrumental theme tune *TSOP (The Sound of Philadelphia)*, performed by the in-house big band MFSB (officially standing for Mother, Father, Sister, Brother, although less family-friendly interpretations exist), whose background presence, in various instrumental permutations, was felt on almost every track the label released at the time. The success of *TSOP* even spawned a mini-industry of lesser imitators, *The Hustle* by Van McCoy and the Soul City Symphony from 1975 being a blatant and depressingly well-received attempt to jump aboard the Philadelphia instrumental bandwagon. Its even cornier sequel, imaginatively titled *The Shuffle,* enjoyed equally widespread airplay and subsequent chart success two years later. Without wishing to in any way undervalue the skill and expertise of Gamble, Huff and Bell, the Philadelphia sound represented an at times uncomfortable alliance between the cutting edge of popular culture and that creative abyss known as 'easy listening'.

Nowhere was this more apparent than in the rise to world stardom of the Three Degrees, whose big hairdos and shiny long dresses even caught the eye of no less an establishment figure than Britain's long-term heir-in-waiting Prince Charles. The fact that HRH had shown no apparent interest in popular music before and has rarely been back there since strongly suggests that the glamorous team headed by Sheila Ferguson (b.1947) were hand-picked as offering a series of high-profile photo opportunities that were unlikely to rock the boat with either the British public or an increasingly inquisitive national and international press. In other words, it seems highly probable this early and profoundly unconvincing attempt to present Charles as a right-on royal was every bit as stage managed as the mildly alluring cabaret routines at which the comely threesome excelled.

But as the middle-aged, middle managers and their dutiful wives smiled with indulgent approval, the teenagers of the house turned away from the TV set in search of new avenues to express their youthful angst...

11

Punk Rock and the New Wave

With the benefit of 20/20 hindsight, perhaps the only surprising aspect of the seismic changes that engulfed rock music from 1976 onwards was that anyone was surprised. The imaginary domestic vignette that closed the previous chapter surely had many manifestations in the real world. From its first flowerings in the 50s, rock music had been a youth culture through which those in their teens and early 20s challenged and provoked the western establishment, into which most of them would eventually be absorbed with the onset of maturity and its associated family and financial responsibilities.

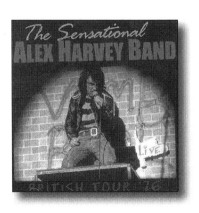

By and large, the heroic figures creating the music and setting the trends were just a few years older than their disciples, although rarely by much more than a decade. Crucially, they were, or at least were seen to be, significantly younger than their fans' parents. Broadly speaking, this remained the case during the 60s and early 70s. Exceptions such as Alex Harvey (1935–1982), whose glory days fronting the Sensational Alex Harvey Band only started as he approached his fortieth birthday, were sufficiently rare as to cause virtually every media profile to record in detail the subject's advancing years.

But as the 70s wore on, the gap finally closed. The fact that rock music had been around for more than two decades naturally meant that many of its first wave of followers now had teenage kids of their own, making it increasingly difficult for the present generation to shock mum and dad with more recent variants on a music that had been central to their own youth. This is not to suggest that the average forty-something couple, whose courtship was launched by jiving to *Rock Around the Clock*, were not a little taken aback by the thrusting sexual imagery of *Whole Lotta Love,* but as the offspring of parents who had actively participated in the 60s of Jimi and Janis gradually entered their own 'difficult' years, the common ground was such that inter-generational domestic squabbles would regularly arise over the ownership of mutually cherished LPs and 45s. Raids on the hi-fi cabinet frequently resulted in carefully preserved Beatle records finding their way to the small bedroom, never to return. Likewise Dylan, the Doors and maybe even some early Zappa. Perhaps dad did not play these albums as much as he used to, any more than he still regularly wore his kaftan, but their timeless qualities shone like a beacon, especially when some areas of rock music were starting to get noticeably tired.

The 70s were, to adopt a favorite soccer managers' cliché, a match of two halves. Of the many world-class musicians to arrive on the scene at the close of the 60s, a sizeable number had served up their finest offerings by 1975 and now seemed destined to spend the rest of their careers reliving past glories, usually with the unquestioning support of a devoted but ageing fanbase. Some of the more accomplished B-list acts, such as Wishbone Ash, proved particularly robust and could still justify the hire of a 1000-seater venue at the turn of the millennium, despite having not had a hit album in twenty years. But WBA, like so many of their lesser and greater contemporaries, had captured the spirit of the early 70s on a ticket that was never to be theirs again. This was equally true at the highest level. Not even the most devoted follower of Page and Plant would seriously claim that *In Through the Out Door* (1979) comes close to equalling the majesty of *Physical Graffiti* (1975), let alone its even more distinguished predecessors. A similar comparison might be made between the adept but lightweight *Going for the One* (1977) and the imposing *Close to the Edge* (1972), both of which were released by a band named Yes but share few other common attributes.

An exception to this general decline was Jethro Tull, whose post-1975 offerings *Songs from the Wood* and *Heavy Horses* (1977 and 1978 respectively) found them on outstanding form, Ian Anderson having by now skilfully transformed his public image from the pop-eyed urban vagrant that had served its purpose admirably in the years leading up to *Aqualung*.

The fact that Tull continued this line of excellence during the 80s and 90s, releasing the superb *Crest of a Knave* in 1987, makes Anderson's seemingly endless creativity one of rock music's most priceless treasures.

But the news from elsewhere was often of increasing mediocrity. Bands whose internal tensions had led to a split often reinvented themselves as a pale imitation of the original. Mainstream British rockers Free, fronted by the darkly charismatic vocals of Paul Rodgers (b.1949) and the subtly understated guitar lines of Paul Kossoff (1950–1976), disbanded in 1973 after just four years in which they had produced the classic *Alright Now*, the almost equally powerful three-minute soundbite *Wishing Well,* plus various high octane blues-based offerings, both live and on vinyl.

As the tragic figure of Kossoff entered the final stages of his drug-fuelled self-destruction, Rodgers formed the competent but relatively unremarkable Bad Company, taking Free drummer Simon Kirke (b.1948) with him and generating half a dozen commercially successful but now largely forgotten albums, plus three UK hit singles, over the remainder of the decade.

A similar tale may be told of the once mighty Deep Purple, whose mid-70s bickering led to a whole series of spin-off ventures, most notably Rainbow (featuring guitarist Ritchie Blackmore) and later Whitesnake (featuring vocalist David Coverdale), decent bands both, but not of a caliber to exceed the precedents set by such triumphant Purple creations as *Smoke on the Water* and *Child in Time.* The prevailing spirit was one of downsizing, possibly reflecting the more modest requirements of a still plentiful but less adventurous audience.

Naturally, some areas of rock prospered amid this ever-expanding creative vacuum, but it tended to be those who placed the least demands on the listeners' ears and intellect that came off best. Increasingly media-savvy solo acts such as Elton John and Rod Stewart went from strength to strength, the fact that Stewart nominally still remained at the helm of pub rockers *par excellence* the Faces being something a large part of his new middle-aged audience probably did not know and most certainly would not have wanted to know. By the time of his 1978 hit *Do Ya Think I'm Sexy?*, Stewart had plumbed the depths of superstar self-parody. This did not pass unnoticed by the anarchic British DJ and satirist Kenny Everett (1944–1995), who featured the song on his national TV show, with Everett in the role of Stewart suffering a bout of flatulence on stage, causing his body-hugging leopard skin trousers to inflate.

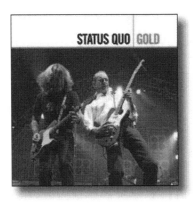

For those who did not think Stewart was sexy and still preferred a little grit in their oysters, Status Quo, having long since abandoned their psychedelic roots, consolidated their long-term role as world purveyors of simple denim-clad twelve-bar boogie. While Quo continued their odyssey of *Rockin' All Over the World*, the neatly-honed and easygoing products of the Eagles continued to gain mass appeal. Maybe dad had not listened to *Sergeant Pepper* or *Blonde on Blonde* for a while, but *Hotel California* was just the thing for winding down after a stressful day at the office. Likewise the latest saccharine offering from the Three Degrees, which was currently climbing the singles' chart alongside similarly syrupy confections from the Carpenters and even our old friend Perry Como who, as he approached pensionable age, was enjoying a new lease of life with his cash-cow cover of Don McLean's *And I Love You So*. People were buying this stuff in huge quantities, and it surely was not only Como's contemporaries.

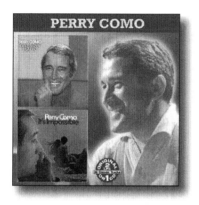 

In short, popular music had become a 'mature' market in every sense of the term, with more and more former rockers trading in their Harley-Davidsons for a mid-range family sedan. This is not to suggest that all of them were listening to Perry Como on the car stereo, but the demand for a less radical product that still came within the broader boundaries of the rock ethos was becoming increasingly evident. Naturally, the smartest movers and shakers in the business got wise to the trend almost before it started, with serious capital being poured into the promotion of accomplished but relatively uncontroversial performers such as Columbia's latest hot protégé, Bruce Springsteen (b.1949).

The situation may also be illustrated by the gradual and not-so-gradual transformation of two established acts from rock's existing hierarchy: Fleetwood Mac and Genesis. As discussed in Chapter 9, the transformation of Genesis from master purveyors of quirky English prog-rock to silver-tongued providers of what might be termed 'new generation middle-of-the-road' took place more or less overnight, following the departure of Peter Gabriel and the subsequent elevation to lead vocalist of Phil Collins.

In the case of Fleetwood Mac, some trace the changes back as far as the departure of Peter Green in 1970, while others would see the turning point as the arrival in 1974 of guitarist Lindsey Buckingham (b.1949) and his then-girlfriend, the singer/songwriter Stevie Nicks (b.1948). But most would surely agree that the shift in direction was fully implemented with the release of the million-selling *Rumours* album in 1977. Gone were the celestial guitar lines of *Albatross,* the troubled introspection of *Man of the World* and the gritty blues-driven hard rock of *Oh Well.*

Instead, there was an album whose content, despite being hailed as 'flawless' in at least one rock encyclopedia, may be summed up by the saccharine aesthetic of its best-known hit song. Built around a monotonous yet curiously seductive two-chord drone, *Dreams* provided the definitive platform for the nasal and girlie vocal style of Nicks, her idiosyncratic delivery of the words resulting in such unforgettable rhetorical distortions as 'When the rain *washezz* you clean, you'll know…', not to mention the classic line 'Thunder only happens when it's raining', which succeeded in being both ungrammatical and meteorologically incorrect within the space of just six words. But even its harshest detractors would gloomily concede that the arrival of *Rumours* was timed to perfection. Like *Bridge Over Troubled Water* less than a decade before, it soon became the album whose presence was required in every plastic record rack in every one of Pete Seeger's *Little Boxes* on every suburban housing estate throughout the Western World. But with all its slick production and superficial air of sophistication, *Rumours* was a million miles from what was happening at the cutting edge of rock music…

Although it will forever be associated with the years from 1976 onwards, the term Punk Rock may be traced back as far as the mid-to-late 60s, when it was perceived as an almost exclusively American phenomenon. In a brief but illuminating article that appeared in the 1973 edition of the *NME Book of Rock*, Nick Logan and Rob Finnis introduce the term as being 'first coined to describe the numerous local white bands who sprang up all over America between 1965-8, a transitional period in [the] development of American rock 'n' roll, the years between the Beatles/Stones-led British invasion and the San Francisco based rock renaissance'. Logan and Finnis go on to depict these 60s punk bands as being 'invariably made up of acned High School heroes. Their sound [was] characterized by Fender and Standell amps, through which one year of guitar lessons were scratched slightly out of tune. One finger played Vox Continental organs on full treble. Drumming was basic Ringo; singing the arrogant whine of a manic Jagger look-alike.' They also note that, in most cases, these bands 'gathered all their talent and inspiration into just one record – few managed a repeat'. The examples cited include *Louie Louie* by the Kingsmen, *Pushin' Too Hard* by Sky Saxon and the Seeds, not to mention the unforgettable *96 Tears* by ? and the Mysterians. Broadly speaking, Logan and Finnis seem justified in categorizing these one-off releases as little more than 'regional successes', although *Louie Louie* became a minor international hit and was later the butt of many a Frank Zappa joke.

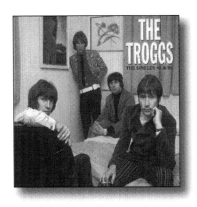

Rather oddly, Logan and Finnis conclude by describing the Troggs as the 'prime British punk band'. Despite their admittedly rudimentary performing skills, the Troggs, fronted by the engaging and rustic figure of Reg Presley (b.1941 or 1943, real name: Reginald Ball), enjoyed a healthy run of national and international hits during the 60s and remain cult figures to this day, Presley having reinvented himself as a noted authority on the phenomena of UFOs and 'crop circles'. All this makes them an essentially different species from the ephemeral figures listed above.

But if Punk Rock 60s-style was peculiar to America, its 70s manifestation was a decidedly bipartite development, spearheaded by the Sex Pistols in the UK and the Ramones in the States. Learning their trade in the basement clubs of New York, the Ramones were among the first bands to publicly promote the new terminology in the songs *Judy is a Punk* and *Sheena is a Punk Rocker,* from the self-titled 1976 debut album and the 1977 release *Rocket to Russia* respectively. In the meantime, on the album *Leave Home* from early 1977, another female acquaintance was celebrated in *Suzy is a Headbanger.* Originally a trio, comprising Joey (Jeffry) Hyman (1951–2001) (drums/vocals), Johnny Cummings (1948–2004) (guitar) and Douglas 'Dee Dee' Colvin (1952–2002) (bass), the band's definitive line-up was completed in 1974 when manager Tommy Erdelyi (b.1952) took over as drummer in order to allow Hyman, soon to become Joey Ramone (alongside 'brothers' Johnny, Dee Dee and Tommy), a greater degree of vocal and visual freedom. Like most punk bands of the new generation, the Ramones were characterized not so much by a lack of musical skill as by an overt and uncompromising rejection of anything that smacked of musical sophistication. With crashing and distorted three-chord riffs, relentless machine-gun drum fills and ranting vocal lines that both addressed and at times glorified such taboo issues as solvent abuse, the world of the Ramones was a long way from the symphonic rock that had held center stage only a few years before. But it was also a world away from the musical soft-furnishings being peddled by Genesis and Fleetwood Mac, giving this dark creative substratum an irresistible allure for a generation of adolescents who, like their parents and older siblings before them, were forever in search of a platform from which to express their own cultural identity. Parallels have even been drawn, by no means without justification, between the Ramones residency at CBGB's in New York's Bowery and that of the Beatles at the Cavern. Although a relatively new venue (founded in 1973 by Hilly Kristal), CBGB's originally targeted the mature 'country, bluegrass and blues' audience, its transformation to a hotbed of punk and the New Wave starting with an early gig by the then-unknown band Television (see later).

Before moving on, it is perhaps worth noting that the Ramones, unlike many other punk bands of the time, displayed a keen awareness of the rich musical heritage that had gone before, one of their most successful singles being an extravagant and disarmingly convincing 1980 cover of the Phil Spector classic *Baby I Love You* produced by the man himself. Against all the odds, the ambitious synthesis of ideas that Spector had failed to fully achieve with Leonard Cohen had hit the spot with Joey Hyman.

Although their rise to prominence was both contemporaneous and in many ways parallel to that of the Ramones, the Sex Pistols are perhaps best seen as a one-off phenomenon that had no exact equivalent on either side of the Atlantic. Originally launched as the Swankers, the band was controlled from the outset by the cynical yet inspired entrepreneur Malcolm McLaren (b.1946), proprietor of London's vintage clothes and record store *Let It Rock* and the cult fashion boutique *SEX*, in partnership with designer Vivienne Westwood (b.1941). Concerned almost exclusively with image, if necessary at the expense of musical expertise, McLaren would routinely fire early members such as guitarist Wally Nightingale (d.1996) for no reason other than their perceived lack of stage charisma. McLaren later drafted in Sid Vicious (1957–1979, real name: John Ritchie-Beverley) as replacement for bass player Glen Matlock (b.1956), despite the new recruit's apparent inability to even hold a bass guitar. But since Vicious had already distinguished himself in the public eye, both as an inventor of the Pogo dance and as an alleged member of a gang who beat up a journalist during a Pistols' gig at the 100 Club, his potential earning power naturally outweighed that of the musically able but less headline-grabbing Matlock. Contrary to popular perception, Vicious was only a late contributor to the band's brief musical odyssey, the definitive line-up being Matlock in the company of vocalist Johnny Rotten (b.1956, real name: John Lydon), guitarist Steve Jones (b.1955) and drummer Paul Cook (b.1956).

For a band whose influence was to reverberate throughout the next decade and beyond, it is ironic that virtually every significant aspect of the Pistols' musical legacy may be experienced on just one album, the famously-titled 1977 release *Never Mind the Bollocks, Here's the Sex Pistols*. Opening with the band's stage anthem *Anarchy in the UK*, this pithy agenda of three-minute assaults plays host to such equally strident creations as the sneering republican rant, *God Save the Queen.* But the most striking aspect of the album is surely the fact that, although the performances are unapologetically raw and unrefined, they are clearly not the work of a team of musical incompetents, the concise and finely-crafted guitar solo on *Anarchy* being a particularly impressive retort to the protracted improvisations of the once celebrated figures who were now being pilloried in the music press as the guitar heroes of yesteryear. Inevitably, stories were soon doing the rounds as to who was really playing on the album. Most prominent of these was that session guitarist Chris Spedding (b.1944), who had worked with the band in preparation for their first demo, had played a greater role than was officially acknowledged. Spedding has always denied this, maintaining in a later interview that the pre-Vicious incarnation of the Pistols was 'very professional in the studio'. Even if uncredited mercenaries really were present during the sessions for *Never Mind the Bollocks,* subsequently released live footage strongly suggests that the Pistols on stage were at least capable of turning in a credible live presentation of the vinyl that bore their name.

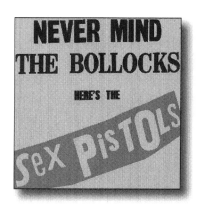

Within less than two years of *Never Mind the Bollocks,* it was all over. Rotten, who had reportedly been reluctant to go along with McLaren's plan to record a song with celebrity fugitive criminal Ronnie Biggs (b.1929), either left or was sacked following the US tour in which he famously taunted the audience with the words 'ever get the feeling you've been cheated?'. Shortly after this, Vicious died of a reported drug overdose while awaiting trial for the murder of his American girlfriend Nancy Spungen (1958–1978).

What little recorded material remained in the can was duly released, including the wonderfully ironic account of the Sinatra classic *My Way*, performed by a contemptuous Vicious. This, and most other post-*Bollocks* fare, is perhaps best experienced in Julien Temple's cut and paste movie *The Great Rock'n'Roll Swindle* (1979) which, although given a lukewarm reception at the time, successfully captures the squalid atmosphere of this brief but profoundly influential episode in the history of rock.

Needless to say, punk did not spring from nowhere, although tracing its precise origins means selecting and distilling a variety of influences spread over the previous two decades. Musically, there were similarities between punk and the most fundamentalist manifestations of heavy metal, a sub-genre that might be termed 'bare metal'. This theory is perhaps borne out in the broad acceptance by punk audiences of Motörhead. But the image projected by the punk rocker was the very antithesis of heavy metal's quintessentially heroic and warrior-like figure, who commanded the devotion of his disciples with superhuman displays of vocal prowess and guitar virtuosity. With punk, the paying public was confronted by a trio or quartet of scowling and scary adolescents whose contempt for any personal accomplishment, be it excellence on the guitar or just winning a place at college, was total. With fitting irony, punk bands were almost always well-received by college audiences.

It has been suggested that punk had a natural precursor in the largely British commercial Glam-Rock scene of the early 70s, although it is difficult to see any paternal links between the Pistols and such vaguely androgynous teen idols as the Sweet and T. Rex. This said, Midlands glam-rockers Slade, with their hectic guitar-driven soundbites, graffiti-style song titles (*Cum on Feel the Noize, Skweeze Me, Pleeze Me* etc.) and the rasping lead vocals of Neville 'Noddy' Holder (b.1946), possibly set a general pattern for the music their pre-teen admirers would grow into as the hormones came to the boil.

At a more sophisticated level of glam-rock, the spiked and vividly colored hairdos of the endlessly talented and productive David Bowie (b.1947, real name: David Robert Jones) during the era of *Ziggy Stardust* and *Aladdin Sane* undoubtedly had an influence on the tonsorial thinking of both genders of punk rocker. Similarly, the macabre shock-rock stage shows of Alice Cooper had set a precedent that presumably did not go unnoticed. Legend has it that McLaren first hired the youth who became Johnny Rotten after listening to him snarl along to a Cooper record on the shop's jukebox.

But the most discernible precedents surely lie in such maverick US acts as Iggy Pop (b.1947, real name: James Newell Osterberg) and the

New York Dolls, the latter having been managed in the pre-Pistols era by none other than Malcolm McLaren.

An isolated figure whose entire career has been spent on the outer fringes of rock, Pop has nonetheless earned the admiration of everyone from David Bowie (who remixed Pop's 1972 album *Raw Power* prior to its release on Columbia) to Glen Matlock who, after his departure from the Pistols, became a member of Pop's backing band, openly acknowledging the enigmatic urban drifter as his hero.

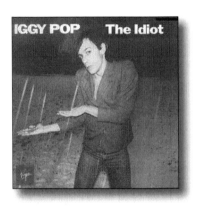

Also influential were the Velvet Underground who, despite their refined artistic associations, showed a marked penchant for some of the most basic and unrefined rock the 60s produced, notably in *Sister Ray*. There was also a sartorial link, visible in the new generation of American punk bands. Early shots of the Ramones, complete with luxuriant fringes, shades and biker jackets could almost be interpreted as a 70s revival of VU fashion statements.

For the British punks, the stylistic inspiration often came from the 50s, the more conservative members of the tribe reinforcing their hair in a manner that resulted in what was essentially an exaggeration of the teddy boy quiff, a look they modernized with a liberal sprinkling of bondage chains and body piercing. Johnny Rotten, in particular, showed an occasional penchant for 50s retro, appearing in one publicity shot sporting drainpipe jeans and a velvet-collared jacket.

The most celebrated and extreme punk hairstyle, the Mohican, had no obvious precedent in the fashion archives, although it is perhaps worth noting that many of the British punk generation would have been entertained in their earlier adolescence by the first of several BBC drama series to bear the title of James Fenimore Cooper's 1826 novel *The Last of the Mohicans,* originally broadcast in 1971.

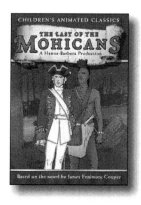

It is curious to note that, although the genesis of punk rock can be directly traced to the USA and that the term 'punk' is in itself an example of quintessentially American slang rarely heard in England before the mid-70s, there were those in the States who saw punk rock in its 70s form as a predominantly British phenomenon. This may be illustrated in a highly illuminating quote from Jaco Pastorius (see Chapter 10), interviewed in 1980 by Damon Roerich: 'I'm a punk from Florida, a street kid. In the streets where I come from, a punk is someone who's a wiseguy...punk is not a bad word. It's sort of someone you respect because he...stick(s) up for himself. It has nothing to do with the punk music movement that's coming out of England now, where people are sticking needles through their noses.'

Pastorius goes on to invoke his own term 'punk jazz', which he claims to have coined ten years earlier and which became the title of one of his own compositions, recorded with Weather Report on the 1978 album *Mr. Gone.* This episode cannot be allowed to pass without noting that fellow bass innovator and perceived rival Stanley Clarke is on record as having once referred to Pastorius, with heavy irony, as 'the Sid Vicious of jazz'.

Although Pastorius is unquestionably understating the contribution of his compatriots to the rise of Punk Rock, it is certainly true that a large number of the most influential 70s punk bands were of British origin, many launching their careers at the same time as the Sex Pistols and almost all surviving longer. To take just one key example, the Damned are widely credited with having released the first commercially distributed British punk single with *New Rose* in 1976. Although not a chart success, this record is also significant in that it was released on the newly launched independent label Stiff Records, home to many an act that would play their part in the post-punk era that became known as the New Wave. With a roster that featured late 70s arrivals ranging from Elvis Costello (b.1954, real name: Declan Patrick McManus, son of big band crooner Ross McManus) to Celtic Punk founding fathers the Pogues, Stiff Records also played host to elder statesman of the New Wave, Ian Dury (1942–2000), former leader of Kilburn and the High Roads (briefly repackaged in the light of his personal fame as Ian Dury and the Kilburns) and by now frontman to Ian Dury and the Blockheads.

Billing itself as 'the world's most flexible record label', Stiff Records provided a vital platform for bands the established labels found too hot

225

to handle. In this respect, like almost all others, the Pistols had charted their own unique course, having been signed and subsequently dropped by both EMI and A&M before *Never Mind the Bollocks* was finally released on Virgin. As a delighted McLaren commented on receiving a £75,000 payoff from A&M, the EMI deal having already netted a reported £40,000 for no returns, 'I keep walking in and out of offices being given cheques!'

Comprising lead vocalist Dave Vanian (b.1956, real name: David Letts), guitarist Brian James (b.1961, real name: Brian Robertson), bass player Captain Sensible (b.1954, real name: Ray Burns) and drummer Rat Scabies (b.1957, real name: Chris Miller), the Damned were a highly professional team whose musical abilities were never in dispute. A major force throughout the heyday of the New Wave, the band remained productive well into the 80s, despite having staged their first of many 'reunions' as early as 1979. Perhaps more than any other punk act, they were masters of the inspired cover version, a frantic account of the Beatles' *Help* appearing as the B-side of *New Rose* and a disarmingly convincing rehash of *Eloise* (originally a melodramatic hit single for Barry Ryan in 1968) reaching UK No.3 in 1986. By this time, Captain Sensible had branched out as a novelty pop act in his own right, reaching the UK No.1 spot in 1982 with a good-natured parody of Rodgers and Hammerstein's *Happy Talk*. This and most other Sensible solo outings were released on the A&M label, whose anxious executives had clearly got over their phobia of punk acts, always given that the listener accepts the jovial and unthreatening Sensible was ever a punk rocker in even the broadest sense of the term. In fact, the Damned never fully conformed to the scary image of the bottle-throwing urban thug that both male and female aficionados of the genre at least attempted to project. Even Vanian's penchant for Munsters/Addams Family clothing and makeup often appeared closer to the world of silent movies than that of Alice Cooper. Only James and Scabies came close to projecting the perceived punk persona, although the latter's wide-ranging wardrobe of shiny trousers seemed to suggest the connection between punk and glam was maybe closer than first suspected.

Although history will forever highlight the Pistols as a unique and defining force, the intervening years have seen the Damned blur into an incidental tripartite alliance with two other enduring British bands: the Stranglers and the Clash. Despite the fact that each band had its own highly individual identity, their histories are routinely confused, with regular pub discussions centering around such questions as which one of the three had an 80s hit with the Kinks classic *All Day and All of the Night*. In fact, it was the Stranglers, although many an otherwise informed party would hesitate to claim this as a gospel truth without first looking it up. Like the Damned, the Stranglers were masters of the cover version, a splendidly audacious hit towards the end of their reign in 1990 being a revival of *96 Tears,* magnum opus of the by now long-forgotten ? and the Mysterians.

Combining ironic humor with an outstanding degree of technical skill, both live and in the studio, it is highly debatable whether or not the Stranglers were ever a punk band, or even anything more than just a time-served class act whose rise to fame happened to take place on the crest of the New Wave. The band was centered on university graduates Hugh Cornwell (b.1949) (vocals, guitar) and Jean-Jacques Burnel (b.1952) (vocals, bass), this erudite pairing being complemented by keyboard player Dave Greenfield (b.1949) and drummer Jet Black (b.1938, real name: Brian Duffy). Originally named the Guildford Stranglers, the band was active from 1974, two years before the first flowerings of British punk. But it was only in 1977, at the height of punk and rise of the New Wave, that the band achieved national prominence with the hit single *Peaches* (UK No.8), its predecessor *(Get a) Grip (on Yourself)* from earlier the same year having languished for four weeks as a 'breaker' in the lower reaches of the chart. With its reggae beat and leering chorus line 'Walking on the beaches, looking at the peaches', the song was as expertly crafted as it was blatantly commercial, that unforgettable bass riff entering the national consciousness at least as indelibly as the unashamedly, and clearly intentionally, puerile lyrics. If this was punk rock, then it was already moving a long way from *Anarchy in the UK.* A global success on what was, for its genre, an unprecedented scale, *Peaches* became one of the first New Wave singles to make its mark in Australasia, a part of the world whose home-grown punk product remained largely unknown at an international level until John Peel's adoption of the Saints.

Although only seen internationally as a cult act, this Brisbane-based team soon acquired friends in high places, an oft-quoted retrospective comment by Bob Geldof, whose own unique musical and humanitarian odyssey will be discussed in the next chapter, being the stuff from which doctoral theses are generated: 'Rock music in the seventies was changed by three bands: the Sex Pistols, the Ramones and the Saints'.

But maybe every punk has his price, this situation being admirably summed up by Johnny Rotten in an unsolicited tribute to his paymaster at Virgin Records: 'I've always liked Richard Branson because, pompous rich twat that he is, he has a great sense of rebelliousness'.

And, despite a long run of chart successes, rebellious the Stranglers would remain, one of their best remembered and most finely hewn songs *Golden Brown* (UK No.2, January 1982) coming within a whisker of radio silence due to suspected drug references. If the Small Faces could get away with it in *Itchycoo Park* and *Here Comes the Nice* during the 60s, then so could the Stranglers more than a decade later, their gently syncopated harpsichord riff giving *Golden Brown* a neo-baroque splendor that no listener, no matter how impressionable, should be denied.

If the Stranglers were incidental beneficiaries from the aftershock of the punk explosion, then the Clash were at its epicenter. Comprising guitarist and lead vocalist Joe Strummer (1952–2002, real name: John Graham Mellor), alongside guitarists Mick Jones (b.1955) and Keith Levene (b.1957), bassist Paul Simonon (b.1955) and drummer Terry Chimes (b.1955, mischievously billed as Tory Crimes on the self-titled debut album, released in 1977 during the first stirrings of Thatcherism), the Clash were arguably the most politically active of all the first division punk bands. The term *Agit Punk* has been applied retrospectively. The band was essentially nurtured from the alliance of Strummer and Jones. It was at Jones' instigation that Strummer had parted company with the then highly regarded 101ers, his exit having reportedly threatened the early survival of his former band.

Like a large number of New Wave acts, the Clash often drew their rhythmic ideas from the enduring resources of reggae, as typified in the their best-remembered song *London Calling,* title track of their 1979 third album. By this time Chimes, who left shortly after recording the first album, had been replaced by Nick 'Topper' Headon (b.1955). Levene had also made his exit, later joining John Lydon in the short-lived post-Pistols venture Public Image Ltd. Despite their capacity to deliver catchy, well-crafted songs and tight, energetic performances, as typified in the hectic *Should I Stay Or Should I Go,* a surprise 'posthumous' UK No.1 in 1991, the Clash's political agenda was already starting to weigh heavily. *London Calling* was a double LP, often described as a 'manifesto', while *Sandinista!* from 1980 was a sprawling three LP set that one rock encyclopedia tartly suggested 'would have been a fair double album and a better single album'. The band's insistence that *Sandinista!* should retail for the same price as a double LP strained their relationship with CBS, the final deal being that the band waived royalties on the first 200,000 sales.

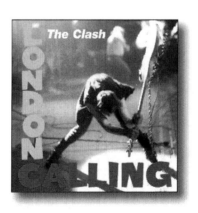

By the time of *Sandinista!,* the Clash were rising more rapidly in the USA than at home, a situation that led to charges that they were gradually becoming the type of 'stadium band' that every punk rocker was programmed to despise. There were also stories of simmering resentments within the band. The situation was not helped when it became known that the unfinished *Combat Rock* album, eventually released in May 1982, had been completed at the instigation of CBS by veteran mainstream producer Glyn Johns (see Chapter 10). Changes of personnel followed, the first departure being Topper Headon, reportedly on grounds of ill health due to years of 24/7 drug usage. With Headon's place taken by Peter Howard, the most dramatic exit was that of Jones, allegedly fired by the alliance of Strummer and Simonon. With the release of *Cut the Crap* in 1985, Strummer, Simonon and Howard had been joined by guitarists Nick Sheppard and Vince White, youthful figures considered so obscure at the time that some contemporary sources do not even mention them by name. The album was poorly received, especially on home territory, the band's subsequent catalog containing mostly retrospective releases. Many Clash scholars maintain to this day that the band was effectively dissolved with the departure of Jones. At the time of his death from what was described as 'congenital heart failure' in December 2002, Joe Strummer had re-emerged as a vigorous campaigner, speaking eloquently and persuasively via the British media on a range of issues, most notably those central to the environmental group *Future Forests* (later relaunched as the *Carbon Neutral Company*). His name has now been immortalized in both the *Strummerville Foundation for New Music* and the *Joe Strummer Memorial Forest* (also known as *Rebel's Wood*) on the Isle of Skye.

As punk evolved into the more broad-based concept of New Wave, a growing inventory of British artists, many of whom would enjoy long and lucrative careers lasting far beyond the inevitably brief reign of punk, experienced their first taste of success. Some, although by no means all, got their first break by signing with Stiff Records, with Elvis Costello, Wreckless Eric (Goulden), the Adverts, Graham Parker, Devo, the Tyla Gang and Kentucky born Richard Hell all striking deals within a short time of the label's launch in 1976.

Of these, Costello proved a particularly intelligent and multi-faceted talent. With his short dark hair, retro-style spectacles and a tight-fitting three-button lounge suit, Costello projected a nerdy stage persona that lay somewhere between Hank Marvin and Buddy Holly, with perhaps even a hint of the sartorially conservative Ron Mael, enigmatic keyboard player with the eccentric yet accomplished American glam pop/rock band Sparks. Musically, Costello owed little to either Marvin or Mael, although the hiccupping vocal style on some of his early recordings was not entirely dissimilar to that of Holly. His first hit single *Watching the Detectives,* released on the Stiff label and reaching UK No.15 in 1977, proved to be yet another manifestation of the reggae influence on the New Wave. Many more Stiff successes followed, one of the early signings being the inter-racial band Madness. It was Madness who, alongside such similar acts as the Specials, the Selector and UB40 would soon spearhead the late 70s Ska movement, centered around the 2-Tone label launched in 1979 by Specials' keyboard player Jerry Dammers.

Costello's stay at Stiff proved brief, although his moves to the Radar, F-Beat and eventually Rykodisc labels yielded more than a dozen UK hits during the period 1978-82. By this time, his backing band, the Attractions, were sharing the billing. Comprising keyboard player Steve Nieve (b.1958, real name: Steve Nason, shown as Mason in some sources), Bruce Thomas (b.1948) (bass) and Pete Thomas (b.1954, no relation) (drums), the Attractions in general and Nieve in particular contributed much to Costello's early sound, even though he has always been perceived as essentially a solo artist. Nieve it was who provided

232

that unforgettable tinkling piano fill, said to have been inspired by the Abba hit *Dancing Queen*, on the evergreen *Oliver's Army* which, after 25 years and numerous re-releases, still remains arguably Costello's best-known song. A diverse and endlessly productive talent, Costello remains active at the time of writing, with more than two dozen albums to his credit. Even *Painted From Memory,* a high-risk 1998 collaboration with Burt Bacharach, proved a triumph for both artists. Costello and Bacharach subsequently appeared as street musicians, performing the Bacharach classic *I'll Never Fall In Love Again*, in the 1999 movie *Austin Powers – The Spy Who Shagged Me.*

Although the New Wave in Britain was largely generated by domestic talent, a number of US performers played pivotal roles. Particularly significant was Television, fronted by the slight but charismatic figure of Tom Verlaine (b.1949, real name: Tom Miller). Rising from the ashes of the Neon Boys, the band comprised Verlaine in the company of bass player Richard Hell (b.1949, real name: Richard Meyers) and drummer Billy Ficca, later to be joined by guitarist Richard Lloyd. Like fellow New York band the Ramones, Television were regular performers at CBGBs, reportedly the first punk band to appear there. A senior figure in the American New Wave, Hell provides a link with punk doyens the New York Dolls, parting company with Verlaine to form the Heartbreakers with ex-NYD Johnny Thunders (1952–1991, real name: John Anthony Genzale). The band's choice of name naturally led to confusion with mainstream US rock stalwarts Tom Petty and the Heartbreakers, whose self-titled debut album came shortly after the launch of the Hell/Thunders alliance. Hell subsequently formed his own band the Voidoids and remained at the helm until their demise in 1984, having by then released two 'official' albums (*Blank Generation* and *Destiny Street*) and a 'posthumous' compilation of unreleased tracks titled *RIP.*

By the time Television released the ground-breaking *Marquee Moon* in 1977, Hell had been replaced by Fred Smith (not to be confused with MC5 guitarist Fred 'Sonic' Smith). Like its 1978 sequel *Adventure*, the *Marquee Moon* album was more enthusiastically received in the UK than the US. It generated two UK hit singles: the title track and *Prove It.*

Running for almost ten minutes in its entirety, the uncut *Marquee Moon* provided still more evidence of the influence of reggae on the New Wave.

The band split shortly after *Adventure*. Verlaine released a string of solo albums, *Dreamtime* (1981) and *Words from the Front* (1982) enjoying critical acclaim but limited sales. Smith continued to work with Verlaine throughout the 80s, co-producing Verlaine's album *The Wonder* in 1990. Lloyd initially went into production, working with New York band Chris Stamey and the Dbs before releasing his first solo album, titled *Alchemy,* in 1979. Its sequel, *Field of Fire*, did not appear until 1985, the long period of inactivity widely believed to have resulted from heavy drug use, followed by a lengthy rehabilitation.

So the New Wave was by no means an exclusively British phenomenon, and nor was it an entirely male preserve. From the earliest days, the format of 'dynamic female singer with predominantly male backing band' was exploited by such acts as Poly Styrene and X-Ray Spex, and Siouxsie and the Banshees.

The latter established that punk fashion and an almost traditional femininity were not necessarily incompatible, with images of the darkly seductive Siouxsie Sioux (b.1957, real name: Susan Janet Dallion) finding their way onto the wall of many an adolescent male's bedchamber. A style icon and an impressive vocal performer both live and on disc, Sioux was an early and alluring exponent of what would later emerge as the craze for Goth fashion. Centered on the creative nucleus of Sioux and bass player Steve Severin (b.1955, also known as Steve Havoc, real name: Steven John Bailey), the Banshees emerged from the notorious Bromley Contingent of hard-core Pistol fans. Their uncompromising debut at a 100 Club punk festival in 1976 comprised a wild 20-minute setting of the *Lord's Prayer,* said to have been interspersed with references to *Twist and Shout, Knockin' on Heaven's Door* and the David Bowie hit *Rebel, Rebel.* A deal with Polydor led to a string of UK hits, of which the first and possibly best known was *Hong Kong Garden* (UK No.7). Staying together for two decades, the band's 1995 swansong *Rapture* is seen by many fans as one of their finest achievements. Although they officially disbanded after the release of this album, a reunion took place in 2002, with the possibility of further revivals anticipated by a still active fanbase.

Female punk instrumentalists were not common on the UK scene, although bass player Gaye Advert (also known as Gaye Atlas), working alongside guitarist and lead vocalist Tim 'TV' Smith, as the key personnel of the Adverts is an exception worth noting, as is Lora Logic (real name: Susan Whitby), occasional sax player with X-Ray Spex. But it was the USA that produced the most significant all-female punk bands, starting in 1976 with the Runaways, an overtly commercial brainchild of veteran producer and entrepreneur Kim Fowley (b.1942), whose mission was reportedly to launch a 'female Ramones'. Later came the Go-Gos, founded in 1978 by guitarist and former fashion designer Jane Wiedlin (b.1958). Although not a particularly distinguished band in their own right, the Go-Gos provided a valuable training ground for singer Belinda Carlisle (b.1958), whose string of international solo hits during the 80s would shine through as genuine quality merchandise in one of pop music's less memorable eras. Interestingly, Carlisle's performances are very clearly the product of a highly trained professional voice, a quality most noticeable on *Circle in the Sand* from 1988, arguably her finest single of all. It is also worth remembering that the Runaways and, to a greater extent, the Go-Gos set a precedent for doyennes of 80s girl-pop the Bangles who, like Carlisle, offered a chink of light in often gloomy times. At the most commercial level, punk found a highly photogenic and televisual ambassador in Miami born Debbie Harry (b.1945, to become Deborah Harry in maturity), lead singer and iconic pin-up of Blondie. Working alongside guitarist Chris Stein (b.1950), Harry launched Blondie in 1974 as a repackaging of her former group the Stilettos.

The original line-up was completed by Fred Smith (bass, again not to be confused with Fred 'Sonic' Smith) and Billy O'Connor (drums), although both had left before the sessions for what became the band's first LP, originally to be titled *Waiting*, but released on the Private Stock label as *Blondie* in 1976. Smith went on to join Television, O'Connor entered law school. They were replaced respectively by Gary Valentine and Clem Burke, keyboard player James Destri being added at an early stage in the *Waiting* sessions. Despite having served the customary American punk apprenticeship at CBGB's, Blondie soon became a chart-focused product, only distantly reflecting the main tenets of punk. Their first major hit *Denis* was an all-commercial confection, in which the title was pronounced *à la français* as 'Denee' in order to match the vocal inflections of the boy-song original, titled *Denise* and recorded by Randy and the Rainbows in 1963. It was a decent slice of late 70s pop, as were the dozen or so hits Blondie produced over the next four years, the media dubbing Harry 'the Monroe of the 70s'. Unlike her putative role model, Harry has survived into late middle age, her voice acquiring a markedly lower *tessitura* on the 1999 hit *Maria*.

Punk achieved an unexpected and far-reaching literary input with the arrival of Patti Smith (b.1946). Born in Chicago and raised in New Jersey, Smith turned thirty on the penultimate day of 1976, making her something of a radical matriarch in a world where anything over twenty qualified for a badge of seniority. Active as a writer since the late 60s, Smith had moved to New York to live with her partner, the photographer Robert Mapplethorpe (1946–1989) in 1967. In 1971, she co-wrote the play *Cowboy Mouth* with actor/playwright Sam Shepard (b.1943), and during the same period submitted articles to *Creem* and *Rolling Stone* at the suggestion of rock critic Lenny Kaye, who has also served as Smith's principal guitarist for much of her career to date. Early collaborations included Smith reciting her own published and unpublished poetry to Kaye's guitar accompaniment at a number of New York venues, including St. Mark's Church in the Bowery. The fact that Smith was a literary figure of some note before she got involved with music is a distinction shared by few and possibly surpassed only by Leonard Cohen. Many years later, when she performed with only an acoustic guitar on the same bill as Bob Dylan, the man himself is said to have remarked, 'she's still the best, you know'.

Skeletal and yet curiously charismatic in appearance, Smith is a songwriter who presents a volatile mix of literary and occasionally biblical references, juxtaposed with expletives and other terminology that, depending on your point of view, may be categorized as 'challenging' or just plain offensive. Her 1974 single *Piss Factory* (coupled with a cover of *Hey Joe*) was an early manifestation of the shock tactics that was to become the core of punk. After signing with the Arista label, she released the *Horses* album in 1976, produced by John Cale and still considered by many to be her *magnum opus*. Although the album is credited as a solo release, she was by now fronting the Patti Smith Group, comprising Kaye alongside Richard Sohl (keyboards), Ivan Kral (bass) and drummer Jay Lee Daugherty. After suffering a serious neck injury in 1977, she took time off to recuperate and write the poetry cycle *Babel,* referred to on the 1978 album *Easter*. This disc also played host to her best known song *Because the Night*, a sexually charged rock anthem co-written with Bruce Springsteen. By the time of the *Easter* sessions, Sohl had been replaced by Bruce Brody. The project with Springsteen was not Smith's first collaboration with the mainstream of rock. Her relationship with Allen Lanier (b.1946) of post-psychedelic middleweight rockers Blue Öyster Cult, known primarily for their darkly compelling 1976 hit *(Don't Fear) The Reaper*, resulted in her contributing the lyrics to several BOC songs, most notably the 1974 anthem *Career of Evil*. But *Because the Night* was the track that gave her worldwide airplay and chart success, although personal circumstances and possibly her own anti-commercial philosophy meant she never fully capitalized on that mainstream breakthrough. After marrying Fred 'Sonic' Smith (1949–1994), she retired from music to raise her two children, only occasionally surfacing during the early part of the 80s. She also had to face a series of personal tragedies. After Mapplethorpe, with whom she had remained on good terms, fell victim to AIDS, Richard Sohl was struck down by a heart attack at the age of 37 in 1990. Fred Smith would suffer the same fate in 1994, and her younger brother Todd Smith, who had provided vital support at the time of her husband's death, was killed by a stroke within the year. On the 1988 album *Dream of Life*, her first since the critically controversial *Wave* from 1979, Fred Smith had played guitar and co-written all the songs. Having survived this truly horrendous period in her life, Smith released five albums from 1996 onwards. Of these, *Gung Ho* from 2000 finds her on particularly impressive form, the war imagery of the controversial Vietnam-inspired title track being one of her most compelling studio creations.

With Patti Smith, punk rock received a vital shot of intellectual depth and maturity. But maturity can strike in many forms...

— 12 —

Adult Rock and the Post-Punk Era

One of the most widely-invoked misconceptions in the world of classical music is the belief that the twelve-tone compositional technique, developed by Arnold Schönberg (1874–1951) and practiced by his disciples Alban Berg (1885–1935), Hanns Eisler (1898–1962) and Anton Webern (1883–1945) of the *Second Viennese School*, had a guiding influence on all 'serious' composers from Schönberg's time onwards. In reality, Schönberg's principles were only ever fully embraced by a small continuum of high profile purveyors of 'minority appeal' compositions. Even now, almost a century after the earliest examples were created, such works have yet to be accepted by large sectors of Segovia's 'philharmonic public'. Segovia himself, despite having single-handedly enriched the guitar repertoire by actively encouraging a huge spectrum of composers to write for the instrument, was never a convert to the cause. In an interview for *Guitar International* magazine published in June 1977, Segovia even announced that his son Carlos Andrés, then just seven years old, 'dislikes dodecaphonic music, as I do'.

Similarly, the influence of Punk Rock and the New Wave, although unquestionably the most significant single development of its time, did not have the capacity to penetrate all sectors of rock music. If Punk had conquered all, then how were the last progenies of UK symphonic rock, most notably Marillion, able to find favor and even fortune in the decade that followed? The mere fact that their name was derived from *The Silmarillion* by J.R.R. Tolkien, whose iconic status among hippies worldwide made his work anathema to every self-respecting punk, showed the band to be swimming against a strong tide. And yet their vintage years, during which they were fronted by a larger than life Scotsman named Fish (b.1958, real name: Derek Dick), yielded a string of highly acclaimed albums, including the 1985 magnum opus *Misplaced Childhood.*

In the US, hirsute Texan blues/rock trio ZZ Top not only survived the 70s but managed to reach an even wider international audience in the 80s. Comprising guitarist/vocalist Billy Gibbons, bass player Joe 'Dusty' Hill and drummer Frank Beard (all b.1949), the band first came to prominence with the 1973 album *Tres Hombres.*

But it was later releases, most notably *Eliminator* (1983) that made them a fully-fledged world force in premium grade fundamentalist rock. As every thumbnail profile points out, the irony of the band's image is that each member except one has cultivated a waist-length beard, the exception to this facial dress code inevitably being Frank Beard.

Similarly untouched by the punk explosion was the slick urban jazz-driven soundscape of Steely Dan. Built around the songwriting partnership of keyboard player/principal lead vocalist Donald Fagan (b.1948) and guitarist/bass player Walter Becker (b.1950), the band derived their collective name from a steam-powered dildo(!) in the William Burroughs novel *The Naked Lunch* (1959). From the mid-70s to the start of their long sabbatical in 1981, Steely Dan had become essentially a studio concept in which Fagan and Becker hired whichever high caliber guest and session musicians they deemed necessary for their latest project. It was this unorthodox but effective policy that, despite the lack of live appearances, yielded the platinum-selling 1977 release *Aja*, considered by many aficionados to be the band's finest album.

In autumn 1975, just as the first rumblings of the punk movement were causing a stir on both sides of the Atlantic, what should hit the UK No.1 spot and stay there for nine weeks but the epic and at times positively grandiose *Bohemian Rhapsody* by Queen? Widely credited as the first global hit single for which an accompanying video was central to the marketing strategy, *Bohemian Rhapsody* could easily have been dismissed as a fitting farewell to the dying genre of symphonic rock, had it not been for the fact that it was this record alone that elevated a previously middle-ranking commercial rock band to superstar status, a level they went on to maintain throughout the punk era and far beyond. Now, as it passes its thirtieth anniversary, *Bohemian Rhapsody* still regularly figures in 'best record ever' polls.

Comprising the extrovert vocalist Freddie Mercury (1946–1991, real name: Faroukh Bulsara) in the company of guitarist Brian May (b.1947), bass player John Deacon (b.1951) and drummer Roger Meddows-Taylor (b.1949, the first barrel of his surname being omitted on most related literature), Queen had first enjoyed chart success just eighteen months earlier with the intricately-woven hard rock single *Seven Seas of Rhye* from the *Queen II* album. Sometimes misleadingly categorized as representing the rearguard of Glam Rock, Queen were, in their early years, neither more nor less than an accomplished and stylish mainstream rock band whose collective title, combined with Mercury's camp stage persona, denied them full recognition in the macho world to which their music belonged. Their third album, *Sheer Heart Attack* (1974), saw the band become increasingly focused on the emerging cult figure of Mercury, the sleazy Parisian imagery of the hit single *Killer Queen* allowing free rein to his unique brand of rock theater.

But his staunchest admirers would willingly concede that Mercury's star could never have fully risen without the creative input of the other members of the band, May in particular. An engaging and resourceful guitarist with a distinctive and gritty valve-driven sound, May was the figure the rock audience turned to on the frequent occasions when Mercury's antics caused them to cringe. Even those who actively loathed *Bohemian Rhapsody* and all it stood for were happy to acknowledge May's finely crafted solo as an all-time great.

As punk attracted ever more converts, Queen continued to prosper. The 1975 album *A Night at the Opera,* from which *Bohemian Rhapsody* is drawn, was said to have been one of the most costly albums of its time, but amply repaid its investors by remaining in the UK charts for almost a year. The follow-up, *A Day at the Races* (1976), continued the Marx Brothers theme and came close to matching the sales success of its by now legendary predecessor. The flow of hit singles continued unabated, although many serious rock fans were beginning to tire of Mercury's seemingly insatiable appetite for the vacuous and gimmicky, the soccer terrace rant *We Are The Champions* (UK No.2, 1977) and the supremely irritating *Radio Ga Ga* (UK No.2, 1984) being impossible to ignore, no matter how hard you tried. But since Queen could by now rely on the regular support of that secret army of casual non-aficionados, whose one record purchase in the year was in all probability going to be one of theirs, the loss of a few long-haired diehards was unlikely to even show on the balance sheet.

By the time Mercury died, at the age of 45, from an AIDS-related illness, Queen were seen as a national institution. In 2002, May opened the Golden Jubilee celebrations of Queen Elizabeth II by performing the national anthem on the roof of Buckingham Palace. In 2005, May and Taylor gave a series of sell-out reunion performances at some of the most prestigious UK venues, with former Free and Bad Company vocalist Paul Rodgers taking on what was effectively the role of a reincarnated Mercury. Deacon was by now retired from the music business, the new line-up being completed by former Blue Öyster Cult bass player Danny Miranda, plus keyboard player Spike Edney and rhythm guitarist Jamie Moses.

What makes this story so remarkable is that, while most old-style rock bands sought to merely ride out the punk era, Queen positively flourished in what should have been a hostile environment, recruiting and retaining a youthful fanbase, while so many other old-style rock bands who remained faithful to the cause became ever more dependent on an ageing and declining audience. Exasperating though their work could surely be, Queen could never be accused of producing the bland musical wallpaper to which certain bands sold out.

As the 70s drew to a close, rock music was broadcasting on several quite distinct frequencies, one of which was a dedicated post-punk channel that will be discussed in later chapters. At the other end of the dial were products aimed directly at the newly defined 'mature' audience, who positively welcomed the repackagings of what had once been Genesis and Fleetwood Mac. The long shadow of Adult Rock (sometimes expanded to Adult-Oriented Rock, or AOR) was covering large and lucrative sectors of the music business.

The 70s had even spawned an unlikely but clearly discernible substratum that might retrospectively be termed Adult Pop. This was spearheaded by the precision-engineered Swedish quartet Abba, whose long period of world dominance had started with victory in the 1974 Eurovision Song Contest. A fact that many Abba devotees prefer not to recall is that 1974 was the group's *second* assault on the Eurovision crown. The song they had fielded the previous year was rejected by the Swedish selectors in favor of a song bearing the English title *You're Summer,* performed by The Nova & The Dolls. As some may recall, The Nova & The Dolls were roundly defeated by Anne-Marie David, singing

Tu Te Reconnaîtras on behalf of Luxembourg, and were never heard of again. Interestingly, Mlle. David later went on to transfer her allegiance to the French Eurovision campaign, losing to Israel in 1979. As for the failed Abba offering, the rejected song was none other than *Ring Ring,* which over the next few years became one of the group's most enduring international hits.

The Swedish selectors soon saw the error of their ways and duly adopted Abba's 1974 offering, the punchy pop song *Waterloo.* First place in the final round was a mere formality, the only other significant contender being the Italian entry, performed by the sultry and alluring Gigliola Cinquetti. One of the most sophisticated Eurovision entries in the history of the event, the Italian song subsequently enjoyed international chart success in its own right, sung by Cinquetti under the English title *Go (Before You Break My Heart)*. As all time-served Eurovision spotters will by now be straining at the leash to point out, Cinquetti was a seasoned practitioner of this unique multimedia discipline, having secured a win for her country with the song *No Ho L'Étà* in 1964. Cinquetti also went on to co-present the 1991 contest, held in Rome.

But it was *Waterloo* that won the day in '74, fully capturing the jocular and at times self-parodying spirit of the contest in its 70s guise. From that moment onwards, Abba's future was assured, the oft-quoted apocryphal statistic being that, at one point in their heyday, they were bringing more overseas currency into the Swedish economy than any other export except Volvo cars. In other words, Abba were apparently earning more on the global market than Sweden's other highly successful car and aircraft manufacturer, SAAB. In addition to the consummate professionalism that was to be the hallmark of all Abba's work from *Waterloo* onwards, perhaps the secret of their lasting success lies in the fact that their product neither targeted nor specifically excluded the notoriously fickle teenage market. It was undoubtedly the more conservative wing of Europe's adolescents that assured Abba's long line of No.1 singles, while the adult market, especially the cash-rich 25-45 age group, kept album sales equally buoyant. You were unlikely to find this week's teen sensation on Mum and Dad's record rack next to *Bridge Over Troubled Water,* but you might well have found Abba.

Besides Abba, genuine examples of 70s Adult Pop are hard to pin down. Slick and professional US acts such as Bread and the Carpenters are obvious contenders, but they differ from Abba insofar as it seems unlikely they ever had a significant foothold in the under-30 market, and are thus better categorized as quality purveyors of 'easy listening'. This said, it should be noted that the growing potential of 'pop records for grown-ups' was identified and acted upon as early as 1965 by the inimitable big band leader James Last (b.1929, real name: Hans Last, often referred to by fans as 'Hansi'). At the time of writing, Last and his strictly regimented team of seasoned pros have sold in excess of 50 million records, starting with the 1965 prototype, *Non-Stop Dancing*.

The formula of grafting together popular tunes of the day in a continuous dance medley successfully captured the party-going ethos of the late 60s and early 70s. It also proved, as Last had doubtless planned from the outset, infinitely adaptable. Everyone from Bach to the Beatles was subject to the Hansi treatment, the capacity of Last and his musicians to pinpoint the requirements of his devoted followers showing an almost military precision. To take just one of numerous examples, the early 70s was the time when Spain became a favored holiday destination for large swathes of the middle-aged Western European market that was Hansi's heartland. He duly responded with a bouncy and sangria-soaked Hispanic concoction, inevitably titled *Olé*. Last's success was made all the more remarkable by a near-absence of hit singles. His only major UK chart success, *The Seduction* from the 1980 movie *American Gigolo,* came fifteen years after the LP production line was up and running. He has also enjoyed considerably less airplay than might reasonably have been assumed. In a recent tongue-in-cheek BBC feature on Last's career, Anglo-American DJ and music pundit Paul Gambaccini (b.1949), whose capacity for storing music-related data is second to none, admitted to having no recollection of any of his BBC colleagues placing a Last recording on their playlist. So it seems that Last's extraordinary success was the direct result of an endless conveyor belt of globally distributed album releases backed up by high-profile live shows, at which the embarrassing spectacle of the 40-plus age group dancing in the aisles and waving 'Super Hansi' banners was routine. Perhaps the 70s really was 'the decade that taste forgot'. But could Last legitimately claim to have set an artistic precedent for the robotic 'dance remixes' of the 80s and 90s?

If textbook exponents of 70s-style Adult Pop are hard to identify, their counterparts in the emerging industry of Adult Rock are numerous. As Genesis, Fleetwood Mac and other established bands eagerly adapted their product to suit the changing market, a whole battalion of new acts entered the frame. From the USA came Toto and Boston, both quality arrivals in what might be termed the 'Springsteen Sector'. In January 1977, just a month after the *Anarchy in the UK* had been stopped in its tracks by EMI's decision to withdraw the single, Boston were at No.22 in the UK singles chart, having earlier reached No.5 on home territory, with the anodyne love lament *More Than a Feeling*.

Named after their Massachusetts city of origin, Boston was the brainchild of guitarist and vocalist Tom Scholz (b.1947), a former designer for the Polaroid corporation who had secured a contract with Epic Records in 1976. He had previously devoted his spare time to painstakingly creating demos of his own songs, on which he played all the instruments. This was a far cry indeed from the colorful early CVs of Messrs. Rotten and Vicious, from which dedicated musical activities were conspicuous by their absence. In the company of Brad Delp (1951–2007) (guitar and vocals), Barry Goudreau (b.1951) (guitar), Fran Scheehan (bass) and Sib Hashian (drums), Scholz steered the band to world prominence with the self-titled 1976 debut album and its 1978 sequel which, like the hugely successful single it yielded, was titled *Don't Look Back*. After these early triumphs and a lengthy tour, Scholz put the band on hold, re-emerging in 1986 with the album *Third Stage*, another US No.1 although less enthusiastically received in the UK. By this time, Scholz and Delp were the only original members, the personnel for the new album being completed by guitarist Gary Pihl and drummer

Jim Masdea. In the meantime, Scholz utilized his earlier technological skills by designing the Rockman range of guitar amplifiers, thus adding to his already considerable personal wealth. High-profile releases after a long period of inactivity were to become a Boston speciality, the last two decades producing *Walk On* (1994) and *Corporate America* (2002), plus the inevitable *Greatest Hits* compilation, complete with its mandatory quota of previously unreleased 'bonus tracks', in 1997.

A thoroughly professional unit whose work often inspires more respect than affection, Boston were purveyors *par excellence* of that elite brand of Adult Rock that still retained sufficient drive to attract the teenagers who were not planning to sport a Mohican and poke safety pins through their ear lobes and elsewhere. It surely speaks volumes that an early publicity shot of the band should find Scholz resplendent in a crisp white jumpsuit of precisely the type favored by Abba.

While Boston were scoring their first wave of chart successes, the sextet of LA session men that would soon become Toto were earning a steady living as one of the West Coast's most respected backing bands. Having successfully toured with such major names as Aretha Franklin and Jackson Browne, the team enjoyed further critical acclaim for their appearances on a series of hit albums by the highly-regarded Texan singer/songwriter William Royce 'Boz' Scaggs (b.1944). The band was fronted by vocalist Bobby Kimball (b.1947), whose real name is sometimes said to be Robert Toteaux, thus providing a possibly more convincing explanation for the band's collective title than the official line that they were named after the dog in the *Wizard of Oz*.

With the twin keyboards of David Paitch (b.1954) and Steve Porcaro (b.1957), plus guitarist Steve Lukather (b.1957), bass player David Hungate and drummer Jeff Porcaro (1954–1992, older brother of Steve), the band released their self-titled debut album in 1978, from which the single *Hold the Line* proved an immediate chart success. The next two albums, *Hydra* (1978) and *Turn Back* (1981) were well-received by the band's established supporters, but it was *Toto IV* from 1982 that fully realized the band's global potential. This was the album that gave them the worldwide hits *Africa* and *Rosanna*, the latter being a celebration of the actress Rosanna Arquette (b.1959), with whom both Steve Porcaro and Steve Lukather were rumored to have had close relationships.

Although the band, amid various line-up changes, remained active well into the 90s, it was the period following *Toto IV* that was to be the high point of their career, their involvement in preparing the backing tracks for the all-star charity single *We Are the World,* recorded in January 1985, underlining the band's international status. Composed by Michael Jackson and Lionel Ritchie at the instigation of 50s heartthrob turned charity activist Harry Belafonte, *We Are the World* was essentially the American music industry's response to the 1984 British charity hit *Do They Know It's Christmas?* masterminded by the unique and tireless figure of Bob Geldof (b.1951).

A native of Dublin, whose brooding Celtic brogue became one of the most recognizable campaigning voices of the 80s and beyond, Geldof's musical career was launched at the start of the New Wave as lead singer with the Boomtown Rats, a name they took from a gang featured in Woody Guthrie's autobiographical work *Bound for Glory.* After a string of relatively minor hits, their single *Rat Trap* reached the UK No.1 spot in 1978 but had limited impact on the US market. The next single, however, could hardly fail to cause a stir on the far side of the Atlantic. *I Don't Like Mondays,* which became the band's second and final UK No.1 of the 70s, tells the story of San Diego schoolgirl Brenda Spencer (b.1962), who went on a shooting spree that resulted in the death of her headmaster and a janitor, plus the wounding of several classmates. Spencer's explanation, as reported by the world press, was that 'I don't like Mondays – this livens up the day'. A tuneful mid-tempo ballad that seemed disarmingly uncontroversial until you checked out the words, *I Don't Like Mondays* was bound to generate a ripple or two when let loose on the US market, its modest peak of No.73 resulting to a greater or lesser extent from an unofficial radio embargo and attempts by Spencer's parents to get the record banned altogether.

With the onset of the 80s, Geldof and his band were widely seen as a spent musical force, their last two Top Ten hits being *Someone's Looking at You* and the prophetically titled *Banana Republic,* both from 1980. Geldof's appearance in the Pink Floyd movie *The Wall* (1982) did little to enhance his street cred. A cynic might suggest, and many did at the time, that his launch of the *Band Aid* project in 1984 could scarcely have come at a better time to rescue a music and media career that was rapidly becoming a busted flush. But the sheer force with which Geldof stressed the urgency of supporting the Ethiopian famine victims silenced most of the dissenting voices, the rallying cry that 'People are dying... now!' becoming one of the defining soundbites of the decade.

Co-written by Geldof and Ultravox frontman Jim 'Midge' Ure (b.1953), *Do They Know It's Christmas?* reached the UK No.1 spot in December 1984 and has made seasonal returns to the national airwaves ever since. It was re-recorded in 2004 with a mainly new team of performers. Some, including teenage blues prodigy Joss Stone, were not even born when proceeds from the song first 'fed the world'. The original 1984 line-up read like a Who's Who of the then current UK music scene, with senior figures like David Bowie and Paul McCartney providing pre-recorded vocal tracks to be dubbed in alongside the contributions of such 80s ephemera as Heaven 17 and vocally challenged girl group Bananarama. Whether or not the huge sums raised by both the record and the ensuing *Live Aid* performances were put to the most effective humanitarian use is a question which world leaders are still debating to this day, but the impact on global awareness is beyond question. If the project also served to boost a few flagging careers, including that of Geldof himself, then so be it.

Charity cover design by Peter Blake

Much the same could be said of the American response, although it must be stressed that both Jackson and Ritchie had long been established as major international stars and thus needed no free publicity. Belafonte, who by now was approaching the age of 60, had already allowed his singing and acting career to wither on the vine in order to focus on his charity work. The following year, he replaced screen legend Danny Kaye as UNICEF's Goodwill Ambassador. If anything, the roster of performers was even more impressive than that of *Band Aid*, with Bob Dylan, Ray Charles and Stevie Wonder appearing alongside the entire Jackson Five (plus sister LaToya and younger brother Randy). Also present were Diana Ross, Paul Simon, Dionne Warwick, Tina Turner, Bruce Springsteen and Willie Nelson, not to mention an overseas guest named…Bob Geldof.

This was more than the satirists could resist, a particularly notable response coming from the ground-breaking British TV series *Spitting Image,* in which anyone who happened to be in the news appeared on the screen as grotesque latex puppets created by the artists Peter Fluck and Roger Law. A hastily assembled but disarmingly accurate choir of spongy caricatures duly performed *We Are the World,* replacing the refrain 'We are the world, we are the children' with 'We're scared of Bob, we're scared of Geldof'.

In 1986, Robert Frederick Zenon Geldof received an honorary knighthood from Queen Elizabeth II in recognition of his charity work. He is often referred to in the media as 'Sir Bob', although his status as a citizen of the Irish Republic, which is not a Commonwealth Realm, makes him ineligible for a full British knighthood. This is a situation he shares with a number of other media figures, including the irreplaceable transatlantic broadcaster Alastair Cooke (1908–2004, real name: Alfred Cooke) who, although born and raised in the north of England, had become a US citizen before being nominated for a knighthood and therefore was unable to style himself 'Sir Alastair'.

Two decades after *Band Aid* and *Live Aid*, Geldof unveiled plans for the international series of *Live 8* charity events in summer 2005. He also caused a timely bout of controversy by publicly encouraging British teenagers to 'bunk off' school in order to join a demonstration for world justice at the G8 summit held in Gleneagles, Scotland in July 2005.

A fellow Dubliner and younger contemporary of Geldof, who appeared on both incarnations of the *Band Aid* single, is the singer Paul Hewson (b.1960), better known as Bono. With award-winning lead guitarist The Edge (b.1961, real name: David Evans), bass player Adam Clayton (b.1960) and drummer Larry Mullen (b.1961), Bono's succinctly named band U2 have been described by one source as 'the last great stadium rock band of the 1980s'. Like Boston and Toto, U2 represent that endlessly marketable brand of Adult Rock whose appeal cuts across the generations. Whether punk had happened or not, these bands or others like them would most likely still have emerged from the pre-punk heritage that accounts for the greater part of rock music as we know it today.

After successfully auditioning with the Irish subsidiary of CBS, the band's debut EP, enigmatically titled *U2:3*, was a chart success in the Irish Republic but not released on the UK mainland. The follow-up, *Another Day*, was also restricted by national boundaries, precipitating a move from CBS to Island. Despite their growing reputation as a live band, the first three Island singles failed to chart, although sales of the debut album *Boy* were relatively encouraging. It was this album that heralded a long and fruitful relationship with producer Steve Lillywhite.

The next single, *Fire*, reached UK No.35 in summer 1981, although the following two, *Gloria* and *A Celebration,* failed to match this relatively modest breakthrough. *New Year's Day* finally made the UK Top Ten in January 1983, and the Martin Luther King tribute *Pride (In the Name of Love)* reached No.3 in Autumn 1984. One of the band's most potent earlier songs, *Pride (In the Name of Love)* was one of an increasing number of excursions by U2 into political territory, proving that Adult Rock could have teeth. In the meantime, album sales were proving to be the band's favored territory. *War* (1983), *The Unforgettable Fire* (1984), *The Joshua Tree* (1987) and *Rattle & Hum* (1988) all reached No.1 in the UK, the last two achieving the same in the US. *The Unforgettable Fire,* released after a brief period of inactivity, was the first major result of an ongoing collaboration with the production team of Daniel Lanois and experimental composer/producer Brian Eno (b.1948).

The arrival of Eno, who was still remembered for his pioneering 70s work with Roxy Music and Robert Fripp, did much to enhance the band's growing status with the serious rock audience for whom the 80s had not always been the happiest of times. Some might even suggest that U2 was one of the few products of lasting quality to emerge from the entire decade. In an era that bestowed stardom upon such comic strip Heavy Metal acts as Def Leppard, it can be hard not to share that negativity. If the 70s was the decade taste forgot, the 80s was the one when music scraped the barrel. This said, other more credible HM bands, such as the unashamedly retro Iron Maiden and US thrash metal megastars Metallica, also forged their careers at this time, the enduring appeal of the HM genre manifesting itself at the time of writing in the extraordinary rise to fame of a positively nostalgic UK team named the Darkness.

After more than 25 years on the road, U2 remain a class act and have successfully maintained a youthful fanbase whose youngest members could not have been around during those early days when CBS failed to spot the full potential. From the mid-80s onwards, the band's campaigning activities continued to grow. In 1986, they joined Lou Reed, Peter Gabriel, Sting and others for the US leg of the *Amnesty International Conspiracy of Hope Tour* and later took part in a benefit for the Irish unemployed, wryly titled *Dublin Self Aid*. In September 2004, Bono addressed the Labour Party's annual conference, urging the British government to 'get real' with the problem of African poverty. The opening remark that he was unaccustomed to performing before such a small crowd did much to break the ice.

The 80s was not a period noted for its distinctive cover designs. This was undoubtedly due in part to the arrival of the CD, resulting in the elaborate creations of such artists as Roger Dean (b.1944), whose striking dreamscapes became synonymous with the albums of Yes during the 70s, being shoehorned at a fraction of their original size into the flimsy plastic receptacle that is the so-called 'jewel case'. It is surely a reflection of the fallibility of human endeavor that such a ground-breaking medium as the CD should find itself housed in a useless thing that falls apart if the user so much as looks at it in a threatening way.

But one iconic image that barely predated the widespread distribution of the CD was the flying resonator guitar on the cover of *Brothers in Arms* by Dire Straits, a band widely acknowledged as a defining force in British AOR. Released in 1985 and reaching the No.1 spot on both sides of the Atlantic, this immaculately produced offering, complete with its clutch of ready-made hit singles (*Money for Nothing, Walk of Life* and that genuinely imposing title track) came more than six years after the band first found success with the slick and robust *Sultans of Swing.* Although a far cry from the typical front man, Mark Knopfler (b.1949) was from the outset a curiously compelling figure, his less-than-heroic appearance and lugubrious vocal style being virtually guaranteed not to divert attention from his capacity to produce wry, perceptive lyrics and, most of all, his intricate and inspired guitar lines. So central was Knopfler to the band's identity that only their most enthusiastic followers were able to name the other members, the original personnel comprising guitarist David Knopfler (b.1952, younger brother of Mark), plus bass player John Illsley (b.1949) and drummer 'Pick' Withers (b.1948). This line-up remained unchanged for the 1978 self-titled debut album and its 1979 sequel *Communiqué,* the latter enlisting a 'ghost' keyboard player named as B. Bear, widely believed to have been co-producer Barry Beckett. By the third release, *Making Movies (1980),* David Knopfler had left and keyboard player Roy Bittan (b.1949) was drafted in. The remainder of the 80s saw innumerable further changes, with Illsley and Mark Knopfler as the only permanent fixtures.

Following the spectacular success of *Brothers in Arms,* Knopfler retreated into a number of less prominent ventures, a shrewd strategy that effectively eliminated the ever-present danger of producing a creditable but ultimately less triumphant sequel. These included the soundtrack for *The Princess Bride* (1987), following up on his success in this field with *Local Hero* (1983). He also expanded his activities as a producer, having previously co-produced the 1983 Bob Dylan album *Infidels.*

Knopfler was by now a headline act in his own right, appearing at the Nelson Mandela 70th Birthday Concert in 1988 and performing in the company of Eric Clapton and Elton John at the 1990 Knebworth Festival. But despite all these blue-chip connections, not to mention his immense personal wealth, it is to Knopfler's eternal credit that he has remained a musician of unblemished integrity with a disarmingly unaffected public persona to match. These are characteristics he shares with a truly extraordinary figure, who briefly entered the periphery of rock music from the rarefied world of the classical guitar...

— 13 —

Classical Crossover –
A Meeting of Great Traditions,
or just "Rock for Wrinklies"?

In the closing months of 1958, a London based 17 year-old Australian classical guitar prodigy completed a series of studio sessions that yielded sufficient material to fill two LPs. Released shortly after on the Delyse label under the titles of *Guitar Recital* and *Guitar Recital – Second Album*, these historic recordings have been reissued, usually on the Decca label, on numerous occasions over the past four decades.

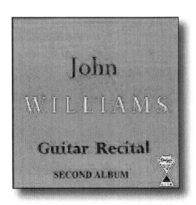

The guitarist was John Williams, and he went on to become one of the most influential classical players of the late twentieth century. Many still see Williams as representing the benchmark of textbook classical guitar technique. Although the media habitually portrays him as a protégé of Andrés Segovia, Williams himself has always been insistent that his true mentor was his father, Len Williams (1910–1987), founder of London's *Spanish Guitar Centre.*

A unique figure on the London music scene, Williams the elder, who brought his family back to the 'old country' from Melbourne in 1952, subsequently sold his interest in the SGC and spent the latter part of his life studying primates in general and Humboldt's Wooly Monkey in particular. His wildlife sanctuary in the Cornish town of Looe became a Mecca for like-minded naturalists worldwide.

Despite his mild-mannered public persona, there can be little doubt that John Williams inherited a large dose of his father's pioneering spirit. After switching labels and releasing *CBS Records Presents John Williams* in 1964, he went on for the remainder of the 60s to record and perform a wide cross-section of the guitar's major concert repertoire, including Rodrigo's *Concierto de Aranjuez* and the mighty Bach *Chaconne* (originally from *Violin Partita No.2 in D minor, BWV 1004).* But as the 60s progressed, his image became subtly yet perceptibly more radical. The 'short back and sides' received less regular maintenance, and the formal evening wear and somber lounge suits gave way to an eye-catching collection of patterned shirts.

By the 1970s, even the horn-rimmed specs had been replaced by the aviator-style 'goggles' that came to define that era's unique taste in face furniture. Insignificant though all this may sound in retrospect, it should nonetheless be emphasized that the Williams makeovers were underway more than two decades before such previously 'straight' classical musicians as the violinist Nigel Kennedy (b.1956) came up with much the same idea, albeit in an 80s post-punk context.

It was in 1970 that Williams threw down the artistic gauntlet by recording with a singer who was neither classically trained in the strictest sense, nor a subscriber to the political neutrality that was still expected to be observed in the public arena by all but the most cutting-edge classical performers.

Maria Farandouri

At the time of the recording, Maria Farandouri (b.1947, also spelt Farantouri) was in exile from her native Greece and had been so since the military coup of 1967. Her mentor, the composer Mikis Theodorakis (b.1925), had been a political prisoner in his homeland for almost three years. His release and subsequent exile took place in April 1970, around the same time that Williams and Farandouri entered the studio to record *Songs of Freedom,* a challenging and superbly presented collection of Theodorakis' songs and instrumentals.

Perhaps the secret ingredient in *Songs of Freedom* was that it is not a crossover recording in the usual sense. Farandouri was appearing in her established role as Theodorakis interpreter *par excellence,* while Williams was providing an intricate and precisely notated backdrop that only a premium grade classically trained guitarist had the skills to handle. So both parties were effectively operating from the heart of their specialist fields. But the very existence of this release led many a pundit to hail John Williams as the quiet yet determined hero who, as a brilliant young classical musician at the gateway to a new decade, was set to apply his creativity in challenging and controversial areas where existing boundaries no longer applied. It was a territory already being investigated by a range of musicians from the other side of the divide, including the early purveyors of Symphonic Rock.

Sadly, things did not turn out quite as anticipated. Although Williams most certainly succeeded in reaching large and lucrative sectors of the non-classical audience, thus venturing far beyond Segovia's stated target of 'the philharmonic public', neither the artistic nor the political force in *Songs of Freedom* has ever been fully recaptured in his later crossover work. Instead, he opted to periodically interrupt his classical career with a series of adventures and misadventures from which, apart from appearing on some classy film scores (not to be confused with those composed by John Towner Williams) and an often overlooked contribution to Frank Zappa's *200 Motels* (1971), few items of lasting merit emerged.

Of the film music, the gently compelling *Cavatina* by Stanley Myers (1933–1993) from the 1971 album *Changes* became a global hit. A highly respected figure with a natural affinity with the guitar's unique voice, Myers had also provided a number of the arrangements used on *Songs of Freedom*. Originally composed for the 1970 movie *The Walking Stick*, where it had languished largely unnoticed, *Cavatina* went on to find a permanent and prestigious celluloid platform in the 1978 box office triumph *The Deer Hunter*.

Williams and Myers duly reconvened for the 1978 album *Travelling*, an all too obvious effort to capitalize on the cash-generating powers of *Changes* and the recent publicity windfall of *The Deer Hunter*. But by this time, the record buying public had been subject to almost a decade of mediocre Williams crossovers, a labyrinthine back-catalog in which everyone from media-savvy jazz singer Cleo Laine (b.1927) to actor, comedian and piano prodigy Dudley Moore (1935–2002) had been invited to the party. Many of these collaborations had enjoyed widespread media attention, but *Travelling* is now only remembered by long haul Williams enthusiasts, the Myers composition *Portrait* being dismissed even at the time as a blatant attempt to forcibly induce the birth of *Son of Cavatina*.

But as *Travelling* concluded its short and uneventful life cycle, Williams was on the starting blocks with a venture that, despite being loathed by large sectors of his classical audience and ignored by almost everyone with an existing interest in rock music, was to bring him a mass media profile that no other classical musician had so far been able to achieve and sustain...

Released in May 1979, *Sky* was the name of both the album and the ensemble that performed on it. In terms of musical content, it was neither more nor less than just another Williams crossover, complete with plugged-in arrangements of the ethereal piano favorite *Gymnopédie No.1* by Erik Satie (1866–1925) and a then widely performed classical guitar miniature known as *Danza*. The whole of Side 2 was occupied by an extended original piece titled *Where Opposites Meet,* this once fashionable format having been abandoned by most rock musicians several years earlier.

But what made Sky so fundamentally different from all earlier Williams crossovers was that all-important concept of image. Instead of just JW and a hired team of session players, Sky was presented to the public as a five-piece 'rock' band, comprising Williams on 'acoustic guitars'; keyboard player and principal composer Francis Monkman; lead guitarist Kevin Peek; bass player Herbie Flowers and percussionist Tristan Fry. Of these, Monkman and Flowers had the most impressive rock CVs, Monkman as a member of the respected early 70s band Curved Air and Flowers as a founder member of Blue Mink, a late 60s pop outfit who had provided a key outlet for the songwriting skills of Roger Cook, one half of the hit-making partnership of Cook and Greenaway.

More important, however, was Flowers' status as a celebrity session man, his most famous studio creation being that unique *portamento* bass-line in *Walk on the Wild Side* by Lou Reed. Fry and Peek also shared a background in session work, with Fry's parallel interest in the outer fringes of contemporary music leading to collaborations with such heavyweight figures as Pierre Boulez (b.1925) and Karlheinz Stockhausen (1928–2007). Peek, a native of Adelaide, had a rather less highbrow address book, his activities as a jobbing guitarist having at various times resulted in gainful employment with Cliff Richard and the New Seekers.

Although the sum total of Sky was unquestionably less than its individual parts, the formula somehow found a vacuum in the market. This first vinyl offering reached an alarming No.2 in the UK Album Chart within a month of release. Its sequel, a double LP that bore the unsurprising title of *Sky 2*, hit the UK No.1 spot in July 1980. It is anybody's guess where it would all have ended, had Monkman not decided to jump ship after the second album. He was replaced by the anonymous figure of Steve Gray. By the time Williams announced his departure in February 1984, three more studio albums were in the shops, not to mention the inevitable *Sky 5 – Live*. Although *Sky 2* was to be the only No.1 album, both *Sky 3* and *Sky 4* (the latter amusingly subtitled *Forthcoming*) reached the UK Top Ten. The *Cadmium* album from December 1983, which was to be his swansong, only made it to No.44, although the immodestly designated *Masterpieces* compilation from 1984 showed all was not yet lost by reaching No.15.

Sky soldiered on minus Williams for a further decade or so, no formal decision to disband having been recorded in the recognized sources. The final chart success was *The Great Balloon Race,* which reached a relatively lowly No.63 in the spring of 1985.

The Sky sound was so bland as to be almost impossible to describe in words. Despite having the capacity to create one of the most strong and focused natural acoustic tones of any guitarist in living memory, Williams in Sky mode stubbornly restricted himself to the thin and 'plastic' sound that characterized the Ovation and Takamine nylon-strung electro-acoustics of the day. This limp soundscape is even retained in the classical duets by Praetorius and Vivaldi, which Williams performs with Peek on *Sky 2*. As for Peek's 'guitar hero' electric solos, one critic of the time described them as sounding midway between a kazoo and the *Stylophone*, a children's electronic instrument promoted in the mid-70s by Rolf Harris. To put it a little less harshly, Peek usually emerged as a competent but formulaic exponent of the 70s 'fuzzy guitar break'. Fry and Flowers were even reduced to the status of novelty acts in such unfunny horrors as *Tristan's Magic Garden* and *Tuba Smarties*, Flowers having been called upon to play the lower instruments of the brass family in his army days. Only Monkman survived with any credibility, his jaunty instrumental *Canonball* from the first album being one of the few *Sky* offerings that do not make the retrospective listener squirm with vicarious embarrassment.

But who was buying the albums and attending the high-profile *Sky* 'gigs' that accompanied those incredible chart conquests? Two decades down the line, it is difficult to imagine anyone more than a few years short of claiming the state pension ever listening to *Sky*. But surely there was too much vinyl flying off the shelves for such an age-specific market profile to provide the full explanation. Maybe those wallet-warming figures really were the result of a uniquely wide age spectrum, in which older listeners played a more decisive role than ever before in the widening church of rock music. Even though many rock encyclopedias conveniently ignore the fact that *Sky* even existed, their historic function, for better or worse, was to raise the age bar significantly in the increasingly cash-rich business of AOR.

By the end of the 80s, Nigel Kennedy's controversial but essentially 'straight' recording of the *Four Seasons* by Antonio Vivaldi (1678–1741) was hitting the national headlines and selling in considerably larger quantities than are customary for a classical disc. From the point of view of the classical music establishment, Kennedy's main crime was that of generating sizeable monetary returns in a field where penury is considered infinitely more respectable, although some of the minor stylistic liberties taken during the recorded performance also raised a few critical eyebrows.

But to the general public, especially those who read tabloid news-papers, Kennedy was seen as an all-conquering iconoclast who sported spiky hair, a newly-acquired Cockney accent and even a long scarf in the colors of the Aston Villa Football Club. Over the next few years, Kennedy skilfully exploited his 'rock star' status with *The Kennedy Experience,* an entire CD devoted to disarmingly successful violin-driven instrumental settings of music by Jimi Hendrix. Later, and rather less convincingly, came a 'concerto' based on music by the Doors.

This new found marketability of classical music or, more specifi-cally, image conscious classical performers, has undoubtedly been a factor in the success of the UK commercial radio network Classic FM, launched in September 1992 and now with corresponding channels throughout the English speaking world.

By the mid-90s, Kennedy was facing a formidable market rival in the Anglo-Oriental former child sensation Vanessa Mae (b.1978, full name: Vanessa Mae Nicholson), whose CD single featuring an electronically enhanced violin arrangement of the famous *Toccata in D minor BWV 565* by J.S. Bach became internationally renowned for its cover shot of the comely soloist wearing a lightly textured dress made all the more floaty by the fact that she was standing waist-deep in water. This new and productive seam of classical 'girl power' was taken up by an all-female string quartet (again with electronic backing tracks) known as Bond and, rather more imaginatively, a raunchy pre-renaissance ensemble styling themselves the Mediaeval Baebes.

At the turn of the millennium, the seemingly endless capacity of John Williams for crossover experiments re-emerged with *The Magic Box,* a celebration of his devotion to the African folk musician and author Francis Bebey (1929–2001). The other featured musician was recorder virtuoso and multi-instrumentalist Richard Harvey, whose ground-breaking work with the pioneering medieval rock band Gryphon had ploughed its own furrow throughout the early 70s, culminating in the possibly unique achievement of the band appearing on all four national

BBC radio channels within the same week. Sadly and yet somehow inevitably, Harvey's performances with Williams, complete with back-slapping on-stage camaraderie, prompted the usual cringes.

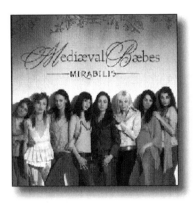

But there was much more to rock in the 80s and 90s than classical musicians fulfilling their not-so-secret dream…

— 14 —

The 80s, the 90s and Beyond

Although Punk Rock was no longer in either the charts or the headlines, many of the more articulate musicians who had first emerged during those explosive years of the mid-70s were able to develop and consolidate their careers throughout the 80s and often well into the 90s. As discussed in previous chapters, British bands such as the Clash, the Damned and the Stranglers all emerged fully intact as the nihilistic and anti-commercial attitudes of fundamentalist early punk gave way to both artistic develop-ment and, let it be said, the need to pay the grocery bills. In the USA, even punk pioneers the Ramones remained at least intermittently active, finally signing off with the 1997 live album *We're Outta Here.* In fact, it now seems that, with such obvious exceptions as the Sex Pistols, remarkably few of the first wave of 70s punk bands disintegrated on impact.

As Punk Rock expanded into the New Wave, other creative forces naturally came into play. It was clear by now that the Jam, a sharp-suited trio from Woking, Surrey, were playing host to a highly talented songwriter in Paul Weller (b.1958), his long and productive solo career making him a father figure to the Britpop movement of the 90s. Like so many British musicians of the time, Weller frequently drew his rhythmic ideas from the subtly compelling language of reggae.

By the end of the 70s, the British fascination with all things Jamaican had fully established itself in such movements as 2-Tone and Ska, represented most prominently by the Specials and Madness (see Chapter 11). In the mainstream of rock, reggae was warmly embraced by big earners including the Police, whose Northumbrian lead singer Sting (b.1951, real name: Gordon Sumner) would later enter that glossy magazine elite of super-rich media-rock celebrities, as typified by the recurring figure of Phil Collins. The smooth and sophisticated reggae textures that characterized such Police hits as *Walking on the Moon* (UK No.1, 1979) were primarily generated by the stylish guitar lines of Andy Summers (or Somers) (b.1942), whose professional career had started in the 60s with Zoot Money's Big Roll Band and its short-lived psychedelic offshoot Dantalion's Chariot.

Founded in 1976 by drummer Stewart Copeland (b.1952), an American citizen raised in the Middle East and who, like Francis

274

Monkman of Sky, had served an apprenticeship with Curved Air, the Police produced some of the most enduring hit singles of the late 70s and early 80s. Despite their relative maturity (Summers was by now in his late 30s), the band successfully appealed to a teenage audience, while keeping close links with the emerging market of AOR.

At street level, the more savvy of the punk survivors carefully re-branded themselves in order to catch the eye of a less fundamentalist market. No transformation was more complete than that of Adam Ant (b.1954, real name: Stuart Leslie Goddard). A former art school student who had been involved with the Malcolm McLaren set from the earliest days, Ant had first come to prominence with Bazooka Joe, whose footnote in rock history was assured when they were once supported by a then unknown band named the Sex Pistols. Johnny Rotten later recalled the Pistols' performance that night as prompting 'not one single hand-clap... (but) we didn't do it to be loved'.

After forming the first incarnation of Adam and the Ants, Ant had to face a somewhat unusual setback when McLaren poached part of the band to form the nucleus of Bow Wow Wow with photogenic singer Annabel Lwin (b.1965, real name Myant Myant Aye – a poetic Burmese appellation translated in most sources as 'cool, cool high').

Ant then joined forces with guitarist and future songwriting partner Marco Pirroni, with whom he cut the single *Car Trouble*. Although initially unsuccessful, this song would later reach the Top 40 in the wake of Ant's subsequent successes. On the advice of McLaren, with whom Ant had stayed on good terms, a comprehensive image makeover was implemented, with Ant's new public persona emerging as a striking amalgam of Native American-style 'war paint' and the colorful militaristic garb of such English dramatic stereotypes as the pirate and the highwayman. The New Romantics had arrived.

A McLaren-negotiated contract with CBS led to the internationally successful 1980 album *Kings of the Wild Frontier.* Three UK No.1 singles followed in rapid succession (*Stand and Deliver, Prince Charming* and *Goody Two Shoes*). By this early stage, Ant had split up the original band, although he took care to keep Pirroni aboard for future ventures. The 1981 *Prince Charming* album was well received on both sides of the Atlantic, as was its sequel *Friend or Foe* the following year. But the bubble was soon to burst, the fact that *Puss 'n Boots* (1983) was produced by none other than Phil Collins showing just how desperate Ant had become to sell records in the mainstream market.

Musically, Ant's sound centered on a pounding tribal beat, said to have been the idea of the ever resourceful McLaren. Parallels were drawn at the time with the synchronized twin drum kits that characterized the early 70s pop hits of Gary Glitter (b.1944, real name: Paul Francis

Gadd, also known in his early career as Paul Raven), whose larger than life stage gear and public persona may also have influenced McLaren's thinking. Although his musical trajectory was short, Ant's sartorial legacy represented one of popular music's most memorable dressing-up crazes. As several fashion websites now acknowledge, the New Romantics were the natural progeny of punk apparatchiks who had always been more interested in the clothes than the music. London clubs such as *Billy's* and *The Blitz* became the catwalk for a growing cast of flamboyant and androgynous figures, while mainstream UK chart bands such as the Birmingham pop quintet Duran Duran eagerly embraced stylish new togs and big hairdos on their evermore exotic videos.

There were certainly some New Romantic bands whose musical offerings left a lasting and favorable impression, most notably Spandau Ballet and Culture Club, the latter fronted by that quintessential 80s gay icon Boy George (b.1961, real name: George Alan O'Dowd). An intelligent and articulate figure who remained a recognized national character long after his brief musical heyday, O'Dowd also boasted a strong and expressive R&B vocal style, as heard on such Culture Club hits as *Church of the Poison Mind* and *Karma Chameleon,* the latter topping the singles charts on both sides of the Atlantic towards the end of the band's run of success in 1983.

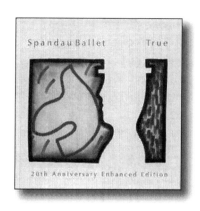

Vocal prowess also became the hallmark of Spandau Ballet, the expressive light baritone of Tony Hadley (b.1960) providing the core of the silky 1983 No.1 *True*. The album bearing the same title, from which the heroic finale *Gold* was also lifted as a single, remains one of the most impressively performed and produced of the era. But there was no escaping the recurring thought that this was a time when style was threatening to eclipse music. Bands and solo artists seemed to come and go with unprecedented rapidity, their appearance often being far more memorable than anything they sang or played.

Despite having had several Top Ten hits during the first half of the new decade, the fashion conscious English duo Soft Cell are now remembered almost exclusively for their precision manufactured cover of the Northern Soul classic *Tainted Love,* recorded by Gloria Jones in 1965.

Incredibly, the Soft Cell version was reissued no fewer than three times over a period of less than five years. Comprising singer Marc Almond (b.1956) and keyboard player David Ball (b.1959), Soft Cell soon established themselves as masters of recycling, material from their 1981 debut album *Non-Stop Erotic Cabaret* resurfacing a year later as dance remixes on *Non-Stop Ecstatic Dancing* – note the presumably unitentional evocation of James Last in the titles. Both albums made the UK Top Ten. Embarking on a solo career from 1984, Almond enjoyed his only No.1 hit, apart from *Tainted Love,* with a 1989 cover of the

Gene Pitney classic *Something's Gotten Hold Of My Heart,* on which Pitney himself appeared as guest vocalist alongside Almond. Despite the disc's UK success, not to mention that fact that both singers emerge with dignity from what could have been a mutually embarrassing alliance, Pitney's management proved reluctant to release the disc in the US, reportedly on the bizarre grounds that their mature and handsome client alongside the diminutive, non-macho Almond could have been mistaken for a gay liaison.

Even bands that stayed for the long haul left a musical legacy that can appear curiously ephemeral with hindsight. To take just one example, the British electro-pop combo Depeche Mode enjoyed an enviable quota of hit singles and albums that continued throughout the 80s and well into the 90s, and yet the most vivid impression many of us have retained is that famous early shot of them all wearing Fair Isle patterned sweaters tucked into their trousers. Compare this with the timeless songwriting tradition of the 60s. As the new millennium progresses, we meet more and more teenagers born of parents who are themselves too young to have directly experienced the Beatles, and yet both generations can often spontaneously quote the opening lines of *Yesterday* and join in the refrain of *Can't Buy Me Love.* Now consider what was in the charts in the early 80s. Unless you happen to have served your adolescence at precisely that time, recollections of the music are likely to be sketchy at best. Although many quality albums and singles were around, few can claim true classic status.

Advances in studio electronics was a defining force in 80s music. For the first time in more than three decades, the keyboard seemed set to threaten the supremacy of the guitar as rock music's principal accompanying instrument. The first generation of electronic and, in the case of the Mellotron, electro-mechanical keyboard instruments had already been a central and often defining force in the soundscape of Symphonic Rock. This had naturally given rise to a dialogue between the fringes of rock and the esoteric world of electronic music, the result being such highly respected keyboard-centered bands as Tangerine Dream and Kraftwerk. The latter had enjoyed unexpected chart success in 1975 with the austere Germanic imagery of *Autobahn,* an extravagant twenty-minute creation that was later ingeniously reduced to the length of a conventional pop single in order to obtain airplay. Evolving from the robotic duo of Ralf Hütter (b.1946) and Florian Schneider (b.1947), whose creative partnership dated back to 1970, Kraftwerk would enjoy further chart success in the hi-tech climate of the 80s.

A short-lived 70s keyboard phenomenon had been that of 'electronic classics', in which a conventional orchestra was replaced by endless banks of state-of-the-art synths. One performer/arranger whose recordings found particular favor was the enigmatic Japanese master of the Moog III analogue synthesizer, Isao Tomita (b.1932). By the time Tomita's Debussy-based extravaganza *Snowflakes Are Dancing* entered the album charts in 1975, to be followed by techno-takes on Mussorgsky's *Pictures at an Exhibition* and Holst's *Planet Suite* over the next two years, the terms Moog and 'synthesizer' had become almost synonymous in the minds of the record-buying public. It was unquestionably a happy coincidence that New York born electronic engineer Dr. Robert Moog (1934–2005) had, like William Henry Hoover before him, been blessed with a surname that so conveniently chimed in with the product. Although Moog scholars insist that the name ought to be pronounced to rhyme with 'vogue', many of the instrument's most eminent exponents, including Rick Wakeman, would habitually enunciate it with the still-customary 'oo' sound. The Moog enjoyed a new surge of popularity in the early 80s as the favored instrument of such newly emerging talents as the hi-tech English singer/songwriter Howard Jones (b.1955), whose still highly regarded album *Human's Lib* yielded no fewer than four hit singles, starting with *New Song* in autumn 1983.

Robert Moog had become increasingly interested in electronic instruments as a teenager in the late 40s. One of his earliest projects was the construction of a *theremin,* named after the long-lived Russian inventor Leon Theremin (1896–1993). Developed during the 1920s, the theremin was a bizarre and unwieldy creation, emitting a note of which the pitch was controlled by waving the hands between two metal rods. As he acquired an impressive string of engineering qualifications, Moog's interest in electronic music never wavered. His first synthesizers were developed in the mid-60s, and the component known as the *Moog Filter* was patented in 1968. By this time, Moog was working in association with such musicians as Herbert A. Deutsch and Walter Carlos (b.1939), later to re-emerge as Wendy Carlos. The historic 1968 Carlos album *Switched-On Bach* was performed on Moog synthesizers and provided the initial inspiration for many later releases in the same sub-genre, including those of Tomita.

But the guitar had nonetheless remained a staple instrument of rock music in the 70s, the occasional appearance of a 'guitarless band', such as jazz-rock icons Weather Report, being sufficiently unusual as to prompt at least a passing comment in the music press. A further example was the British prog-rock quartet Greenslade, fronted by the twin keyboards of Dave Greenslade and Dave Lawson. As was noted at the time, this layout gave an exceptional degree of visual prominence to bass player Tony Reeves, neither Greenslade nor Lawson having shown aspirations to emulate the stage acrobatics of Keith Emerson.

Unlike their US precedents in the 60s, where basic single manual organs were regularly in evidence, 70s-style punk rock bands rarely drifted far from the traditional line-up of voice/guitar/bass/drums. As punk broadened into the New Wave, keyboards and occasionally saxophones entered the frame, although not often to the exclusion of the ever-present rhythm guitar.

By the start of the 80s, all this was changing. One of the most accomplished bands of the time comprised a fixed personnel of just two, only one of whom claimed full credits as an instrumentalist. Rising from the ashes the Tourists, whose brief heyday in the late 70s is best remembered for a competent but essentially imitative cover of the Dusty Springfield hit *I Only Want To Be With You,* Eurythmics (whose fans insist on not referring to them as *the* Eurythmics) were powered by the vocal excellence of Annie Lennox (b.1954) and the endlessly imaginative instrumental input of Dave Stewart (b.1952). Interestingly, Stewart's background was mainly in the remote sphere of Folk-Rock, his earlier associations being with renaissance-inspired troubadours the Amazing Blondel and a now forgotten band named Longdancer, said to have been related in spirit to the proudly regional folk-rock of Newcastle-upon-Tyne's only recently disbanded Lindisfarne. Stewart hailed from the nearby North Eastern town of Sunderland.

But although many shots of Eurythmics on stage show Stewart playing an acoustic or electric guitar, their principal soundscape was unquestionably electronic and consequently keyboard-driven. After first reaching the Top Ten with *Sweet Dreams (Are Made Of This)* in early 1983, they enjoyed a string of hit singles, culminating in the 1985 summer No.1 *There Must Be An Angel (Playing With My Heart)*, which featured a celebrity guest appearance by Stevie Wonder on harmonica. This song also found Lennox at her most vocally commanding, the outstanding range of pitch and expression drawing the attention of many a listener who had previously kept the band's work at arm's length. Visually, Eurythmics naturally focused on the unique androgynous allure of the crop-haired Lennox, whose highly individual post-punk wardrobe contained everything from floaty evening dresses to men's suits. The more conventionally attired Stewart, often hiding behind a large pair of shades, provided a suitably enigmatic Svengali-like figure. To a greater extent than almost any other chart act of the time, Eurythmics showed that genuine creative talent could still make itself heard, even in the often sterile climate of early 80s chart pop.

A pioneering figure from the early post-punk years who undoubtedly helped shape the emerging culture of electronically generated urban imagery was London born Gary Numan (b.1958, real name: Gary Anthony James Webb). Originally guitarist and vocalist with the Lasers, who later re-emerged under the more evocative title of Tubeway Army in 1977, Numan's growing interest in the remote and emotionless textures created by German bands such as Kraftwerk and Can drew him more towards the keyboard as his solo career took shape. Reaching the UK No.1 spot with *Are 'Friends' Electric?,* while still trading as Tubeway Army in the spring of 1979, Numan replicated this early success with his best-known song *Cars* later the same year. This song would also break Numan's solo career in the US, its creator's dark fascination with the secure environment offered by motor vehicles bearing little resemblance to that far-off teenage world of hot rods and beach buggies.

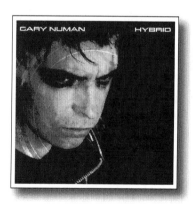

But as the mainstream of music prepared for the era of power dressing, the ever-inquisitive John Peel was investigating a vital new substratum…

Having played reluctant bridesmaid to its Merseyside neighbor throughout the 60s, the Northern English city of Manchester suddenly and unexpectedly came into its own during the death throes of the 70s. The precise moment of inception of what would presently acquire the inevitable and unfunny title of the 'Madchester' Scene is difficult to pinpoint, although most scholars operating in this field place post-punk pop band the Buzzcocks in pole position. Despite only reaching a modest No.12 in the autumn of 1978, the catchy and energetic *Ever Fallen In Love (With Someone You Shouldn't've)* has become one of the best remembered songs of its time. It recently resurfaced as the title music for *The Grimleys,* a better-than-average British TV sitcom set in the 70s.

Formed in 1976, the Buzzcocks were centered on the key figures of Howard Devoto (b.1955, real name: Howard Trafford) and Pete Shelley (b.1955, real name: Peter McNeish).

The latter, incidentally, should not be confused with the portly contemporaneous apparition known as Peter Shelley. Entering the public arena in the early 70s as producer of Rock & Roll retread Alvin Stardust (b.1942, formerly Shane Fenton, real name: Bernard William Jewry), this elder Shelley went on to have two hit singles in his own right. The second, *Love Me, Love My Dog* (UK No.3, spring 1975), found the man himself miming to his own sugar-coated performance on *Top of the Pops,* complete with canine companion. Whatever undesirable acts the

285

Buzzcocks may have committed at other times, they are innocent of this grave musical offence against *TOTP* viewers and the animal kingdom.

The role of the Buzzcocks in providing honest entertainment, while at the same time drawing national attention to their region's emerging musical identity, is beyond dispute. But they were never a band geared up to maintaining the support of the famously high-minded listeners to the late night John Peel show. This role was fulfilled by a succession of more cerebral Manchester bands, starting in 1977 with Joy Division, who would reform three years later as New Order. Previously known as Stiff Kittens and Warsaw, Joy Division provided a songwriting and performing platform for the tragic figure of Ian Curtis (1956–1980). Significantly, Curtis was, like Gary Numan, an admirer of Kraftwerk and Can, the austere and Germanic textures providing a sympathetic backdrop for his own often bleak writing.

In the company of Bernard Albrecht (b.1956, real name: Bernard Dicken) (guitar/keyboards), Peter Hook (b.1956) (bass) and Steven Morris (b.1957) (drums), Curtis had a short but influential creative innings. A long-time sufferer from epilepsy, who was also rumored to have developed clinical depression resulting from marital difficulties and the impending burden of fatherhood, Curtis was found hanged in May 1980. With bitter irony, the band's best-known song *Love Will Tear Us Apart* was later described as 'the most beautiful song ever written' by fellow Rock & Roll casualty, Kurt Cobain (1967–1994).

By this time, a pivotal figure had entered the frame. Anthony H. Wilson (1950–2007), then still known as Tony Wilson, was already familiar to the Manchester public as an oh-so-clever young news anchor on local TV. But despite his irritating on-screen personality, Wilson can justly claim credit for giving vital support and publicity to Manchester's talented but impecunious musicians, first by applying his broadcasting contacts and expertise to launching the pioneering regional music show *So It Goes.* Casting himself by now as Manchester's most hip impresario, Wilson went on to devote his new-found entrepreneurial flare to launching Factory Records and the Factory Club, forerunner to the much discussed Hacienda Club. While Joy Division were still appearing as Warsaw, Wilson was one of several media figures present at a 'battle of the bands' organized by the Stiff and Chiswick record labels. Legend has it that Curtis stormed over to Wilson and berated him for failing to support deserving local bands such as Warsaw. The result was not only a contract with Factory Records, but also a management deal with Rob Gretton (1953–1999), who happened to be present in his role as the venue's resident DJ.

Following the death of Curtis, the band reformed with Albrecht, by now using the name Bernard Sumner, as frontman. Keyboard player Gillian Gilbert was added to the instrumental backdrop, and the collective title New Order was adopted. The disturbing connotations of both the old and the new names led to a re-run of some hostile press comments: the expression 'New Order' or *Neue Ordnung* will forever be associated with the social and political aims of the Nazi party during the 30s and 40s, while Joy Division (as featured in the 1955 publication *The House of Dolls* by Holocaust survivor Yehiel De-Nur, using his Auschwitz prison number Ka-Tzetnik 135633 as a pen-name) was a reference to areas of the concentration camps where women prisoners were forced to have sex with German soldiers.

The relaunched band's best known song *Blue Monday* (no relation to the Fats Domino song of the same name) linked the Orwellian atmosphere of Joy Division to an incessant yet distinctive disco beat, said to have been discovered by chance during a programming session in the studio. As British journalist and 'Madchester' authority Richard Luck points out, it was this dance-friendly aspect of New Order that 'offered up something vivid and exciting' at a time when, as Luck notes, disco music meant the Bee Gees (in their late 70s *Saturday Night Fever* mode) and KC and the Sunshine Band. Several years down the line, Ian McCulloch of the post-punk Liverpool band Echo and the Bunnymen would characterize the New Order ethos as one of 'intelligent dance music'. Like Joy Division before them, New Order enjoyed the active support of John Peel, the *Peel Sessions* from June 1982 entering the UK charts as an EP in 1986.

The next major Manchester band to secure Peel's patronage was the Smiths, fronted by Steven Patrick Morrissey (b.1959), who was known from the outset by his surname only. Forming a quartet in 1982 with guitarist Johnny Marr (b.1963, real name: John Martin Maher), Andy Rourke (b.1964) (bass) and Mike Joyce (b.1963) (drums), Morrissey was an instantly controversial figure with an apparently unwavering belief in his own future potential.

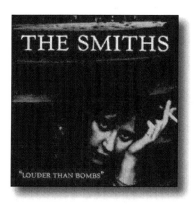

In an early encounter with Wilson, Morrissey is said to have categorically informed the Factory boss that he was going to be famous. Unconvinced, due largely to the singer's nerdy appearance, Wilson later commented that he 'didn't think Steven would be able to keep away from his bedroom long enough to become a success'. Wilson realized his mistake soon enough, although not before the Smiths had signed with the rival Rough Trade label. The debut single *Hand in Glove* had limited impact, but its follow-up, *This Charming Man,* reached UK No.25 and earned the band an appearance on *Top of the Pops.* The songwriting partnership of Morrissey and Marr proved fruitful, although differences between the two central figures led to Marr's departure in 1987. Various Marr solo ventures followed, starting with some sessions for Talking Heads, patrician US purveyors of upmarket New Wave. Over the next few years, Marr went on to work with a wide range of bands. These included commercial providers of soft punk the Pretenders; economically named British band The The; New Order spin-off Electronic and, most surprising of all, former Roxy Music singer and debonair lounge lizard crooner Bryan Ferry. By this time, Marr had emerged as a rare example of a star instrumentalist in the post-punk era, his light and transparent textures often being described as harking back to the 60s folk-rock of the Byrds. This is not to suggest that the 80s did not produce its own crop of old-style celebrity axe warriors, although such figures, to be discussed later in this chapter, typically inhabited the pre-punk worlds of hard rock, heavy metal and contemporary blues. Marr was never perceived as a guitar hero in this sense of the term, although his playing was, and remains, widely admired.

The elaborate public image cultivated by Morrissey was drawn from several identifiable sources. Most bizarre of all was his adoption of a hearing aid, apparently as a reference to the emotional 50s pre-rock singer Johnnie Ray (1927–1990). Another favorite Morrissey stage prop was a bunch of gladioli, said to be a floral tribute to the ever quotable writer, wit and posthumous gay icon Oscar Wilde (1854–1900). The contrast of personalities between Morrissey and Marr could be difficult to reconcile, even for the band's followers. A published letter to the editor of *Private Eye,* revered senior organ of British political satire, famously hailed Marr as a 'restrained and talented player', while in the same sentence dismissing Morrissey as a 'pretentious prat'.

As Richard Luck points out, the significant but not always earth-shattering record sales achieved by the Smiths perhaps do not fully reflect the mark they left. This said, their unfailing capacity for spotting a good soundbite has undoubtedly resulted in a whole sequence of headline-grabbing titles remaining in the memory long after the song itself is forgotten. A glance down any Smiths discography reveals such timeless gems as *Heaven Knows I'm Miserable Now, Shoplifters of the World Unite* and *Girlfriend in a Coma.*

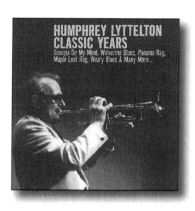

This last title resurfaced almost two decades after its release in, of all places, the BBC Radio Four spoof panel game *I'm Sorry, I Haven't a Clue,* chaired by the wonderfully sardonic old Etonian jazz trumpeter Humphrey Lyttelton (1921–2008), who on this occasion invited a hapless contestant to sing the words of *Girlfriend in a Coma* to the tune of *Tiptoe Through the Tulips.* As Elvis Costello later observed, possibly referring more to Morrissey's subsequent solo career, '(he) comes up with the greatest song titles in the world, only somewhere along the line he seems to forget to write the song'.

But as Luck goes on to conclude, also citing the words of Jonathan Kennaugh writing in the *Rough Guide to Rock,* the historic role of the Smiths was essentially to bring Manchester's musical identity to wider national attention, thus creating a portal for several later bands, two in particular...

Throughout the second half of the 80s and the first years of the 90s, Manchester's music scene was dominated by the combined forces of the Stone Roses and the Happy Mondays. Formed in 1980 as the Patrol and rumored to have briefly adopted the name English Rose, the Stone Roses comprised Ian Brown (b.1963) (vocals), John Squire (b.1962) (guitar), Gary 'Mani' Mounfield (b.1962) (bass) and Alan 'Reni' Wren (b.1964) (drums). When they first relaunched themselves under the new collective title in 1985, the line-up also included guitarist Andy Couzens and bass player Pete Garner, predecessor to Mounfield. In a latter-day echo of the notorious press dismissal of Uriah Heep (see Chapter 8), one critic summarized their self-titled 1989 debut album as 'the worst elements of 1980s independent rock, rolled into a shapely ball'. They also earned the soubriquet 'Sex Pistols of the 1990s' following various public displays of disorderly conduct, including a rumored conviction for criminal damage after trashing the offices of their former record company. In retrospect, the critical assault quoted above was perhaps less damning than apparently intended. The band's early work was recognized even by their staunchest disciples as being discernibly influenced by such existing Indie bands as Primal Scream and the Jesus & Mary Chain. A much raised question that still remains unresolved is that of whether or not *Made of Stone* by the Stone Roses was directly derived from *Velocity Girl* by Primal Scream.

The term Indie had by now entered the lexicon, referring to virtually any band not under contract to a major international label. Inevitably, the term 'major international label' is open to a wide range of interpretations, although most sources restrict it to the so-called Big Four, namely Warner, Universal, Sony-BMG and EMI. At the time of writing, it is by the exclusion only of these labels that the UK based NME (*New Musical Express*) Indie Charts are calculated. Although the term Indie is long established as a stamp of artistic integrity, the question of how many Indie bands would choose to remain so if offered a passport to the world of country mansions with guitar-shaped swimming pools is as intriguing as it is unanswerable.

Entering the lower reaches of the UK charts with *She Bangs the Drums* in summer 1989 and hitting the Top Ten with the double A-side *Fool's Gold* and *What the World is Waiting For* later the same year, the Stone Roses kept the Manchester flag flying well into the next decade. A remix of *Fool's Gold,* one of several known to exist, reached No.25 as recently as March 1999. When Squire was interviewed by *Time Out* in May 2005, the possibility of a Stone Roses reunion was not ruled out, thus further fuelling the speculation that had existed more or less since the band's demise in 1996.

The Happy Mondays were officially launched in 1984, although they were said to have been rehearsing informally since c.1980. Their arrival brought about what many commentators agree was the Factory label's finest hour (the Stone Roses recorded first on Silvertone, later on Geffen). Either a quintet or a sextet, depending on your point of view, the definitive line-up was centered on lead vocalist Shaun Ryder (b.1962), plus his younger brother Paul Ryder (bass), Mark 'Moose' Day (guitar), Paul 'PD' Davis (keyboards) and Gary 'Gaz' Whelan (drums). The sixth man was Mark 'Bez' Berry (b.1964), whose role has variously been described as that of dancer, occasional percussionist and 'vibe master'. In 2005, long after the rest of the band had disappeared from the mainstream public radar, Bez appeared before a nationwide audience as a contestant in the reality TV horror *Celebrity Big Brother.* He won.

After taking part in a 'battle of the bands', in which Wilson had allegedly informed them in advance they would be victorious, the Happy Mondays released their debut LP in 1987 under the often abbreviated title of *Squirrel and G-Man Twenty Four Hour Party People Plastic Face Carnt Smile (White Out)*. This marked the first appearance of the defining term *Twenty-Four Hour Party People* that later provided the title of Wilson's book and its much discussed movie in 2002. Although Bernard Sumner of New Order had overseen a number of earlier Happy Mondays recordings, the album was produced by John Cale, whose time with the Velvet Underground had taken place while the Ryder brothers and their colleagues were still primary school kids in the Manchester suburb of Little Hulton. By now a reformed heroin addict, Cale's puritanical stance on the use of recreational substances caused immediate conflict, one theory being that Shaun Ryder's reaction against Cale's regime precipitated Ryder's graduation from marijuana to smack.

The sequel to *Squirrel and G-Man,* the more succinctly titled *Bummed* was produced by Martin Hannett (1948–1991, also known as Martin Zero), a familiar figure on the 'Madchester' scene and one of Wilson's partners in the Factory enterprise. The others were Alan Erasmus, Rob Gretton and Peter Saville. Some sources credit Wilson and Erasmus as the founders, with a fifty per cent stake each, although others suggest all five partners had an equal twenty per cent stake from the outset. Hannett is said to have been portrayed in a ten-line sequence from the Happy Mondays song *Tart Tart,* even though the band had not met him at that stage.

It was on the *Bummed* album that the influence of the Beatles became more apparent, an earlier song titled *Desmond* having been withdrawn from *Squirrel and G-Man* because of its resemblance to the Lennon and McCartney-penned *Ob-la-di, Ob-la-da.* The 'donor' song had been a UK No.1 hit in 1968 for Scottish pop band the Marmalade, and large sectors of the population would doubtless have recalled that its central character was a market trader named Desmond.

Pills 'n' Thrills and Bellyaches, released in November 1990, gave the band their greatest mainstream chart successes. The album peaked at UK No.4 and the single drawn from it, *Kinky Afro,* reached No.5. But by now, Shaun Ryder's drug intake was becoming an expensive and time-consuming factor that almost scuppered the next studio album. A live disc recorded at the Elland Road soccer stadium in Leeds was released in September 1991 and kept fans happy for the time being, reaching No.21 in the UK charts. But Wilson was to regret his decision to despatch the band to Barbados, where they were to work on the next album alongside Chris Frantz and Tina Weymouth from Talking Heads. With crack cocaine available and affordable anywhere on the island, Shaun Ryder's descent into serious addiction is said to have been rapid and spectacular. Against all the odds, the resulting album *Yes Please!* was released in October 1992 and charted at UK No.14. In the meantime, there had been much sun-soaked tragicomedy, with stories of Ryder breaking into the studios of producer Eddy Grant (still remembered by British audiences as guitarist and principal songwriter with 60s pop band the Equals) with a view to stealing two sofas (!) to trade for drugs. Shortly after, an increasingly desperate Wilson had arrived on the island and a few days later was alarmed to see a local drug dealer known as Bobby the Diver strolling along the ocean front wearing his (Wilson's) Armani jacket and trousers. With Ryder in rehab, the Happy Mondays had folded by the end of 1993.

Ryder returned to music in 1995 with Black Grape, an all-new band whose first album, bearing the provocative title *It's Great When You're Straight... Yeah!* was a success in its own right and spawned no fewer than three hit singles. The 1997 sequel, titled *Stupid, Stupid, Stupid,* was less successful, although it did contain the hit single *Marbles.* The band disintegrated shortly after.

At the time of writing, a new incarnation of the Happy Mondays has been seen at a number of UK venues. On at least one occasion, the support band was reportedly Domino Bones, featuring the indefatigable Bez.

One major Manchester band that emerged in the mid 80s and yet was never perceived as being closely associated with the scene around Factory Records and the Hacienda Club was the slick multi-racial soul combo Simply Red. This said, there was one rumored episode when Shaun Ryder and Bez were late for a Manchester gig and, on reaching the venue, dashed through the auditorium and made a leap for the platform. They found themselves standing next to Simply Red lead singer Mick Hucknall (b.1960), the Happy Mondays having been booked to appear elsewhere in the city.

In the company of Sylvan Richardson (guitar), Fritz McIntyre (keyboards), Tony Bowers (bass), Tim Kellet (keyboards, trumpet) and Chris Joyce (drums), Hucknall's vocal prowess is used to impressive effect on their 1985 debut album *Picture Book.* The album's main hit single, *Holding Back the Years* (UK No.2 in spring 1986), was a stylish and sumptuous creation, despite being constructed on a simple two-chord *ostinato.* Almost a year earlier, the album had yielded its first hit single in the shape of *Money's Too Tight (To Mention)* (UK No.13 in summer 1985), an inspired cover of a song first recorded by Ohio based soul duo, the Valentine Brothers. Two other tracks from the album, *Jericho* and *(Open Up The) Red Box,* were also released as singles, although neither reached to Top 40.

From the outset, Hucknall and his team displayed a penchant for retro that would result in the 1987 cover of the Cole Porter standard *Ev'ry Time We Say Goodbye.* Anyone reading the small print on *Picture Book* will spot a credit for one Ronnie Ross, who plays baritone sax on three tracks. No further details are given, but this would appear to be referring to the veteran London jazzman Albert Ronald Ross (1933–1991). Although he had previously rubbed shoulders with the world of rock music as a onetime sax teacher to David Bowie, Ross was by this late stage in his career an impressively patrician figure to be working alongside a then virtually unknown band of twenty-something Mancunians. But despite all this, together with an increasingly suave collective stage image, Hucknall's immediate background was in the latter phases of punk rock. Most discographies note that, although the arrangement was extensively revised for *Picture Book, Holding Back the Years* was first recorded by Hucknall's previous and more gritty band, the Frantic Elevators.

But from *Picture Book* onwards, Simply Red have remained an upmarket act with at least one eye fixed on the AOR sector, such quality single releases as *Stars* from 1991 and *Fairground* from 1995 earning valuable airplay on the BBC's erstwhile easy-listening channel Radio 2. This said, Radio 2 has come a long way since the days when it was known as the Light Programme and its staple weekday broadcast was *Housewives' Choice.* One of its current presenters is none other than the ever-knowledgeable and informative Bob Harris, whose once concealed interest in country music has served him well in his new surroundings. It is a sobering thought that the irreplaceable John Peel might also have finished up broadcasting from that previously uncharted area of the BBC headquarters, although most of his long-standing supporters would presumably prefer to think not.

But while Simply Red ploughed a creative furrow that was essentially separate from the 'Madchester' scene and its associated 'baggy' fashion conventions, Luck and other commentators see a direct historic line leading from 'Madchester' to 90s global sensation Oasis. As famous in the media for their turbulent private lives as their musical activities, the brothers Noel and Liam Gallagher (b.1967 and 1972 respectively) have become tabloid celebrities whose faces are known to legions of middle-aged suburbanites with little or no interest in actually hearing what the band sounds like. This is their loss, since Noel Gallagher has emerged as a songwriter of enviable resources, while his famously pugnacious younger brother combines a natural vocal talent with a commanding, if at times rather surly, stage presence.

The elder Gallagher is also said to display the type of old-fashioned leadership that, although at times authoritarian, certainly gets the job done. Dates and details vary between accounts, but the most widely told version of events is that Noel, at the age of 26 in 1993, offered to work with Liam's band The Rain on the strict understanding that Noel was given total artistic control from that moment onwards. The terms were accepted and a recording deal secured, reportedly after Oasis had gate-crashed an event at the Glasgow venue *King Tut's Wah Wah Hut,* where Boyfriend and 18 Wheeler, recent signings with the Creation label, were performing. The story goes that Creation boss Alan McGee, mindful that Oasis had arrived with a large entourage of inebriate supporters, allowed them a spot and was impressed by what he heard. A contract was duly offered, and Oasis remained with Creation until its dissolution in 1999. Although it retained the status and kudos of an Indie label, Creation entered into a working relationship with Sony around the time Oasis signed. This naturally caused a few raised eyebrows amongst the Indie purists, but the effect on budgets and distribution was presumably to the promotional advantage of the bands involved, including Oasis.

By the time their debut album *Definitely Maybe* was released in August 1994, a line-up had been established, comprising the Gallaghers plus Paul 'Bonehead' Arthurs (guitar), Paul 'Guigsy' McGuigan (bass) and Tony McCarroll (drums). McCarroll was replaced by Alan White during the recording of the hugely successful second album *(What's the Story) Morning Glory* (1995). The core personnel remained otherwise unchanged for *Be Here Now* (1997), although both Pauls had quit before the next album, *Standing on the Shoulders of Giants* (2000). In the meantime, a B-side compilation titled *The Masterplan* had been released in November 1998. In the final mix of *Giants*, any studio footage involving the two departed members had reportedly been re-recorded at Noel Gallagher's instigation by their replacements, Colin 'Gem' Archer and Andy Bell.

A pleasing historical coincidence is that the names Creation and Oasis had both been used before. Veteran impresario Robert Stigwood had launched a label named Creation Records in 1967, although this soon disappeared with the advent of the longer-lived RSO (Robert Stigwood Organisation) label. A band bearing the name Oasis had briefly existed c.1984, comprising Welsh singer and erstwhile Eurovision hopeful Mary Hopkin, classical cellist Julian Lloyd Webber (brother of West End theater tunesmith Andrew), singer/composer Bill Lovelady and croaky Lancastrian crooner and pianist Peter Skellern. Some sources also record the presence of session guitarist Mitch Dalton. A debut LP was released on Warner, although evidence relating to live performances has proved elusive. One internet article categorizes the band's tiny recorded legacy as that of a 'simpergroup'.

Archive trivia aside, it has been suggested on more than one occasion that the Oasis of the Gallagher brothers can sound uncomfortably close to a kind of reheated Beatles, a charge further fuelled by Liam Gallagher's decision to name his first child Lennon Francis Gallagher (born 13 September 1999). However, any back-to-back musical comparison tends to produce little objective evidence, other than a very approximate vocal parallel between the younger Gallagher and his publicly acknowledged idol.

The Rutles

Unfortunately, there are a number of times when Noel Gallagher's songs have been linked to disturbingly similar existing compositions.

The melodic and harmonic parallels between the 1994 single *Whatever* and *How Sweet To Be An Idiot* from *The Rutles,* a 1973 TV feature and accompanying LP parodying the Beatles, are difficult to ignore. This did not go unnoticed by *Rutles* creator Neil Innes, previously of the satirical Bonzo Dog Doo-Dah Band, who is now credited as co-writer of *Whatever.*

When the song *Step Out* was withdrawn at the last minute from the second Oasis album, due to a reported similarity to the Stevie Wonder classic *Uptight,* spotting the next Oasis alleged rip-off became almost a national sport. One of the most bizarre findings resulted from various re-examinations of the first album, an approximate parallel being noted between the song *Shakermaker* and the Coca-Cola jingle *I'd Like To Teach the World To Sing*, a global hit in 1971 for the New Seekers. Another unhappy encounter with a 'simpergroup'?

But few would disagree that Noel Gallagher at his most inspired is a songwriter of force and integrity, the hit singles *Wonderwall* and *Don't Look Back in Anger* from *(What's the Story) Morning Glory* holding legitimate claim to the title of latter-day rock classics.

By the time Oasis arrived, the 'Madchester' scene was in its death throes. But competition soon appeared from other parts of the British Isles. As specific to the London area as Oasis were to the north-west, Blur were soon placed alongside Oasis as prime movers in the emerging category to be known as Britpop, an openly chauvinistic term invoked more frequently by Britain's downmarket 'red top' tabloid newspapers than by the serious music press. Representing a quasi-Victorian expression of national pride, combined with a knee-jerk reaction against the US-led forces of Grunge, Britpop would presently become enmeshed with the national embarrassment of Cool Britannia, a further tabloid term provoked by the mercifully short-lived efforts of the New Labour government under Tony Blair (elected with a landslide majority in May 1997) to cosy up to newsworthy aspects of the music business. It all went haywire at the annual media circus that is the British Phonographic Industry or 'Brit' Awards in 1998, when Danbert Nobacon (real name: Nigel Hunter) of the anarchist-leaning band Chumbawamba poured a jug of water over the Rt. Hon. John Leslie Prescott MP, otherwise known as Blair's Deputy Prime Minister. The motivation behind Nobacon's attack was apparently to protest on behalf of the Liverpool dockers, who were involved in a long-running industrial dispute.

Fronted by the distinctive 'Cockney' vocal style of Damon Albarn (b.1968), whose father had managed British jazz-rock pioneers Soft Machine during the 60s, Blur can be traced back to 1989 and thus pre-date Oasis by a small margin. With Albarn doubling on keyboards, the remaining personnel comprised a classic rock/pop line-up of Graham Coxon (guitar), Alex James (bass) and Dave Rowntree (drums). They first entered the charts with *She's So High* and *There's No Other Way* in autumn 1990 and spring 1991 respectively. Both were taken from the debut album *Leisure* and were released on the Parlophone-associated Food label. Critical comment was favorable, although the band's sound, despite their regional origins, led them to be categorized on the fringes of the now declining 'Madchester' movement. In what was seen as an attempt to move away from this stereotyping, and from the teenage following that the singles had earned them, the band took the drastic move of joining the 1992 Rollercoaster Tour, in which many commentators saw them as coming off second-best to such hard-edged post-punk acts as the Jesus & Mary Chain, My Bloody Valentine and Dinosaur Jr.

Further chart singles followed, although another Top Ten success eluded them until *Girls and Boys,* a No.5 hit from the highly successful *Parklife* album in spring 1994. The previous album *Modern Life is Rubbish* (1993) was well received but did not match the No.7 chart success of *Leisure.* By this time, an earlier perceived rivalry with Britpop trailblazers Suede had been replaced by what the media gleefully portrayed as a head-to-head conflict between Blur and Oasis. This reached its zenith in the summer of 1995, when the Blur single *Country House,* from the recently completed *Great Escape* album, was released to coincide with the Oasis single *Roll With It* from *(What's The Story) Morning Glory.* Any notion that the bands were unwilling participants in this commercial trench warfare may be substantially weakened by listening to the lyrics of *Country House,* the second verse opening with the line: 'He's got morning glory, life's a different story, everything going *Jackanory',* the reference of which is surely obvious. The term *Jackanory,* possibly introduced into the song as nothing more than a convenient rhyme, refers to the low-budget children's TV show launched by the BBC in the 60s, in which a 'resting' actor or actress appeared as a 'talking head' reading a story to camera, with occasional cross-fades to static illustrations.

Initially, the marketing gamble paid off, with *Country House* beating Oasis to the UK No.1 spot and providing Blur with their first chart-topping single. Both *Parklife* and *The Great Escape* reached No.1 in the UK album charts, although the even greater success of *(What's The Story) Morning Glory* took some of the shine off the earlier victory.

With the turn of the millennium and the declining fortunes of Britpop, the band entered a period of apparent semi-retirement, with speculation about disagreements between Albarn and Coxon suggesting the end was in sight. Various solo ventures followed, Albarn travelling to Mali on behalf of the Oxfam charity and producing the fund-raising album *Mali Music*. This led to rumors of a possible Blur reunion for *Live 8* in summer 2005, although it hit the buffers when Albarn spoke out in the lead-up to the event as one of its harshest critics, his complaints being due in part to the small number of black and African performers.

At the 1996 Brit Awards, Jarvis Cocker of senior Britpop practitioners Pulp had stormed the stage in order to ridicule the messianic stage routine of Michael Jackson. His efforts, like those of Nobacon two years later, were widely appreciated. By this time, Jackson's star on this side of the Atlantic was on the wane. The British public, who in the 70s had warmed so easily to the handsome teenager with the big natural Afro frizz and had been equally welcoming of the slick 'grown-up' Jackson of the 80s, were now becoming increasingly uncomfortable with the ghoul-like apparition that was emerging from endless sessions of cosmetic surgery. Cocker's intervention prompted a public reaction that ranged from quiet indulgence to vociferous acclaim, although it also earned him a visit to the local police station on the extraordinary grounds that his impromptu gyrations of the posterior had somehow constituted an assault on a number of children who were on stage with Jackson. Video footage revealed no evidence to support these allegations, although some sources record that one child appeared to have been accidentally struck a glancing blow by a bouncer dressed as a monk. You couldn't make it up...

Although Pulp were by no means the first act to benefit from the Britpop craze, they were unquestionably one of the longest established. Some sources trace their origins back as far as 1978. Having fronted the band from the outset, Cocker (b.1963) was into his 30s before they enjoyed national prominence. Despite an early invitation to record a session for, unsurprisingly enough, John Peel, major commercial success eluded them throughout the 80s. Various changes in line-up and artistic direction had taken place before they finally entered the lower reaches of the UK singles chart with *Lipgloss* in autumn 1993. By now, the personnel had settled as Cocker with Russell Senior (guitar, violin, acoustic bass), Candida Doyle (piano, keyboards), Steve Mackey (bass), Nick Banks (drums, percussion). With the No.2 hit *Common People* in the summer of 1995, Pulp had finally come up with the imaginative slice of social observation that was to become an anthem not only for the band but for the Britpop era as a whole. Cocker's sensitive eye and ear for the disappointments and missed opportunities experienced by the 'everyman' narrator reaches its triumphant highpoint in *Disco 2000* (UK No.7 in the winter of 1995), the song's central character of Deborah bearing a poignant resemblance to someone almost every heterosexual male had once covertly worshipped. The final chorus ironically quotes the title of *What Are You Doing Sunday?*, a cheesy 1971 hit for Tony Orlando and Dawn that would have been known to Cocker's contemporaries, although perhaps not his younger target audience.

One highly significant UK band of the era who were never perceived as exponents of Britpop, and yet are said to have directly influenced such current post-Britpop acts as Coldplay and Travis, was Radiohead. Comprising Thom Yorke (b.1968) (vocals/guitar), Ed O'Brien (b.1968) (guitar/vocals), Colin Greenwood (b.1969) (bass), his younger brother Jonny Greenwood (b.1971) (guitar/keyboards) and Phil Selway (b.1967) (drums), the nucleus of the band was established when Yorke, O'Brien and the elder Greenwood met in the mid-80s as pupils at Oxford's prestigious Abingdon School. Despite a break in continuity while individual members studied at various different universities, the above line-up was to prove permanent. Originally bearing the collective title *On a Friday*, the only day on which they could rehearse while still at school, they rebranded themselves as Radiohead in response to criticism of the original name in the Oxford based *Curfew* magazine. The new name inevitably led to confusion with the long established and then still active Talking Heads, the irony being that it was taken from the title of the David Byrne song *Radio Head* on the 1986 *True Stories* album by none other than Talking Heads. After a modestly successful 1992 debut EP, Radiohead took off big time with the 1993 album *Pablo Honey,* its escalating impact on the world market causing the gruelling promotional tour to enter its second year. From this point onwards, the band was seen as more rock than pop, with albums rather than singles as the preferred medium. This said, the song *Creep* from *Pablo Honey* reached UK No.7 in the autumn of 1993, with a handful of further chart hits to follow over the remainder of the decade.

Spring 1995 saw the release of *The Bends,* a rock-centered album regarded by many as the band's anti-commercial response to the possibly unexpected mainstream popularity of *Creep.* The album was produced by the patrician figure of John Leckie, who had previously been associated with projects including *All Things Must Pass* by George Harrison, the debut album by the Stone Roses and *The Dark Side of the Moon* by Pink Floyd which, despite its possible shortcomings in other areas, displays a quality of production that even its harshest critics have to acknowledge. Having apparently settled into a cycle of one new album every two years, Radiohead released in June 1997 what many consider to be their masterpiece. *OK Computer* found the band in a newly experimental phase, incorporating such fringe techniques as *Ambient* and *Noise.* Still figuring in *Best Album* polls a decade after its release, *OK Computer* is seen by many commentators as the high-point in 90s British rock, an honor often justifiably shared with *Urban Hymns,* the 1997 valedictory album by the Verve, fronted by the darkly charismatic figure of Richard Ashcroft (b.1971).

Formed in 1989 near the Lancashire town of Wigan, the Verve originally comprised Ashcroft in the company of guitarist Nick McCabe, bassist Simon Jones and drummer Peter Salisbury. A second lead guitarist, Simon Tong, was added following McCabe's departure in 1995 and remained aboard after McCabe rejoined. Like Radiohead, the Verve displayed an air of artistic maturity that set them apart from the epicenter of Britpop. However, *Urban Hymns* spawned no fewer than three UK chart singles. The looped sample of an orchestral version of the Rolling Stones song *The Last Time* that was used in the production of the No.1 hit *Bitter Sweet Symphony* led to a lawsuit from ABKCO Music, owners of the Stones' back catalog. The result was that Ashcroft shared the writing credits with the exalted company of Mick Jagger and Keith Richards, but also had to hand over the royalties to veteran pop mogul and ABKCO supremo, Allen Klein (b.1931).

During the prosperous and materialistic climate of the Reagan and Thatcher years, the slick stage routines and high-budget videos of Michael Jackson (b.1958) had naturally found favor with the acquisitive and sharply dressed young bankers and brokers, who ended their working day around smoked glass tables in the stylish wine bars of the world's wealthiest capitals. It was the growth of this increasingly visible social class that led to the term *Yuppie* (young urban professional), popularized by the US columnist Bob Greene but apparently first cited by R.C. Longworth in a 1981 article for the *Chicago Tribune*. The British contingent of yuppies, in particular, was eager to flash its cash after the prolonged economic instability and industrial unrest of the 70s. Trade Union power would shortly meet its Nemesis with Thatcher's spectacular defeat of the *National Union of Mineworkers,* led by the uncompromising figure of Arthur Scargill. As the British writer Richard Ingrams, former editor of *Private Eye,* commented as Thatcher unleashed her deadly endgame, large sectors of the British populace had come to relish the daily ritual of seeing Scargill receive 'another custard pie in the face', even though the situation was no joke for the nation's mining industry and its workforce.

But those who prospered under Thatcher and her overseas counterparts often did very well indeed, the increasingly upmarket product that was Michael Jackson giving voice and vision to the achievements and aspirations of the 20-40 sector. Newer figures on the music scene also flourished in this cash-driven climate, with songs such as *Material Girl* by Madonna and the silken-textured Sade hit *Smooth Operator* emerging as enduring anthems of the era.

From its earliest days, Michael Jackson's career had been the triumphant outcome of shrewd marketing strategies and, let it be said, outstanding talent. As the youngest and most featured member of the original Jackson 5 (subtly rebranded the Jackson Five circa 1973 and later to become the Jacksons, as younger family members were added to the roster), his pre-pubescent soprano naturally matured into a light tenor which, combined with the lilting falsetto at which so many male soul singers excel, gave the maturing Jackson a wide and expressive vocal range.

Despite their overt teenybopper appeal, the Jackson 5 successfully maintained a wider fanbase than many of their peers, the mere fact that they recorded on the Tamla Motown label allowing them the soul credentials that raised their status above that of most 70s bubble gum ephemera. Even the Rankin & Bass cartoon series, that ran from 1971-73 and used likenesses of the band designed by artist Paul Coker, proved less of an embarrassment than might reasonably have been feared. All this good fortune, together with a healthy repertoire of such quality soul-pops as *I Want You Back, ABC* and *Skywriter,* made for an early success story to be both admired and envied.

The advent of a potential rival team in the shape of the Osmonds had only limited impact, the girls-only appeal of the wholesome white boys from Utah apparently leaving most Jacksons fans profoundly unmoved. A backhanded compliment paid to the Jacksons in many a schoolyard at the time was a terse observation to the effect that 'at least they're better than the Osmonds'. Can we possibly imagine any self-respecting Jackson risking his hard-earned reputation with the Little Jimmy Osmond anti-classic *Long Haired Lover from Liverpool?*

As a solo artist, Michael Jackson's early career ran parallel with the heyday of the Jackson 5, his first global chart success with *Got To Be There* coming in the first weeks of 1972 when he was 13 years old. As success bred success, Jackson's career outside the family unit was consolidated by appearances alongside such big hitmakers as longtime Jackson 5 supporter Diana Ross and, a few years later, Paul McCartney. Herein lies a recurring formula in the Jackson strategy: the prestige collaboration that also yields credible musical results. Anyone performing alongside Ross was no longer perceived as 'just a kid', while McCartney, despite the mediocrity of much of his post-Beatle output, had nonetheless claimed his rightful place at popular music's highest tables while Jackson was still learning his first dance steps.

Jackson also kept exalted company in the control room, the 1979 album *Off The Wall* being co-produced with soul and jazz legend Quincy Jones (b.1933). With the release of *Thriller* in 1982, Jones remained a guiding presence behind the mixing desk. As every Jackson fan eagerly reminds us, this album became the best-selling disc of all time, with up to 60 million copies out there at the last count. Of the various mega-hit singles to emanate from *Thriller,* arguably the most significant of all was the frantic but grit-free pop rock of *Beat It,* home of the masterful guitar solo by guest star Eddie Van Halen.

In terms of audience recruitment, this was one of Jackson's smartest moves to date. As the 80s unfolded, he had successfully retained large numbers from his original early 70s fanbase, many of whom were by now nearing the age of 30, while attracting new support from the more conservative teens. As was suggested earlier, his gold-encrusted image went down well with the yuppies, while his role as a world style icon was becoming increasingly central. But the rock audience had always kept his work at arm's length. Now, with the release of *that* guitar solo, they could ignore him no longer. This is not to suggest that every seasoned rocker suddenly diverted his beer money to the purchase of the entire Jackson 5 back catalog, but how many copies of *Beat It* were surreptitiously placed on the record rack next to some well-worn vinyl by Motörhead et al?

By the time Eddie Van Halen (b.1955) played his starring role on *Beat It,* his permanent position with the band bearing his surname was well established. Based on an instrumental nucleus comprising Dutch born Van Halen, plus older brother Alex Van Halen (b.1953) (drums) and Michael Anthony (Sobolewski) (b.1954) (bass), Van Halen the band was first formed in California c.1974. Despite Anthony's legendary vocal prowess, earning him the nickname 'Cannon Mouth', the band employed what has since been described as a 'rotating list' of lead singers. Of these, the first and arguably best remembered was David Lee Roth (b.1954), whose earliest connection with Van Halen was as the owner of their rented PA system. Roth featured on the first six albums, starting with the self-titled debut release in 1978 and remained aboard up to and including the 1984 release titled, appropriately enough, *1984*. In the meantime *Van Halen II* (1979), *Women and Children First* (1980), *Fair Warning* (1981) and *Diver Down* (1982) had rolled off a production line with the impressive yield of one album every year or so. After his departure in 1985, which some commentators reported as an effective dismissal resulting from differences with other members of the band, Roth was replaced by the equally dynamic figure of Sammy Hagar (b.1947), culled from the highly respected but less prominent Californian hard rockers, Montrose. Hagar stayed for the next eleven years, a less productive era in terms of album releases, but one in which Hagar won a coveted Grammy award for *Best Hard Rock Performance* on the Van Halen album *For Unlawful Carnal Knowledge* (1991). Escalating tension with the Van Halen brothers led to Hagar's exit in 1996, followed by a brief reappearance by Roth that resulted in two newly recorded songs being added to the 1996 compilation *Best of Van Halen Vol.1*. But despite rumors of a permanent reunion, auditions continued for Hagar's replacement, the front runner at the time being the emerging but still relatively unknown Mitch Malloy. It has been said in retrospect that Malloy's decision not to join the band stemmed from Roth's appearance with his former colleagues to present one of the 1996 *MTV Video Music Awards*, thus fuelling speculation that the old line-up was set to reform and making the position of any lead vocalist who was not Roth untenable.

This being the case, it represents a creditable piece of level-headed thinking on the part of Malloy, his career as a solo artist remaining active at the time of writing, albeit on a relatively modest scale. The MTV episode, despite being greeted with a standing ovation, is believed to have precipitated a further manifestation of the alleged capacity of Roth and Eddie Van Halen to get on each other's nerves. Roth subsequently mounted a media campaign, in which he claimed to have been the unwitting participant in a cynical strategy to sell more copies of the compilation album. The Van Halen brothers responded by stating that there had never been any likelihood of Roth being permanently reinstated, and that they had never suggested otherwise either to the media or to the man himself.

The post of lead vocalist was eventually taken by Gary Cherone, formerly of the by now defunct Boston band Extreme. Cherone stayed for just one album, the 1998 release *Van Halen III* which, despite its titular reference to the now classic late 70s recordings, found the band in a newly spiritual and even ethereal mode. Sales, however, were disappointing compared with earlier albums. Cherone made a quiet and reportedly amicable departure in 1999, subsequently launching his new band Tribe of Judah. After several years of inactivity, Van Halen toured again in 2004 with Hagar on lead vocals. By this time, the increasingly fragile figure of Eddie Van Halen had undergone a hip replacement and treatment for cancer of the throat. A highly publicized 2-CD compilation album, titled *The Best of Both Worlds,* was released to coincide with the tour, complete with three new songs featuring Hagar. Although sales almost inevitably achieved platinum status, the response from longstanding fans was mixed. In particular, many were unhappy with the policy of mostly alternating Roth songs with Hagar songs, as opposed to the more logical sequence of allowing each singer a disc to himself. Few seemed unduly concerned by the absence of any material from *Van Halen III.*

Musically, Van Halen occupied the center ground between old school Heavy Metal and the even more overtly theatrical 70s subgenre of Glam Metal as practiced almost exclusively by US bands, most notably Kiss. The band's most lasting legacy, however, is Eddie Van Halen's status as guitar hero and technical innovator. Van Halen delivered a spectacular menu of 'dive bombing' (descending *glissandos,* usually created by forcing the whammy bar) and 'tapping' (virtuosic flourishes resulting from the use of both the left and the right hand on the fingerboard). Although Van Halen has often been credited with inventing the latter technique, earlier examples of tapping are easily found, one frequently cited pre-Van Halen exponent being Steve Hackett of Genesis. From a wider historical perspective, there is even an indirect precedent in the pioneering violin compositions of Niccolo Paganini (1782–1840). But there can be little doubt that it was Van Halen's consummate mastery of the technique that brought it to wider public attention and spawned innumerable adolescent imitators throughout the 80s and 90s.

Other guitarists who emerged around the same time were travelling down the same route and would more than likely have reached the same destination with or without Van Halen's lead. Most notable of all is jazz-fusion maestro Stanley Jordan (b.1959), whose intricate textures are seen by many as taking the technique to its logical conclusion.

It is also worth noting that the Chapman Stick, an instrument specifically designed for tapping, was developed by Emmett Chapman as far back as the early 70s, the first commercially produced examples going on sale in 1974. Even the Chapman Stick had several precursors, including the double-necked Touch Guitar built by the father and son team of Joe and Dave Bunker in 1955 and patented by them as the Duo-Lectar in 1961. According to Dave Bunker's own published recollections, the style that would become known as tapping was used occasionally by Merle Travis and further refined by Jimmie Webster (1908–1978), who also produced what appears to have been the first dedicated tutor book titled *Touch System* in 1952.

Although tapping can only be applied to a limited extent on the nylon-strung classical/flamenco guitar, a number of outstanding exponents on the metal-strung acoustic guitar have emerged in recent years. Most emanate from the US, including such outstanding figures as Michael Hedges (1953–1997) and Preston Reed, although a notable British exponent has now appeared in the hugely talented Anglo-Irishman Clive Carroll, a recent collaborator with the veteran Australian guitar virtuoso and master showman Tommy Emmanuel.

But the fact remains that Eddie Van Halen is the first name that springs to mind on the frequent occasions in music-related discussions when tapping is invoked. By identifying the potential of what was previously a peripheral skill and applying it to the heart of rock music, Van Halen was one of several key figures who ensured the enduring cult of the guitar hero, once seemingly threatened by the explosion of punk, would survive and thrive through the 80s and 90s. It was a role he shared with such dazzling virtuosi as Joe Satriani (b.1956), former Zappa protégé Steve Vai (b.1960, a one-time pupil of Satriani) and the much-mourned Texas blues star Stevie Ray Vaughan (1954–1990). Van Halen also represented a further shift in the trend towards the guitarist assuming the status of principal band member, outranking the traditionally central figure of lead singer. In many cases, of course, the guitarist and lead singer had been one and the same person, even though from the 60s onwards his instrumental supremacy would often be complemented by relatively modest vocal powers. An obvious example is Jimi Hendrix, although many would argue with good reason that the Hendrix voice, despite its limited scope in terms of pitch and dynamic, more than compensated for this deficit in its sheer expressive force. By the mid-to-late 70s, as established bands split either temporarily or for keeps in order to pursue solo ventures, it was natural enough that some of the new teams would carry the name of their mute axe warrior. Even though the first post-Deep Purple ensemble involving Ritchie Blackmore was officially titled Rainbow, the fact that Blackmore was the only member of the original line-up anyone had heard of surely made it inevitable that the debut album was titled *Ritchie Blackmore's Rainbow* and that the band should be referred to as such ever after.

Prior to this came the singular success story of the Robin Trower Band, in which the hunched and twitching figure of ex-Procol Harum guitarist Trower (b.1945) wove kaleidoscopic Hendrix-influenced guitar lines around the gruff and compelling vocal lines of bassist James Dewar (1942–2002), ably supported by drummer Bill Lordan (preceded in the original 1973 line-up by Reg Isidore). A hugely underrated talent, Dewar's death from pneumonia at the age of 59 is still lamented by a select fraternity of devotees. But while Trower's professional career was rooted in the 60s and flourished after he first went solo in the early 70s, only the corporate 80s could have created the precision engineered product that was, and remains to this day, Yngwie J. Malmsteen (b.1963), that central initial apparently being included to avoid confusion with any other musician who happened to be named Yngwie Malmsteen. In fact, the original moniker was Lars Yngve Johann Lannerbäck, his mother's maiden name of Malmsteen having apparently been adopted by Yngwie and his brother Bjorn (but not his sister Ann Louise, also known as Lolo) following their parents' divorce. Born in Stockholm and imported to the US by Mike Varney of Shrapnel Records in 1982, it has been said on more than one occasion that Malmsteen is every bit as quintessentially Swedish as Abba, the Volvo 240GL and the contents of the IKEA catalog. All were created to meet the requirements of an existing and lucrative market, and all met those requirements with an accuracy that would humble the finest heat-seeking missile.

Dripping gold and resplendent in an extravagant but formulaic wardrobe of stage outfits, Malmsteen is the gift wrapped *Action Man* of high-earning rock stars. But it has to be acknowledged that his mastery of the guitar is consummate. From the instrumental *Black Star,* complete with obligatory twenty second 'classical' prelude, that opened his debut album in 1984, it was clear that Malmsteen was a finger-crunching fret-burner of the type that is idolized predominantly by those who yearn to achieve the same. It also became clear from this album, and its sequels, that Malmsteen's compositions were little more than empty vessels in which to transport that phenomenal skill to his growing legions of admirers and aspiring imitators. The same imagery could even be applied to the members of his band, whose names and roles were known only to those who make a habit of reading the small print. Amid an ever-changing roster of able but obscure Americans and Scandinavians, the sharp-eyed reader will spot such familiar names as Jethro Tull drummer Barriemore Barlow and, on later releases, former Rainbow vocalist Joe Lynn Turner (b.1951, real name: Joseph Linquito), who by that time was en route to joining one of the 90s incarnations of Deep Purple. In fact, Turner played a vital role in one of the more memorable items in Malmsteen's back catalog: a scorching cover of the Hendrix classic *Spanish Castle Magic* on the 1989 album *Trial By Fire: Live in Leningrad.* An honest and compelling tribute to one of Malmsteen's most distinguished creative forefathers, this item alone shows what he has the potential to achieve when playing music other than his own.

Almost as celebrated as Malmsteen's manual dexterity is the revolutionary design of Fender Stratocaster that now bears his name. Instantly recognizable by its scalloped fretboard, the *Malmsteen Strat* is a concept that reportedly first took root when the adolescent Malmsteen was employed as a guitar repair man by a music store in his native Stockholm. In an interview with Joe Lalaina, quoted in the liner notes to a 1991 compilation titled *The Yngwie Malmsteen Collection*, Malmsteen recalls the store acquiring a 'lute from the 1600s' and that 'instead of having frets, the wood was carved out on the neck, so the top of the wood was the fret. It looked really cool...'. Since lutes built in the sixteenth and seventeenth centuries usually had flat fingerboards to which strands of gut were tied in order to create the frets, the date Malmsteen gives is maybe a little early. Lutes with fixed metal frets are now a common sighting, a famous example being the lute built for Julian Bream by the English craftsman David Rubio (1934–2000). Several lutes of the Rubio design survive, one having recently surfaced at the Early Music Centre in the Northern English city of Bradford. But it seems most likely that the instrument Malmsteen saw was a hybrid guitar-lute, of the type built mainly in Germany during the nineteenth century. These instruments had six single strings like a conventional guitar and typically had scalloped frets similar to those of the *Malmsteen Strat*, usually with a narrow band of metal fretwire inserted at the highest points.

As the 80s drew to a close, popular music and its associated cultures had become more diverse than at any other time in history. The mixed media genre of Hip Hop, although seen by most commentators as having its earliest manifestations in the 70s or even the 60s, enjoyed its first major flowerings in the late 80s. It is perhaps more than just a coincidence that Hip Hop, with its widely acknowledged debt to the itinerant West African poet/musician known as a griot, should be taking center stage in global youth culture during the same era in which World Music became a recognized catch-all sub-genre and a fashionable topic of conversation within the more radical sectors of the 30 plus age group. How many erudite 80s dinner parties took place amid the strains of the Paul Simon blockbuster *Graceland* from 1986? Featuring Simon in the company of the South African vocal ensemble Ladysmith Black Mambazo and projecting the group's leader Joseph Shabalala (b.1941) to instant cult status, there can be little doubt that *Graceland* was the *Bridge Over Troubled Water* of its time. Although the album also entered Cajun and Hispanic territory, not to mention a guest appearance by the Everly Brothers, it was unquestionably the high-profile African content that fired the public imagination, especially at a time when social justice appeared to be finally gaining a foothold in that troubled part of the world.

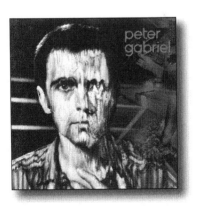

This growing mainstream appetite for World Music proved instrumental in the revitalized 80s career of Peter Gabriel, whose rich and varied personal odyssey since leaving Genesis made it hard for his younger fanbase to believe he had ever been associated with what had by now become a middle-of-the-road corporate enterprise. After scoring a surprise early solo hit with *Solsbury Hill* in the spring of 1977, Gabriel entered a period of prolonged musical experimentation and personal soul-searching before resurfacing in the singles chart with the similarly quirky yet inspired *Games Without Frontiers* at the start of 1980. As British audiences knew only too well, the title of this song was an ironic reference to the 1970s Europe-wide television tournament *Jeux Sans Frontières,* re-branded *It's a Knockout* by the BBC, presumably for the benefit of its monoglot viewers. Staged at open-air venues throughout the continent, *JSF* comprised teams of amateur athletes entertaining themselves and an excitable crowd by playing elaborately staged outdoor party games, usually involving large quantities of water. Compared with this televisual garbage, the *Eurovision Song Contest* was a cultural event of the highest refinement. In the meantime, Gabriel had embarked on the series of four solo albums that were all to be titled simply *Peter Gabriel*. As well as working alongside such high-ranking names as Robert Fripp, who appears on the first three albums from what fans now term the 'untitled era', Gabriel also used this period to road test his earliest collaborations with the young and reclusive English singer/songwriter Kate Bush (b.1958), who is widely believed to have made an anonymous contribution as backing singer on *Games Without Frontiers*. Bush it was who would go on to appear alongside Gabriel, by now with equal billing, on the 1986 hit *Don't Give Up*. Gabriel and Bush subsequently triumphed as *Best Male Solo Artist* and *Best Female Solo Artist* at the 1987 Brit Awards, the latter decoration mischievously described by some commentators as a victory of silence over sound, since Bush appears to have released no new solo recordings between *Hounds of Love* (1985) and *The Sensual World* (1989).

An idiosyncratic but often compelling talent, Bush scored her first hit single at the age of nineteen with *Wuthering Heights* (UK No.1 at the start of 1978). Despite the song's undeniable flair and originality, the single version was almost brought to its knees by an affected and little girlish vocal style, at least an octave above Bush's pleasant natural soprano, thus rendering the literary references in the song virtually unintelligible. Appearing on *Top of the Pops* in diaphanous Victorian-style dresses and indulging in the most extraordinary displays of eye-popping and other facial contortions, Bush's early stage persona appeared to owe more to the disturbing figure of Miss Havisham, created by Charles Dickens in the novel *Great Expectations,* than to the Emily Brontë character of Catherine Earnshaw from whose point of view the song is supposedly written. Bush appeared to acknowledge these youthful distortions of her own creation by releasing an alternate take of *Wuthering Heights* with a more mature vocal on the 1986 compilation *The Whole Story.* Ironic though this album title was doubtless intended to be, the notoriously unproductive Bush went on to release all of three new solo discs over the next two decades, *Aerial* (2005) coming some twelve years after its 1993 predecessor *The Red Shoes.*

Having signalled his interest in the African situation with the minor UK hit *Biko* in 1980, Peter Gabriel became a key figure in kick-starting the World Music phenomenon with his logistical and financial support of the WOMAD (World of Music, Arts and Dance) festival in 1982. Despite its noble artistic objectives, the event failed to recoup Gabriel's investment, a one-off Genesis reunion being organized to help cover his personal losses. A more lasting venture in this field was Gabriel's launch of Real World Studios and its eponymous record label, both of which have survived beyond the millennium. His career as a solo artist also enjoyed a second flowering in the years following the WOMAD venture, the 1986 hit *Sledgehammer* being remembered as much for its award-winning video as for its equally enduring musical content. Despite having spent much of the 90s away from the public gaze, Gabriel remains a cutting edge figure to this day, one of his recent activities being a collaboration with Brian Eno on the online distribution of music. Projects include the recent launch of an organization known as MUDDA (Magnificent Union of Digitally Downloading Artists), a co-operative for the protection of musicians' copyright.

Like in the UK, mainstream rock in the USA survived the 80s wholly intact, senior acts including Aerosmith being joined by young and eye-catching ensembles such as Guns N'Roses and Bon Jovi. These last two names are seen by many as representing the two extremes of US rock in the late 80s, the big-haired and media savvy ethos of Bon Jovi always being in stark contrast with the punk-like relish with which Guns N'Roses, who in the early days had allegedly toyed with the idea of adopting the collective title of AIDS, challenged established taste.

One respected commentator has even drawn a parallel with the dichotomy that existed in the 60s between fresh-faced teen bands like Herman's Hermits and such hard-nosed R&B acts as the Animals. Driven by the audio-visual double act of lead singer W. Axl Rose (b.1962, real name William Bruce Rose, but often said to have been raised under the name of Bill Bailey) and British born lead guitarist Slash (b.1965, real name: Saul Hudson), Guns N'Roses were first active in the Los Angeles area around 1985. With the original line-up completed by rhythm guitarist Izzy Stradlin (b.1962, real name: Jeff Isabelle), bassist Michael 'Duff' McKagan (b.1964) and drummer Steven Adler (b.1965), the band enjoyed early regional success with a single released independently on the Uzi Suicide label before signing a deal with Geffen Records, the enterprising figure of David Geffen (see Chapter 10) remaining at the cutting edge throughout the post-punk era. Slash and Adler had respectively replaced early band members Tracii Guns and Rob Gardner, apparently on the rather curious grounds that neither Guns nor Gardner had been willing to tour outside the LA area. Guns, whose surname inspired the first half of the band's name, had formerly been a driving force behind the highly skilled and relatively mainstream LA Guns, with whom Rose had also spent a brief early stint. In the meantime, Rose had worked alongside Izzy Stradlin in the short-lived Hollywood Rose, an immediate precursor to what was to become Guns N'Roses.

GN'R's 1987 debut album *Appetite For Destruction* topped the US charts with 18 million copies sold. Early copies featured Robert Wilson's notorious 'robot rape' painting on the front of the sleeve and are now highly collectable. The album also reached No.15 in the UK, its success, especially on home territory, undoubtedly assisted by the bands energetic touring schedule and growing reputation for memorable stage antics. Having first come to public attention supporting such established acts as Iron Maiden and LA glam rockers Mötley Crüe, it took little time for GN'R to attract their own vociferous crowd. The 1988 EP *GN'R Lies* enjoyed a prominence almost equal to that of its predecessor, although it was to be another three years before the band built on these early achievements with the 1991 double release of *Use Your Illusion I* and *Use Your Illusion II*, both of which reportedly sold in excess of five million on the US market alone. By this time, the band's status as a live act was unassailable, although the release of new material on disc was to remain an infrequent occurrence. In fact, *The Spaghetti Incident?* from 1993 was to be the only other original recorded offering of the decade, *Use Your Illusion* (1998) being a US only single disc distillation of material from the two 1991 releases. In the meantime, the band also found favor in the singles charts, with *Sweet Child O' Mine* (1988) and *Paradise City* (1989) heralding a string of bestsellers on both sides of the Atlantic. Several of these, including the apparently self-parodying cover of Bob Dylan's *Knockin' On Heaven's Door* from *Use Your Illusion II*, achieved higher chart positions in the UK than at home. By the time this inimitable performance was dominating the British airwaves, the *GN'R* line-up was undergoing a series of changes that started with the departures of Adler and Stradlin in 1990 and 1991 respectively. Despite becoming an increasingly marketable figure in his own right, Slash remained aboard until 1996. McKagan chose not to renew his contract in 1997, leaving Rose as the sole surviving member from the classic 80s line-up.

Amid the tortuous personnel changes of the 90s, one-off guest jams in live shows became a regular feature, with guitar icons Ronnie Wood, Brian May and Lenny Kravitz all appearing on the roster.

Despite their ongoing penchant for the outrageous and the controversial, which many saw as reaching its zenith with the inclusion of the song *Look At Your Game Girl* by serial killer Charles Manson as a 'hidden track' on *The Spaghetti Incident?*, GN'R have always remained respectful of the band many perceive as their chief source of inspiration.

That band is Aerosmith, whose song *Mama Kin* appeared as a cover on that early Uzi Suicide disc by GN'R. Formed in Boston, Massachusetts, at the start of the 70s, the two-man central force of lead singer Steven Tyler (b.1948, real name: Stephen Victor Tallarico) and guitarist Joe Perry (b.1950, real name: Anthony Joseph Pereira) were accused in the early days of casting themselves as Mick Jagger and Keith Richards respectively in an attempt to create an all-American Rolling Stones for the new decade. This was due primarily to a discernible and never-denied musical influence, but perhaps it also had something to do with Tyler's remarkable visual resemblance to the rubber-lipped English icon of 60s R&B.

With Tyler and Perry working alongside guitarist Brad Whitford (b.1952) (replacing early member Ray Tabano), bass player Tom Hamilton (b.1951) and drummer Joey Kramer (b.1950), the band was signed by Columbia in 1972. This followed an often impecunious early career, during which they gave free performances outside Boston University when no paid work was on offer. Their 1973 self-titled debut album reached No.21 in the US charts, although the 1974 sequel *Get Your Wings* peaked at a relatively modest No.74, despite having apparently matched the sales of its predecessor.

But it was the third release, *Toys in the Attic* (1975) that everyone remembers, partly due to the multi-layered references in the title and partly due to its having remained in the US charts for almost two years, including 31 weeks in the Top 40. By this time, Aerosmith was a major force in the US, although their growing cult status with the British audience would only bear its full fruit later in their career. *Toys in the Attic* also yielded two US hit singles, with *Sweet Emotion* charting in 1975 and *Walk This Way* in 1977. In the meantime, a re-issue of *Dream On* from the first album had reached US No.6 in 1976, its initial release on single having only been a minor hit. The band built on the *Toys in the Attic* breakthrough with *Rocks* (1976) and *Draw the Line* (1977), although the completion of *Night in the Ruts* (1979) was delayed by Perry's decision to leave the band while the album was being recorded. Whitford made his exit in 1981, the respective replacement guitarists being Jimmy Crespo (following a brief innings by Ritchie Supa) and Rick Dufay. In a remarkable turn of events, Perry and Whitford both rejoined after attending an Aerosmith concert on Valentine's Day 1984, the re-assembled original line-up apparently still remaining in place at the time of writing. The path to the release of *Done With Mirrors* (1985), which was to be the first studio album after the much-publicized reunion, was not entirely smooth, with both Tyler and Perry having cause to enter drug rehabilitation programs along the way.

Tyler's narcotic habits indirectly give rise to mention of one of rock music's most celebrated paternity sagas. It is now universally known and acknowledged by all parties that Steven Tyler is the biological father of actress Liv Tyler (b.1977), despite the fact that she spent the first eleven years of her life as Liv Rundgren, having been led to believe her rock star father was not Steven Tyler but Todd Rundgren. Already a patrician figure in US rock by the time of the child's birth, Rundgren (b.1948) had been frontman to Nazz, quality purveyors of late 60s pop, before launching a solo career that yielded such worldwide hits as *I Saw The Light* from the 1972 double album *Something/Anything?* By the late 70s, Rundgren's parallel activities as producer and studio impresario occupied a large part of the agenda, his collaboration with hi-tech arranger Jim Steinman resulting in the massive commercial success of the 1977 'Wagnerian Rock' extravaganza *Bat Out Of Hell* by the highly marketable but then largely unknown Meat Loaf (b.1947, real name: Marvin Lee Aday).

The truth about Rundgren's family circumstances only emerged when the pre-adolescent Liv Rundgren/Tyler noticed a striking resemblance between herself and Mia Tyler (b.1978), Steven Tyler's acknowledged daughter by a different mother and now a successful plus-size model and aspiring actress in her own right. When Steven Tyler's erstwhile partner Bebe Buell (b.1953) was challenged on the paternity question, her reported response was that she had named Rundgren as her daughter's father on the grounds that living with Tyler was 'like going to Peru and back every day', the picturesque reference to Tyler's once-copious drug intake being all too obvious.

Aerosmith's eventual breakthrough in the UK singles chart came when formative New York Hip Hop trio Run-D.M.C reached UK No.8 in 1986 with a cover of the earlier Aerosmith US hit *Walk This Way,* both Tyler and Perry appearing as guests on this radical reworking. From that point onwards, Aerosmith have made regular forays into the UK charts in their own right, starting with *Dude (Looks Like a Lady)* in autumn 1987. But it is as a long-serving US force that the band will forever be known. 2001 saw their induction to the Rock & Roll Hall of Fame. Although located in Cleveland, Ohio, this hallowed institution has, since 1986, held annual ceremonies in New York City, in which newly selected performers, songwriters and producers are formally welcomed aboard. For performers, it is usually required that their first record was released at least 25 years earlier.

One band whose marketability recognizes no national boundaries is the team once witheringly referred to as 'New Jersey soft rock overlords, distrusted by purists as *false metal*'. Formed in 1983, Bon Jovi comprised lead singer Jon Bon Jovi (b.1962, original spelling: John Bongiovi), guitarist Richie Sambora (b.1959), keyboard player David Bryan (b.1962, full name: David Bryan Rashbaum), bass player Alec John Such (b.1956) and drummer Hector 'Tico' Torres (b.1953). Signing with Phonogram and releasing a self-titled debut album in 1984, the band enjoyed instant success with a Gold Disc in the US and polite critical reception in the UK. The 1985 sequel, titled *7800o Fahrenheit,* suffered a less smooth passage, its progress in the UK being hindered by a subtly worded *Kerrang!* review that summarized the album as 'a pale imitation of the Bon Jovi we have got to know and learnt to love'. But it was *Slippery When Wet* (1986) that projected the band to world stardom, achieving US sales of 12 million and yielding no fewer than four hit singles over the next two years: *You Give Love a Bad Name; Livin' On a Prayer*; *Wanted Dead or Alive* and *Never Say Goodbye.* Interestingly, the last of these was more successful in the UK, reaching No.21 in the summer of 1987. The 1988 album *New Jersey* was a further commercial triumph and remains a 'fan favorite' as home of such staple live numbers as *Bad Medicine* and *Lay Your Hands On Me.* The ensuing tour allegedly put a strain on the working relationship between Jon Bon Jovi and Richie Sambora, resulting in a period of downtime at the start of the 90s while Sambora completed his solo album *Stranger In This Town*. The band reconvened for *Keep the Faith* (1992), after which Such announced his departure. Curiously, most sources agree that he was never officially replaced, even though his role was effectively taken over by Hugh McDonald (b.1950). Subsequent studio offerings have been infrequent, although *These Days* (1995) and *Crush* (2000) have both found favor with fans past and present, the latter album yielding the world-wide hit single *It's My Life*.

Bon Jovi participated in *Live 8* in July, 2005, unveiling a new song titled *Have a Nice Day* alongside repertoire standards as *Livin' on a Prayer* and *It's My Life*. The 2004 boxed set *100,000,000 Bon Jovi Fans Can't Be Wrong*, a self-celebrating reference to the 1959 compilation *50,000,000 Elvis Fans Can't Be Wrong*, generated further munificent revenue while providing new ammunition for the band's detractors.

While LA remained the most active smelting plant for rock's ever-increasing array of metallic elements, a more soft-focus aesthetic was emanating from the town of Athens, Georgia. Formed at the University of Georgia in 1980, REM was one of a new breed of 80s rock band that revived gently psychedelic lyrics against a backdrop of the 'jangly' folk-rock guitar style most readily associated with the Byrds. Comprising singer Michael Stipe (b.1960) and guitarist Peter Buck (b.1956), who were later joined by bass player Mike Mills and drummer Bill Berry (both b.1958), the band soon gave up their university courses in order to build a musical career that, although not an overnight success, would bring them world stardom by the end of the decade and beyond. After serving their apprenticeship with eighteen months of gigs around the Southern States, the band entered the Drive-In Studios owned by producer Mitch Easter. The result of this session was the single *Radio Free Europe,* whose title refers to the US-funded post-war broadcasting network. Released in 1981 on the independent Hib-Tone label, the initial pressing of just one thousand copies drew sufficient public acclaim to be voted *Best Independent Single* in the annual poll organized by the *Village Voice.* Moving to the larger indie label IRS, the band released the *Chronic Town* EP in 1982, followed less than a year later by their debut album *Murmur,* the latter including a re-recorded version of *Radio Free Europe. Murmur* went gold in the US, as did all REM albums until sales reached platinum with *Document* in 1987.

Variously described as 'jangle pop' or 'college rock', the 60s retro elements that have always characterized the textures created by REM have often led their work to be categorized alongside that of the loosely defined group of 80s LA bands that became known as the Paisley Underground. Although many of the band's scholars insist that their collective title, which replaced the pre-*Radio Free Europe* name Twisted Kites, was chosen from a random series of letters. The 'official' explanation that it stands for Rapid Ear Movement, derived from the dream state known as Rapid Eye Movement, is arguably more convincing.

The second album *Reckoning,* released in April 1984, made it to the lower reaches of the UK charts, with all subsequent 80s releases enjoying increasing chart success on both sides of the Atlantic. A five-album deal signed with Warner Brothers sealed the band's elevation to superstar level, the first Warner album *Green* (released November 1988) enjoying universal critical acclaim and double-platinum sales. A regular flow of worldwide hit singles followed, with such inspired and imaginative songs as *Losing My Religion, Shiny Happy People, Man on the Moon* and *The Sidewinder Sleeps Tonight* achieving classic status. Album mega-sales continued throughout the 90s, with *Out of Time* (1991), *Automatic for the People* (1992) *Monster* (1994) and *New Adventures in Hi-Fi* (1996) all going platinum several times over.

Berry's decision to leave the band in October 1997 must rate as one of the most civilized departures in the history of music, with the exhausted and reportedly depressed drummer offering to stay aboard if his exit threatened to precipitate the band's demise. It is also said that Berry even offered to continue to appear on studio sessions, Stipe's oft-quoted public response being that 'I just love the guy too much to see him sad'. Continuing as a three-piece and using various guest and session drummers, most notably Barrett Martin (formerly of the Screaming Trees), REM have released four albums in the post-Berry era. Their decision to part company with long-time producer Scott Litt and replace him with Patrick McCarthy was questioned by many supporters, although any negative impact on sales figures appears to have been minimal.

But despite their early folk-rock leanings, the increasingly eclectic REM of the 90s had several close encounters, most notably in the *Monster* album from 1994, with elements of a far from folksy all-American genre that emanated from Seattle at the start of the decade...

Although not exclusive to the city of Seattle, most sources agree that the rise of Grunge was geographically rooted in the Pacific Northwest states of Washington and Oregon. Generally regarded as a loose amalgam of heavy metal, hard-core punk and that catch-all 80s term Alternative Rock, Grunge will forever be associated with the demographic concept known as Generation X and in particular with the 1991 novel *Generation X: Tales for an Accelerated Culture* by the Canadian writer and social commentator Douglas Coupland (b.1961). Emerging out of the Northwest 80s punk culture represented by bands such as the Fartz, the U-Men and the Accused, the Grunge soundscape was characterized by 'dirty' guitar riffs, a pounding drum beat and markedly slower tempi than those associated with punk. It was the prominent use of this last stylistic trait that led some commentators of the time to disagree over whether or not influential bands such as the Melvins and the Wipers should be categorized as 'late punk' or 'early Grunge'. Some researchers have also detected an indirect influence on Grunge by such 60s Northwest bands as the Wailers (no Bob Marley connection) and the Sonics.

The coining of the term 'Grunge' is generally attributed to Mark Arm (b.1962, real name: Mark McLaughlin), vocalist with Green River and later Mudhoney. Although Arm's description of Green River's sound as 'pure grunge' appears on the surface to be a negative self-evaluation, most followers of the genre perceive it more as an honest summing-up of the music's gritty 'warts and all' ethos. Either way, Green River, whose history dated back to the pre-Grunge days of 1983, were seen as founding fathers of an identifiable school of rock music that would reach world attention almost a decade later with the rise to prominence of such bands as Alice in Chains, Pearl Jam, Soundgarden and, most famously of all, Nirvana. Of these, Soundgarden first came together within a year or so of the formation of Green River, the others all becoming active by the end of the 80s. But it was not until the early 90s that Grunge finally emerged as a world force. Up to then, it was essentially a regional genre, promoted by such Pacific Northwest indie labels as Sub Pop, K-Records and the alarmingly named Kill Rock Stars. Of these, Sub Pop was especially active in distributing the music to a wider audience, the ironically titled *Sub Pop Singles Club* mailing out newly-minted discs by local bands to its subscribers on a monthly basis. Sub Pop founders Bruce Pavitt and Jonathan Poneman also scored an early publicity coup by co-operating with the British music magazine Melody Maker in an article on what was then still uncharted waters for most of the readership.

It was, however, the instant success of the second Nirvana album *Nevermind* (1991) and its first of four single releases *Smells Like Teen Spirit* that finally broke the ice on a global scale. By this time, the band were signed to, once again, Geffen Records, their first studio album *Bleach* having been released on Sub Pop in 1989.

As fans of Pearl Jam are apt to point out, their debut album *Ten* was released a month before *Nevermind*, although sales figures only appear to have taken off after the success of the latter had stimulated interest in the Northwest scene as a whole. History would prove that the uncompromising textures generated by Nirvana were precisely what the turn-of-the-decade market was looking for, their penchant for the 'soft verse, hard chorus' format seen by some as being inspired by 80s cult band the Pixies. Nirvana singer/guitarist and principal songwriter Kurt Cobain (1967–1994) is known to have been a Pixies fan, revealing in a Rolling Stone interview that he regarded *Smells Like Teen Spirit* as his own failed attempt to write a song in the style of the Pixies. In fact, Cobain is known to have shown admirable generosity in crediting his musical influences, often using high-profile interviews as a platform to invoke the names of favored musicians whose own careers were unlikely ever to equal the status of his own. It is also believed that Cobain was instrumental in the reissue of deleted albums by such bands as the Raincoats and the Vaselines. The latter band's guitarist and singer Frances McKee is widely believed to have been the inspiration behind Cobain's decision to name his daughter Frances Bean. The child's middle name was reportedly a reference to the way she had appeared to her father during early scans, a somewhat embarrassing soubriquet to carry in later life, but by no means the most excessive example of its type in the nomenclature of rock offspring.

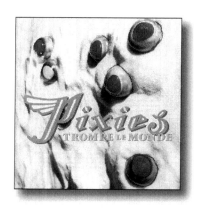

Fronted by the two-man powerhouse of Cobain and bass player Chris (or Krist) Novoselic (b.1965), Nirvana had worked with various short-term drummers, including Aaron Burckhard and Dale Crover, before finally settling on Chad Channing (b.1967) in the period prior to *Bleach*. Although Channing was officially in harness at the time of the album's release, Crover appears on three of the tracks. A somewhat shadowy fourth man, also billed as playing on that first album, even though he apparently did not, is guitarist Jason Everman, the generally accepted reason for the silent credit being that it was Everman's $606.17 that financed the studio time. By the time of the *Nevermind* sessions, Channing had made his exit, to be replaced by hardcore punk veteran Dave Grohl (b.1969). Unsurprisingly, the name Nirvana had been used before, most notably in the rather more obvious context of a now long-forgotten British psychedelic ensemble, whose main claim to fame was that they had supported the High Numbers (later to become the Who) before having a minor hit single with *Rainbow Chaser* in the spring of 1968.

Although projected sales of *Nevermind* were a relatively modest half a million, the album was certified triple platinum (in excess of three million sales) within six months of release. A deeply symbolic moment came in early 1992, when the album replaced *Dangerous* by Michael Jackson at the top of the Billboard chart, an event seen by many as sealing the triumph of 'alternative' music in its various guises over the failing dominance of mainstream pop.

Incesticide (1992), a retrospective compilation of B-sides and previously unreleased studio material kept fans happy in the period of preparation that finally resulted in the September 1993 release of *In Utero,* the band's third and final studio album with Cobain at the helm. Although Cobain had emphasized that this album, for which the band worked with former Pixies producer Steve Albini (b.1962), was aimed primarily at the band's core punk and indie fanbase, sales nonetheless went on to exceed even those of *Nevermind,* the final tally earning platinum status five times over.

The tragic circumstances of Cobain's death have been picked over down to the finest detail, as has his turbulent marriage to Courtney Love (b.1964, real name: Courtney Michelle Harrison), erstwhile singer with the mixed gender Indie band Hole. It was his union with Love that produced Frances Bean Cobain in August 1992, the couple having married in the February of that year. Not always popular with Nirvana fans, Love has often been cast as a Yoko-like figure, who allegedly used her relationship with Cobain to further her own talent-starved musical ambitions. It has even been suggested that Cobain wrote most of the songs on the Hole breakthrough album *Live Through This* (1994), even though the only concrete evidence Cobain was involved in the album at all is his acknowledged presence as a backing singer on an alternate take of one of the tracks.

On April 8 1994, Kurt Cobain was found shot dead in a room over the garage at his Lake Washington home. A few days earlier, he had left a drug rehabilitation center in California, where he was being treated for heroin addiction. The shotgun that had caused the fatal head injury was found at his side, the autopsy report concluding that Cobain's death was the result of a 'self-inflicted shotgun wound to the head'. Despite the official findings, rumors immediately started to circulate that Cobain had, in fact, been murdered, the main thesis being that the high level of heroin recorded in the toxicology report would allegedly have made Cobain physically incapable of rolling down his sleeve, putting away the needle and spoon, and then pulling the trigger. Doubt has also been cast on the authenticity of what appeared to be a suicide note found at the scene, due largely to a change of handwriting style in the closing lines. But no murderer has ever been found and the case remains officially closed at the time of writing.

Public response to Cobain's death was dramatic to the point of excess, with high schools on both sides of the Atlantic reportedly organizing special assemblies and even counselling sessions to support traumatized fans. Most bizarre of all was the wideley reported decision of British journalist and broadcaster Bernard Levin (1928–2004), an opera fan and stalwart of the BBC's pompous and flatulent classical music quiz show *Face the Music*, to go out and buy a Nirvana CD in order to discover 'what all the fuss was about'. Informed and perceptive though he invariably was when writing on home territory, it seems rather unlikely that Levin's readership found themselves greatly illuminated as a result of his morbid curiosity about this alien topic.

Despite his self-destructive lifestyle and the often combative nature of his music and lyrics, Kurt Cobain is a figure with whom it is difficult not to sympathize. His public and private support of fellow musicians is well-documented, and it was surely a genuine devotion to his wife and child that prompted the potentially embarrassing episode at the Reading Festival in 1992, when Cobain successfully persuaded the crowd to yell in unison 'We love you, Courtney', in celebration of the recent arrival of Frances Bean. On a darker topic, few would now question the sincerity of Cobain's outrage on hearing that two men had raped a woman while chanting the words of *Polly* from *Nevermind*. Said to have been inspired by a news story about a 14-year-old rape victim in Tacoma, the song is written from the standpoint of the rapist and was always destined to be one of Cobain's most shocking creations.

Music critic Greil Marcus has suggested that the song was possibly descended from the traditional murder ballad *Pretty Polly*, recorded in 1927 by Dock Boggs but believed to have been at least a century old by that time. In an apparent sequel to *Polly*, the later Nirvana song *Rape Me* from *In Utero* is written from the victim's point of view and infuriated feminists, even though Cobain always maintained that it was an anti-rape song. Cobain's public response to the real-world *Polly* rape was recorded in the notes to the US release of *Incesticide*, where he condemned the protagonists as 'two wastes of sperm and eggs…I have a hard time carrying on knowing there are (sic) plankton like that in our audience'. Grotesque imagery, but unquestionably the words of an artist whose anger and even fear at the damaging potential of his own creativity is genuine. This said, it could equally be argued that it was Cobain's own choice to take his music into such dangerous terrain, and that to release songs that were so clearly open to evil misinterpretation showed a certain naivete on his part.

Although the mainstream popularity of Grunge was not destined to survive through the 90s, the demise of Soundgarden in 1997 being seen by many as the final death knell, aspects of the genre lived on is such bands as the Smashing Pumpkins.

Formed in Chicago in 1988 and fronted by singer and guitarist Billy Corgan (b.1967), the band's penchant for panda-like eyeliner has often led them to be portrayed as latter-day standard bearers of the often ill-defined subgenre of Gothic Rock.

Dating back at least to the 70s, Gothic Rock is typically character-ized as a visual as much as a musical distillation of Glam Rock and Punk, perhaps with some later dashes of the New Romantic. Alice Cooper and his various antecedents are often credited as founding fathers, while evocative use of cosmetics alone usually guarantees a mention for such image-conscious punk bands as Siouxsie and the Banshees.

Some published definitions are more specific than others, although most are agreed that the concept of Gothic Rock was first established following the release of the 1979 single *Bela Lugosi's Dead* by the short-lived British band Bauhaus, their collective title derived from the 1920s German school of art and architecture known as Staatliches Bauhaus.

Popular culture in the 90s maintained the eclecticism of the latter part of the previous decade. The most senior bands, such as the Rolling Stones and the Who, retained their capacity to fill the largest venues whenever they chose to tour again. Their audiences were by no means limited to an ageing population of lifelong disciples, the 20-40 age group often accounting for a significant percentage of ticket sales. Sadly, the assassination of John Lennon had long since barred any possibility of the Beatles ever rising from the ashes and thus forming a 'big three' with their southern English counterparts. The acceptance of rock musicians into the media establishment was now demonstrated by the fact that such world figures as Michael Jackson, Paul McCartney and Mick Jagger were considered newsworthy regardless of what they happened to be doing or not doing on the musical front.

This was equally true, on home territory at least, for Elton John, his 2005 'gay wedding' to longtime partner David Furnish being trumpeted throughout the British airwaves as the most lavish public celebration of the recent liberalization of UK civil law.

At the other end of the dial, the growing influence of all aspects of Hip Hop culture during the 90s saw leading international Rap artists enjoy an ever-increasing celebrity status with younger audiences from all ethnic backgrounds. For the first time in maybe three decades, it had become common for teenagers to swear allegiance to neither rock nor pop, with even the most mildly rebellious adolescents heaping ridicule on Jagger *et al* in much the same way as their forbears had sneered at James Last.

Occupying the center ground was a seemingly endless conveyer belt of talented new rock bands that appeared to be set for the long-haul, alongside manufactured pop acts that clearly were not. The unsurpassed creativity of the LA music scene has been further enhanced by such quality bands as the Red Hot Chili Peppers, whose enduring level of musicianship enabled them to build on the groundbreaking success of *Mother's Milk* (1989) with such 90s classics as *Californication* (1999).

Other California bands, including the post-punk trio Green Day, found fame in the 90s and have remained active beyond the millennium. With the 70s emergence of punk now three decades old, those who dismissed it as a passing phase have long been silenced.

Significantly, the three core members of Green Day, namely guitarist/lead vocalist Billie Joe Armstrong, bass player Mike Dirnt (real name, Michael Pritchard) and drummer Tré Cool (real name, Frank Edwin Wright III) were all born in 1972, making them too young to have been fully aware of the early culture from which their music derives. But in much the same way as Noel and Liam Gallagher of Oasis retrospectively absorbed the influence of the Beatles in general and John Lennon in particular, Green Day have become contemporary representatives of the music that would have been around them in early childhood. In fact, the sixth Green Day album *Warning:* (2000) is seen by some commentators as displaying elements of the Beatles and even the Kinks, the title track sometimes being compared with the vintage Kinks song *Picture Book* from the *Village Green Preservation Society* album of 1968.

Digging still deeper into the roots of mainstream rock is the currently celebrated Detroit duo the White Stripes, comprising guitarist/lead singer Jack White (b.1975, real name: John Anthony Gillis) and drummer Meg White (b.1974). Often mistaken for a brother and sister team, the Whites appear to have been at one time a married couple, with Jack choosing to adopt Meg's more marketable surname. Their divorce was announced in 2000, although their artistic relationship remained fully active. Their fundamentalist musical philosophy has led them to be hailed as post-millennium exponents of Garage Rock, a 60s US expression used to describe the raw but endlessly enthusiastic teen bands who would rehearse in the family garage, a training ground for many a future star.

Precise definitions vary, but many see Garage Rock in its original form as being closely linked to the US-only 60s form of Punk Rock, referred to in Chapter 11. It should also be emphasized that the 90s revival of the term Garage Rock is in no way related to the largely British variant of electronically-driven Dance Music that is sometimes referred to as Garage.

Releasing their self-titled debut album in 1999, later described by Jack White as 'the most raw, the most powerful, and the most Detroit-sounding record we've made', the duo built on early critical acclaim with *De Stijl* (2000). The album's title is taken from the 1920s Dutch art movement seen by many as a precursor to the essentially post-World War II multi-media genre of Minimalism. Although the album's cover uses a *De Stijl* inspired design, and the band's preference for stage outfits in only red, white and black shows distinctly minimalist sartorial leanings, the music of the White Stripes can only be described as minimalist insofar as it strips the textures down to their most basic rock elements. But minimalism in a musical context, as pioneered by such works as *In C* by Terry Riley and later developed by John Adams, Philip Glass, Steve Reich and others, is not directly reflected in the work of the White Stripes, even though the notion that their 'back-to-basics' creative philosophy is spiritually linked to minimalism in its widest sense seems plausible enough.

Interestingly, the use of the term 'minimalism' appears to have come late to music as a whole, an early reference being a 1968 review by the composer Michael Nyman of a now largely forgotten composition by Cornelius Cardew (1936–1981) based on the philosophical work *The Great Digest* by Confucius.

It was with the release of *White Blood Cells* (2001) and its sequel *Elephant* (2003) that the White Stripes became a major force in both the UK and the US. Although much of the acclaim has been British-led, the September 2002 issue of the UK monthly Q magazine rating them No.12 in a list of *50 Bands To See Before You Die,* the US media has been quick to follow suit. By the time *Get Behind Me Satan* was selling by the truckload in 2005, Rolling Stone had published the oft-quoted soundbite that 'if you happen to be a rock band, and you don't happen to be either of the White Stripes, it so sucks to be you right now'.

A potent testimony to the duo's enduring talent, but also a significant comment on the state of rock music in the early twenty-first century. After more than half a century of experimentation and cross-pollination, one of the most celebrated bands of the new millennium still draws much of its musical vocabulary from those pioneering days of the 50s and 60s. It was even announced, at the time of its release, that all the instruments used on *Elephant* were older than the band members.

Surely proof positive that rock music is now a fully mature artistic genre, whose most able current practitioners take pride in the legacy of which they are the present custodians...

— 15 —

Coda

On 13 November 2005, British 70s cult band Van Der Graaf Generator gave a concert at the Bridgewater Hall in the center of Manchester, England. It was their last British date on a Europe-wide reunion tour that was to end in the Netherlands six days later. First opened in September 1996, the Bridgewater Hall replaced the Free Trade Hall, famous as the scene of the Bob Dylan 'Judas' episode. With its precision acoustic engineering, the Bridgewater Hall is, to a greater extent than the Free Trade Hall, perceived as a purpose-built classical music venue.

Although never destined to become a major commercial force, VDGG gained a loyal fanbase during the heyday of progressive rock, the darkly poetic lyrics and dynamic vocal style of frontman Peter Hammill making them one of the most highly regarded live acts of the era. With the virtuosic flute and saxophones of David Jackson and driving harmonic and rhythmic backdrop from Hugh Banton (keyboards) and Guy Evans (drums), their densely woven sound was unusual for its time in that it was not guitar centered, even though Hammill used both electric and acoustic guitars as accompanying instruments. Needless to say, their most faithful supporter on the national airwaves was John Peel. The Manchester concert had an added poignancy in that Hammill had put together the first incarnation of VDGG while still a student at Manchester University in 1967.

This Sunday evening performance was particularly memorable for two reasons. Firstly, it became clear from the opening accounts of *The Undercover Man* and *Scorched Earth* from *Godbluff* (1975) that Hammill and this quintessential VDGG line-up had lost none of their vocal or instrumental prowess in the intervening years. Nor had Hammill's uniquely compelling stage persona shed any of its magnetism as he approached late middle age.

But secondly, there was the curiously reverential atmosphere that emanated from the auditorium. From a mostly male audience with what appeared to be an average age of around fifty, the pre-concert chatter was polite, often highly knowledgeable, and muted to little more than a whisper. In other words, all who attended the event were observing the strict audience conventions of a classical concert.

A breathtaking set was duly afforded a standing ovation of the type we might reasonably expect after a successful orchestral performance, and rather less demonstrative than is customary at the opera.

Van Der Graaf Generator remain the same commanding musical force they were three decades ago, but the manner in which the mature rock audience receives and appreciates their work could scarcely have changed more dramatically...

Select Bibliography

Blake, Stephen and Andrew John. *The World According To Heavy Metal.* London: Michael O'Mara Books Ltd, 2002

Bromberg, Craig. *The Wicked Ways of Malcolm McLaren.* London: Omnibus Press, 1991

Brown, Tony, Jon Kutner and Neil Warwick. *The Complete Book of the British Charts.* London: Omnibus Press, 2002

Buckley, Jonathan, Orla Duane, Mark Ellingham and Al Spicer, ed. *Rock – The Rough Guide.* London: Rough Guides Ltd, 1999 – second edition

Dannemann, Monika. *The Inner World of Jimi Hendrix.* London: Bloomsbury, 1995

Dorman, L.S. and C.L. Rawlins. *Leonard Cohen – Prophet of the Heart.* London: Omnibus Press, 1990

Friedman, Myra. *Janis Joplin – Buried Alive.* London: Star Books, 1974 – revised 1975

Hopkins, Jerry and Danny Sugerman. *No One Here Gets Out Alive – A Biography of Jim Morrison.* London: Plexus Publishing, 1980

Johnstone, Nick. *Patti Smith – A Biography.* London: Omnibus Press, 1997

Knight, Curtis. *Jimi.* London: Star Books, 1974

Logan, Nick and Bob Woffinden, ed. *The Illustrated NME Encyclopaedia of Rock.* London: Salamander, 1979 – third impression

Logan, Nick and Rob Finnis, ed. *NME Book of Rock.* London: Star Books, 1973

Luck, Richard. *The Madchester Scene.* Harpenden: Pocket Essentials, 2002

MacDonald, Ian. *The People's Music.* London: Pimlico, 2003

Scully, Rock with David Dalton. *Living with the Dead.* London: Abacus, 1996

Shapiro, Harry and Caesar Glebbeek. *Jimi Hendrix – Electric Gypsy.* London: Mandarin, 1990 – revised 1992

Shelton, Robert. *No Direction Home – The Life and Music of Bob Dylan.* Harmondsworth: Penguin, 1987

Stump, Paul. *The Music's All That Matters – A History of Progressive Rock.* London: Quartet Books Ltd, 1997

Tobler, John, ed. *Who's Who in Rock & Roll.* London: Hamlyn, 1991

Wilson, Anthony. *24 Hour Party People – What the Sleeve Notes Never Tell You.* London: Channel 4 Books, 2002

Young, James. *Nico – Songs They Never Play On The Radio.* London: Bloomsbury, 1992

Zappa, Frank and Peter Occhiogrosso. *The Real Frank Zappa Book.* New York: Picador, 1989

Index

Casey Jones And The Engineers, 102
Cash, Johnny, 77, 176, 177, 191
Catherine, Philip, 152
Cat Mother And The All-Night
    Newsboys, 101
Cavern Club, 60, 218
CBGB's, 218, 237
CCS (Collective Consciousness
    Society), 114
Cedrone, Danny, 15, 29, 93
Chandler, Bryan 'Chas', 96, 100
Channing, Chad, 335
Chapman, Emmett, 314
Chapman Stick, 125, 314
Charles, Ray, 201, 255
Checker, Chubby, 205
Cher, 189
Cherone, Gary, 313
Chicago (band), 166
Chiffons, 65
Chimes, Terry, 229, 230
Chinmoy, 167, 169
Chipmunks, 100
Chris Stamey and the Dbs, 234
Chumbawamba, 300
Cinquetti, Gigliola, 247
Clapton, Conor, 107
Clapton, Eric, 56, 58, 66, 102, 103,
    104, 105, 106, 107, 108, 112,
    190, 260
Clark, Dick, 205
Clarke, Michael, 178
Clarke, Stanley, 170, 171, 225
Clash, 227, 229, 230, 273
Classic FM, 270
Clayton, Adam, 256
Cleuver, 151
Clinton, William Jefferson
    (Bill), 200

Cobain, Frances Bean, 334, 336, 337
Cobain, Kurt, 286, 334, 336, 337, 338
Cobham, Billy, 167, 170
Cochran, Eddie, 26, 27
Cocker, Jarvis, 303, 304
Cocker, Joe, 63, 112
Cohen, Leonard, 76, 197, 198, 219, 237
Cohen, Michael, 183
Coker, Paul, 308
Coldplay, 305
Cole, Nat 'King', 79
Collins, Allen, 187, 188
Collins, Judy, 179, 198
Collins, Phil, 106, 115, 147, 149,
    150, 172, 215, 274, 276
Colvin, Douglas 'Dee Dee'
    (Ramone), 218
Comets, 15
Commander Cody and his Lost
    Planet Airmen, 181
Como, 19, 22, 214
Concert for Bangladesh, 66
Confucius, 343
Cook and Greenaway, 266
Cooke, Alastair, 255
Cooke, Sam, 56, 201
Cook, Paul, 219
Cook, Roger, 266
Cool, Tré (Frank Edwin
    Wright III), 341
Cooper, Alice, 119, 222, 227, 339
Cooper, James Fenimore, 224
Copeland, Stewart, 274
Copland, Aaron, 131
Cordwell, John, 42
Corea, Armando Anthony
    Chick, 167, 169, 170
Corgan, Billy, 339
Cornick, Glen, 132

Everly, Don, 27
Everly, Phil, 27
Everman, Jason, 335
Extreme (Gary Cherone band), 313

F

Faces, 55, 76, 213
Factory Club, 286
Fagan, Donald, 243
Fairport Convention, 44, 157, 158, 159, 180
Falling Spikes, 80
FAME (Florence Alabama Music Enterprises), 190
Fame, Georgie, 56, 96, 165
Family, 104
Farandouri, Maria, 263, 264
Fariña, Richard, 180
Farlowe, Chris, 57
Farrar, John, 30
Fartz, 332
Fayed, Mohammed al, 141
Felder, Don, 192
Feliciano, José, 83
Felix, Julie, 94
Fender Stratocaster, 42
Ferguson, Sheila, 206
Ferry, Bryan, 289
Ficca, Billy, 233
Fiddler, John, 138
Finnis, Rob, 216
First National Band, 183
Fish (Derek Dick), 242
Flack, Roberta, 38
Flamingo (Club), 48, 49, 56
Fleetwood Mac, 108, 214, 218, 246, 249
Fleetwood, Mick, 58
Flowers, Herbie, 266, 268

Fluck, Peter, 255
Flying Burrito Brothers, 178, 191
Flynn, George, 154
Focus, 150, 151, 152
Fogerty, John, 181
Fontana, Wayne, 150
Fosdick, W.W., 18
Four Seasons, 67
Fowley, Kim, 130, 235
Fox, Lucas, 117
Franklin, Aretha, 88, 251
Franklin, Erma, 88
Frantic Elevators, 296
Frantz, Chris, 294
Fratto, Russ, 20
Free, 116, 212, 246
Freed, 20, 21
Free Trade Hall, 42, 345
Frey, Glenn, 191
Friedkin, William, 141
Fripp, 122, 123, 125, 257, 320
Fry, Tristan, 266, 267, 268
Furay, Ritchie, 182
Furnish, David, 339
Future Forests, 231

G

Gabriel, Peter, 146, 147, 149, 172, 215, 258, 320, 321
Gaines, Cassie, 188
Gaines, Steve, 188
Gallagher, Lennon Francis, 299
Gallagher, Liam, 297, 299, 341
Gallagher, Noel, 297, 299, 300, 341
Gallo, Joey, 41
Galway, James, 195
Gambaccini, Paul, 249
Gamble and Huff, 205
Gamble, Kenny, 205

Garcia, Jerry, 86, 181
Gardner, Rob, 323
Garfunkel, Art, 42
Garner, Pete, 291
Gaye, Marvin, 201
Geffen, David, 183, 191, 323
Geldof, Bob, 66, 228, 252, 254, 255
Genesis, 123, 146, 147, 149, 150,
         172, 214, 218, 246, 249, 313,
         320, 322
Gibbons, Billy, 242
Gibson ES-335, 22
Gilbert, Gillian, 287
Giles, Michael, 122, 128
Gillan, Ian, 127, 128
Gillespie, John Birks Dizzy, 163
Gilmour, Dave, 137
Giltrap, Gordon, 161
Glass, Philip, 342
Glebbeek, Caesar, 100
Glitter, Gary, 276
Glover, Roger, 127, 128
Goffin, Gerry, 196
Go-Gos, 236
Gong, 111
Goodman, Jerry, 167
Gordon, Jim, 105
Gordy, Berry, 76, 202
Goudreau, Barry, 250
Graham Bond Organization, 50, 103
Graham, Davy, 161
Grand Ole Opry, 177
Grant, Eddy, 295
Grant, Marshall, 177
Grant, Peter, 112
GratefulDead, 10,80,86,110,181,197
Gray, Steve, 267
Grech, Ric, 104
Green Day, 340

Greene, Bob, 307
Greenfield, Dave, 228
Green, Peter, 58, 108, 215
Green River, 332
Greenslade (band), 282
Greenslade, Dave, 282
Greenwood, Colin, 305
Greenwood, Jonny, 305
Gretton, Rob, 287, 294
Grisman, David, 181
Grohl, Dave, 335
Gryphon, 270
Guildford Stranglers, 228
Guitar International
         (UK magazine), 241
Gunn, Trey, 124
Guns N'Roses, 322, 323
Guns, Tracii, 124, 323
Gurley, James, 87
Guthrie, Woody, 36, 193, 252

H

Hacienda Club, 286, 295
Hackett, Steve, 123, 147, 148, 313
Hadley, Tony, 278
Hagar, Sammy, 312, 313
Haley, Bill, 15, 21, 22
Hall, Rick, 190
Hamilton, Frank, 37
Hamilton, Tom, 325
Hammer, Jan, 167
Hammill, Peter, 345, 346
Hammond, Albert, 69
Hammond (-Hammond), Jeffrey, 133
Hammond, John, 40, 96
Hammond Organ, 136, 165, 166, 173
Ham, Peter, 63
Hannett, Martin, 294
Happy Mondays, 291, 292, 293, 295

Incredible String Band, 45, 160
Indie Charts, 292
Ingrams, Richard, 307
Innes, Neil, 300
Iommi, Tony, 119
Iron Butterfly, 74, 113
Iron Maiden, 257, 324
Isidore, Reg, 316
Isle of Wight Festival, 193
Isley Brothers, 96, 201
Isley, Ernie, 201, 202
Isley, Kelly (O'Kelly), 201
Isley, Marvin, 202
Isley, Ronald, 201
Isley, Rudolph, 201

J

Jackson, David, 345
Jackson Five, 255, 308, 311
Jackson, LaToya, 255
Jackson, Lee, 126
Jackson, Michael, 252, 254, 303, 307, 308, 310, 335, 339
Jackson, Randy, 255
Jacqui McShee's Pentangle, 159
Jagger and Richard(s), 53, 57
Jagger, Mick, 50, 55, 65, 216, 307, 325, 339, 340
Jam, 274
James, Alex, 301
James, Brian, 226, 227
James Gang, 192
Jan and Dean, 31
Jansch, Bert, 159, 161
Jasper, Chris, 202
Jefferson Airplane, 87
Jefferson Starship, 87
Jenkins, Johnny, 204
Jennings, Waylon, 186

Jenson, Marianne, 197
Jesus & Mary Chain, 52, 291, 301
Jet Black, 228
Jethro Tull, 132, 134, 135, 142, 151, 211
Jewell, Derek, 148
Jimi Hendrix Experience, 96, 202
Joe Strummer Memorial Forest, 231
Johanson, Jai Johnny, 189
John, Dr., 48
John, Elton, 192, 196, 203, 213, 260, 339
John Evan Band, 133
Johns, Cathy, 189
Johns, Glyn, 191, 231
Johnson, Alphonso, 171
Jolson, Al, 13
Jones, Brian, 50, 54
Jones, Gloria, 278
Jones, Howard, 281
Jones, John Paul, 112, 113, 116
Jones, Kenny, 76
Jones, Mick, 229, 231
Jones, Paul, 50
Jones, Quincy, 310
Jones, Simon, 306
Jones, Steve, 219
Jones, Tom, 112
Joplin, Janis, 87, 95, 200
Jordan, Stanley, 314
Joyce, Chris, 295
Joyce, James, 198
Joyce, Mike, 288
Joy Division, 286, 288

K

Ka-Tzetnik 135633
    (Yehiel De-Nur), 287
Kaye, Danny, 255

Mason, Nick, 137
Mastelotto, Pat, 124
Matching Mole, 172
Matlock, Glen, 219, 223
Matson, Vera, 19
Matthews Southern Comfort, 180
Maxwell, Robert, 141
Mayall, John, 57, 58, 106, 108
May, Brian, 244, 324
Mayhew, John, 146
McCabe, Nick, 306
McCarroll, Tony, 298
McCarthy, Patrick, 331
McCartney, Paul, 32, 60, 64, 66, 96,
    141, 254, 310, 339
McCulloch, Ian, 288
McDevitt, Chas, 33
McDonald, Hugh, 329
McGee, Alan, 297
McGhee, Brownie, 48
McGuigan, Paul 'Guigsy', 298
McGuire, Barry, 41
McIntyre, Fritz, 295
McKagan, Michael 'Duff', 323, 324
McKee, Frances, 334
McLaren, Michael, 219, 222, 226,
    275, 276, 277
McLaughlin, John, 165, 166, 167,
    168, 169, 170, 171, 172
McLean, Don, 19, 214
McManus, Ross, 225
McPhatter, Clyde, 30
McShee, Jacqui, 159
Meaden, Peter, 71
Meat Loaf, 327
Mediaeval Baebes, 270
Medicine Head, 138
Meeks, Johnny, 183
Meisner, Randy, 191

Mellotron, 280
Melvins, 332
Mercury, Freddie, 244, 245
Messina, Jim, 182
Metallica, 257
Meuhliesen, Maury, 194
MFSB, 205
Miles, Buddy, 99
Miller, Roger, 200
Mills, Mike, 329
Milne, A.A., 54
Minimalism, 342
Miranda, Danny, 246
Mitchell, John 'Mitch', 96, 97, 99,
    104, 129
Mitchell, Joni, 94, 179, 193
Monkees, 182
Monkman, Francis, 266, 267, 268, 275
Monster Raving Loony Party, 72
Monterey Festival, 32, 75, 97
Monteverdi, Claudio, 151
Montreux Jazz Festival, 155
Montrose, 312
Moody Blues, 125
Moog Filter, 282
Moog, Robert, 281
Moog Synthesizer, 280, 282
Moon, Keith, 11, 71, 72, 76, 113
Moore, Dudley, 265
Moore, Scotty, 18
Morad, Luciana Gimenez, 55
Morave, Rushton, 116
Moraz, Patrick, 145
Morrison, Jim, 81, 82, 83, 84, 180
Morrison, Sterling, 80
Morrison, Van, 68
Morrissey, 288, 289
Morris, Steven, 286
Moses, Jamie, 246

W

Wagner, Robert, 197
Wailers (US band), 332
Wakeman, Rick, 131, 144, 145, 281
Walker, Cindy, 175
Walker, Luise, 94
Wallis, Larry, 117
Walsh, Joe, 192
Ware, John, 183
Warhol, Andy, 80
Warlocks (Grateful Dead), 86
Warlocks (Velvet Underground), 80
Warsaw (Joy Division), 286, 287
Warwick, Dionne, 255
Waters, Muddy, 20, 48, 49
Waters, Roger, 137
Watson, Bernie, 58
Watts, Charlie, 49, 51
Weather Report, 171, 224, 282
Weavers, 36
Webber, Andrew Lloyd, 127, 299
Webber, Julian lloyd, 299
Webern, Anton, 241
Webster, Jimmie, 314
Weedon, Bert, 29
Welch, Bruce, 30
Weller, Paul, 274
West Coast Pop Art Experimental
    Band, 86
Westwood, Vivienne, 219
Wetton, John, 124
Wexler, Jerry, 47
Weymouth, Tina, 294
Whelan, Gary 'Gaz', 293
While, Kellie, 160
Whiskey, Nancy, 33
White, Alan, 145, 298
White, Jack, 341, 342
White, Lenny, 170

White, Meg, 341
Whitesnake, 212
White Stripes, 341, 342, 343
White, Vince, 231
Whitford, Brad, 325, 326
Whitman, Slim, 177
Who, 10, 71, 72, 73, 74, 75, 76, 112,
    113, 339
Wiedlin, Jane, 236
Wilde, Oscar, 289
Wilke(r)son, Leon, 187
Williams, Hank, 174
Williams, John, 95, 261, 262, 263,
    264, 265, 266, 267, 268, 270
Williams, John Towner, 265
Williams, Lamar, 189
Williams, Len, 262
Williamson, Robin, 45, 160
Williamson, 'Sonny Boy', 102
Williams, Tony, 167
Wilson, Brian, 32
Wilson, Jackie 96
Wilson, Robert, 324
Wilson, Tom, 43
Wilson, Tony, 286, 288, 293, 294
Winwood, Steve, 98, 104
Wipers, 332
Wirral International Guitar
    Festival, 154
Wishbone Ash, 144, 211
Withers, 'Pick', 259
Wonder, Stevie, 201, 255, 283, 300
Wood, Natalie, 196, 197
Wood, Ronnie, 55, 324
Woodstock, 76, 99, 107, 110, 166, 185
Wreckless Eric (Goulden), 231
Wren, Alan 'Reni', 291
Wright, Richard, 137
Wyman, Bill, 51

Made in the USA
San Bernardino, CA
04 March 2017